W9-BQL-641

Adult Learning: A Design for Action

A Comprehensive International Survey

Adult Learning:
A Design for Action:
A Comprehensive International Survey

International Conference on Adult Education and
   Development, Dar es Salaam, 1976.

Edited by

B. L. HALL

and

J. R. KIDD

International Council for Adult Education, Toronto

CARRIE RICH MEMORIAL LIBRARY
CAMPBELL UNIVERSITY
BUIES CREEK, NC

PERGAMON PRESS
OXFORD · NEW YORK · TORONTO · SYDNEY · PARIS · FRANKFURT

U.K.	Pergamon Press Ltd., Headington Hill Hall, Oxford OX3 0BW, England
U.S.A.	Pergamon Press Inc., Maxwell House, Fairview Park, Elmsford, New York 10523, U.S.A.
CANADA	Pergamon of Canada Ltd., 75 The East Mall, Toronto, Ontario, Canada
AUSTRALIA	Pergamon Press (Aust.) Pty. Ltd., 19a Boundary Street, Rushcutters Bay, N.S.W. 2011, Australia
FRANCE	Pergamon Press SARL, 24 rue des Ecoles, 75240 Paris, Cedex 05, France
FEDERAL REPUBLIC OF GERMANY	Pergamon Press GmbH, 6242 Kronberg-Taunus, Pferdstrasse 1, Federal Republic of Germany

Copyright © 1978 Pergamon Press Ltd.

All Rights Reserved. No part of this publication may be reproduced, stored in a retrieval system or transmitted in any form or by any means: electronic, electrostatic, magnetic tape, mechanical, photocopying, recording or otherwise, without permission in writing from the publishers.

First edition 1978

British Library Cataloguing in Publication Data

International Conference on Adult Education and
Development, *Dar es Salaam, 1976*
Adult learning.
1. Adult education - Congresses
I. Title II. Hall, B L III: Kidd, J R
IV. International Council for Adult Education
374 LC5209 78-40283
ISBN 0-08-022245-5 Hardcover
ISBN 0-08-023007-5 Flexicover

CARRIE RICH MEMORIAL LIBRARY
CAMPBELL UNIVERSITY

In order to make this volume available as economically and as rapidly as possible the authors' typescripts have been reproduced in their original forms. This method unfortunately has its typographical limitations but it is hoped that they in no way distract the reader.

*Printed in Great Britain by William Clowes & Sons Limited
London, Beccles and Colchester*

Contents

Restructuring Adult Education

Case Studies

158231

Issues for Development

Conclusions

Preface and Acknowledgements

The book is a product and an example of ideas and actions for the carrying out of a design for development that recognizes the centrality of adult education and of the participation of the people in development decisions. In this sense it is a text that reflects and illuminates the new initiatives of the expanded, human-centred concept of development.

The book consists of 24 papers contributed and used by participants in the <u>International Conference on Adult Education and Development</u> held in Dar es Salaam, Tanzania, in June 1976, under the auspices of the International Council for Adult Education. The Conference — and this book of selected papers — results from the efforts and commitment of many nations, organizations and individuals.

The contribution of Tanzania to the Conference is recognized particularly while acknowledging the wide support in terms of money, material and services from foundations, intergovernmental agencies and regional organizations. The International Institute for Adult Literacy Methods in Iran made possible the distribution of plenary papers at the Conference and the subsequent Conference Report in the Winter 1976-77 issue of <u>Literacy Discussion</u>.

In total, the Conference generated 65 papers for advance study, for presentation at the Conference, for group discussion, for follow-up. The task of selection was not easy. Many excellent papers are not included, usually because they dealt with subjects of particular rather than general interest. However, we acknowledge the contribution of all the authors to the success of the Conference, and a list of all papers has been included. Some of the papers in the book have been edited and reduced in length to give focus to their arguments. We have tried to ensure that they retain their own style and natural idiom.

The Editors have been aided substantially by Clif Bennett, Helen Callaway, Margaret Gayfer, Rebecca Kabwasa, Jacqueline Sullivan and Dorothy Thomas.

J. R. Kidd   Toronto
Budd L. Hall   October 1977

An Urgency: Adult Education in and for Development

J. R. Kidd

The seminar on education for development is
in India. A Vice Chancellor says: "Go to
the village. Treat the village as your guru."
Unlike many university men in India, he has
done so himself and has learned much from the
villagers. Paulo Freire enjoins all teachers
to begin their work by listening to the
learners.

But if the villagers of India or of the world could solve their
own problems with their own wisdom, experience and resources,
there would no longer be a thousand million rural poor and dire
prospects of pestilence and mass starvation.

Fantastic changes have come to India. Factory and farm production as well as the GNP have soared and over the past year the
country has had a favourable balance of trade. But few of the
economic gains are reaching the rural poor. This harsh fact is
also true in a majority of the countries that are sovereign
members of the United Nations. The next five-year plan in
India will concentrate on research, trained personnel, distribution and delivery systems to ensure that some results of the
national productivity will reach the disadvantaged five hundred
million. And India is exceptional only in the fact that the
discrepancy between national growth and the participation of
the masses in development has been officially recognized and
that some serious action will follow.

Practitioners in adult education often use the term development
almost as often as the word democracy. The paradox is that a
theme seldom absent in speeches and essays appears less frequen-
tly in actual programs. Activities in adult education have
been initiated for a hundred purposes — to help people to make
money, to dress better, to have nutritious meals, to use well
their leisure or avoid boredom — but infrequently to bring
about balanced development at home or internationally. Do you
doubt that assertion? Scan the courses offered in adult education classes in a hundred countries. Or review the names of
those who participated in the great international meetings on

1

development — UNCTAD IV, Habitat, Food, Population, the New
Economic Order, and the others — and note how few adult educationists were even present.

But the situation is changing.

In 1976 the largest international meeting on adult education
ever assembled met far away from the usual conference haunts,
in a developing country, Tanzania. More than five hundred participated, representing 82 countries. They came from every
region: from Vietnam, Iran and India and Sri Lanka in Asia;
from countries in the Pacific; from Peru and Venezuela and
Costa Rice in Latin America; from the Caribbean; and from
countries in Africa that speak Portuguese, French and English
as well as African languages. Transportation costs have been
soaring but this event was so important that people found the
means to attend. They were attracted by the theme, Adult
Education for Development, by the record of Tanzania in utilizing adult education for development, and because of the leadership of President Julius Nyerere. He did not disappoint them.
He began proceedings with an incisive statement about the goals
of development:

> But Man can only liberate himself or develop
> himself. He cannot be liberated or developed
> by another. For Man makes himself. It is
> his ability to act deliberately, for a self-
> determined purpose, which distinguishes him
> from the other animals. The expansion of his
> own consciousness, and therefore of his power
> over himself, his environment, and his society,
> must therefore ultimately be what we mean by
> development.
>
> So development is for Man, by Man, and of Man.
> The same is true of education. Its purpose
> is the liberation of Man from the restraints
> and limitations of ignorance and dependency.
> Education has to increase men's physical and
> mental freedom — to increase their control
> over themselves, their own lives, and the
> environment in which they live. The ideas
> imparted by education, or released in the mind
> through education, should therefore be liber-
> ating ideas; the skills acquired by education
> should be liberating skills. Nothing else
> can properly be called education. Teaching

> which induces a slave mentality or a sense of
> impotence is not education at all — it is
> attack on the minds of men.

And the delegates, coming from so many different cultures and
circumstances, were quickly able unanimously to accept this
statement of objectives as a <u>Declaration of Dar es Salaam</u>.

Of course, this meeting did not just happen, nor was it just
another conference. It was a stage in a process that will continue into the 1980's and it had been planned for over a year.
People in many countries has helped. The first draft of the
issues had been made in Ottawa with the help of staff members
of the World Bank, ILO, UNESCO, FAO, WHO issues of development
as seen from their experience and perspectives. In the months
following, meetings were held in centres of development in four
countries, social scientists and education planners added their
insights and 60 papers and studies were prepared to ensure that
debate about the issues and necessary action would be well
founded.

As in the case of many international conferences, there were
messages from heads of state such as Pierre Trudeau, Prime
Minister of Canada, from regional organizations such as the
Arab League, and from advocates of special interests. But these
were not ritual statements only; they dealt directly and rele-
vantly with <u>development</u>. The message from Maurice Strong, first
Executive Director of the United Nations Environmental Program,
typifies the tone and substance of all:

> The Stockholm Conference on the Human Environment,
> and the United National General Assembly Resol-
> utions which followed, created the structure for
> a world action plan towards the protection and
> enhancement of Man's Environment at a time when
> his resources are being over-exploited and the
> gap between rich and poor is apparently becom-
> ing wider. At a moment in time when the real-
> ization that man is heading blindly towards his
> own ultimate destruction has become the dramatic
> cornerstone for urgent action, the creation of
> the United Nations Environment Programme in
> Kenya — the first occasion in the history of the
> United Nations that a world headquarters of an
> important component of the United Nations system
> has been located in a developing country —

became the mirror of Man's conscience;   his
environmental conscience. The task of UNEP is
to find solutions to the many-faceted and interacting problems which, in the course of development, affect the environment;   and which must
involve all disciplines, and every human being,
bringing together the children and the adults,
the ignorant and the wise, the developed with
the developing nations, in a cultural setting
which has the goals of social and economic
development in an environmentally-sound manner.
The outer limits of the planet, in the light of
the quantum of population growth, are rapidly
being reached. It is thus the moment for serious
re-appraisal of the development process itself.

The creation of a critical mass of environmen-
tally-aware leaders to guide the public and the
key administrators towards environmental progress, is an essential characteristic of the
action plan which the Stockholm conference recommended as an imperative for man's protection
and well-being. In this context, therefore,
the education of the masses towards environment
linked with development, is the *sine qua non*
of our endeavours, and must be the goal of all
who believe in humanity and its ecological relationship with nature, and the need to conserve
our resources and manage them in the interests
of all. This is a-political;   this is a means
whereby people, irrespective of religions, cultures, political ideologies, economic and social
dimensions, physical and geographical differences, can strive together towards a better and
more fullsome life.

It is with the deepest recognition of its value
for man's future, therefore, that I extend my
sincerest appreciation and best wishes to the
success of the present conference on Adult
Education and Development. The fact that UNEP
is participating in this conference indicates
the importance attached to adult education.
UNEP, in collaboration with UNESCO, has embarked
on a major programme for environmental education
and related training;   not only at the three
pedagogic levels of primary, secondary and uni-

versity education, but also at the levels of
children and youth, and adult education. A
major international conference on Environmental
Education is to take place next year where policy
recommendations will be made which, when implemented, will enable governments to allocate resources towards the achievement of the overall
objectives. This is a major problem which will
require the total involvement of all key educators and all institutions. I am sure that the
initiatives and recommendations to be made at
this Conference in Dar es Salaam will provide a
major thrust towards aligning influential decision makers in the overall attempt towards educational development including environmental
dimensions.

One of the key documents studied was the UNESCO Recommendation
on Adult Education which was subsequently adopted unanimously
at the 1976 General Conference. Representatives familiarized
themselves with the terms of the Recommendation and took counsel
together about implementing the Recommendation in all countries.

Of course, the working documents did not all come from heads of
state or from intergovernmental organizations. The range of
authorship was wide. The total number of documents generated
exceeded 60 and the papers were of many kinds: statements of
concept and issue, case studies of specific applications of
adult education to development, papers prepared to generate
discussion in study groups, papers on methods and media specially suited to development, papers analyzing strategies. The
authors came from 38 countries, including Guinea Bissau, Mozambique, Vietnam, Burundi, Antigua, Papua-New Guinea, countries
that have infrequently been heard from in the past.

Fields of work represented went far beyond governments and universities and included some not always well represented at adult
education meetings. One example is workers' education, particularly the newer programs for rural workers associated with
the International Labour Organization. This initiative, which
seems so logical and so necessary, and aligns workers' education
with the masses of the rural poor, was welcomed as an innovation
of enormous potential consequence. Another field that received
special attention was that of the "short cycle colleges" now
found in many countries under such names as "community colleges",
"junior colleges", "colleges of applied arts and technology".

The range of special interest was wide — libraries and museums,
indigenous arts, languages for education, participatory research,
and there were many unscheduled informal sessions. The emphasis,
however, was not on separate interests but on development.

One conference participant prepared no advance paper, and took
part only once in the plenary sessions, yet his presence dominated many sessions and his counsel was sought again and again:
Paulo Freire.

What is here presented includes roughly one-third of the papers
that were prepared. The editors found the task of choosing,
and thus of eliminating extremely burdensome: excellent papers
have not been presented because there was no room for all, because the subject they presented might have been treated in part
in another paper, because while significant the writer's topic
might have been more local in emphasis than of general interest,
or because the paper was developed for discussion rather than
for a reading audience. Several of the additional papers are
case studies of particular countries and regions. Some have to
do with languages and development. One notable paper by Professor Mubange E. Kashoki is "Cultural Pluralism and Development
in Zambia". Dr. Kashoki is Director and Research Professor of
African Languages, Institute for African Studies, University of
Zambia. He rightly points out that developing countries often
give precedence to economic and political decisions affecting
development while decisions affecting cultural development are
postponed.

> Developing countries which are preoccupied with
> economic development are simultaneously pre-
> occupied with another type of development —
> cultural development ... These national goals
> are not necessarily compatible, let alone easily
> harmonized, and they are often in conflict ...
> It would certainly be in the national interest
> if economic development took place in step and
> in harmony with cultural development. It is
> precisely the conspicuous absence of such a
> policy in almost all the developing countries
> that should be of primary concern.

Other writers and speakers sounded the same note: the matter
is of such consequence that it must be taken up directly in
conferences, papers, research and development.

We regret all of these omissions but many have been reprinted
in journals. The entire collection has been placed in several
repositories. A list of all papers is appended and individual
papers can be obtained on loan from the International Council
for Adult Education.

However, careful planning, advance studies and excellent documents assist but do not guarantee success of an international
meeting. The annals of international conferences in the mid-
seventies show many dismal failures, with whole days wasted in
political manoeuvering. HABITAT, just a month before, based on
four years of preparation and with a budget 100 times greater
than that available to the Dar es Salaam planners, had been dis-
rupted again and again by political struggle and the results
fell far short of expectations. However, the mood at Dar es
Salaam was affirmative; the representatives exerted themselves
to find measures of agreement. The environment in a developing
country impelled the participants to talk together, to learn
from each other, to reach some understandings on goals and urgencies, to accept and respect honest differences and to concentrate
on a design for action.

Other international meetings have fractured or foundered on dis-
agreements about the meaning of development. When this notion
is coupled with that of adult education, the possibilities of
confusion and dissension are compounded. Of course, many differences in semantics and substance did surface but that did
not prevent the achievement of accord on central issues. Everyone accepted some notion of "balanced development"; that there
is a component or aspect of adult education in every economic
or social or political project, that adult education can never
remain neutral about the issues of development, that the institutions of adult education should enlarge and focus their energies on development tasks which are of such importance that delay
cannot be tolerated.

There has been the emergence of a growing concensus about the
goals of adult education. This process has been going on for
a number of years through a series of international gatherings,
notably the UNESCO world conference in Tokyo, conferences at
ILO and OECD, and an international seminar on literacy at Persepolis. The latter group unanimously approved a Declaration
dealing with the structures that must be built for the development of lifelong learning and the kinds of actions that must be
taken:

Those which from the political point of view
tend to bring about the effective participation
of every citizen in decision making;

Those which from the economic point of view aim
at harmonious development of society and not at
blind and dependent growth;

Those which from the social point of view do
not result in making education a class privilege
and a means of reproducing established hierar-
chies and orders;

Those that from the professional point of view
provide communities with genuine control over
the technologies that they wish to use;

Those which from the institutional point of view
favour a concerted approach and continuing cooperation among all authorities responsible for
basic services (agriculture, welfare, health,
etc.).

The Declaration of Persepolis, the Declaration of Dar es Salaam
of Julius Nyerere and the UNESCO Recommendation on Adult Education all attest to the fact that adult education is now seen,
not as something occasional and peripheral, but in the main
stream of economic, social and political advance, or if you
will, in the centre, the very core of development.

At Dar es Salaam attempts to reach further coherence were
speeded up. The representatives accepted unanimously a statement of first principles by the Conference Raporteur General,
Professor Lalage Bown of the University of Lagos:

This Conference believes that mass poverty and
mass ignorance and illiteracy are recognized by
most governments and their citizens as among
the major problems of the present day and that
most governments have assumed responsibility
for combating them through development plans
and programmes;

That education, and in particular that part of
education involving adults, is an essential
factor (though not the only one) in promoting
development processes; adult education can
moreover contribute decisively to the full participation of the masses of the people in their

own development and to their active control of
social, economic, political and cultural change;

That all development planning, including educational planning, is influenced by the political
environment, which may be more or less favourable to the work of adult education; but it is
convinced that adult education can almost always
play some role in raising the people out of
apathy and marginality;

That once there is commitment of any sort by
government and citizens to promote adult education it is necessary to organize structures
and provide resources to carry that commitment
into action;

All development programmes and all educational
programmes should set out with the prime goal
of benefiting human beings in their lives and
in their communities, should be centred on man
and should be based on respect for the individual's worth, intelligence and competence to
solve his or her own problems;

And that any development programme, to be man-
centred must be inspired and carried through by
the people "at the grass roots" in their communities and organization.

The Conference then went on to identify strategies to achieve
these goals:

Since adult education is only one element in a
strategy to promote development, it is essential
that there be close inter-relationship between
adult education agencies and other development
agencies; and this Conference calls for a coordinated approach, in which adult education
workers are trained and encouraged to work with
and to consult other development specialists
and in which development workers are encouraged
to contribute to adult education.

This Conference, recommended, as essential elements in a strategy of adult education for development based on the principles
expressed above:

mass participation in both planning and

implementation of programmes;

mass orientation towards development;

structures to provide work and opportunities
to learn new working skills;

decentralized systems of production;   mechanics
to enable the people to control their environment;   processes leading to increased equality
and social justice.

Specific recommendations for adult education followed:

The Conference wishes to affirm the obvious
but often forgotten truths that no individual
can learn for or on behalf of another and that
learning is sterile unless it leads to action;
and that therefore the most valuable types of
adult education are those designed to:

a) help individuals to become more creative
    and productive;

b) become collectively aware of their present
    situation and of the changes which they are
    actively involved in bringing about;

c) take initiatives, make choices and find
    free and responsible solutions.

In the light of these principles, this Conference calls for a radical shift on the approaches
to planning, to education as a whole and to
adult education in particular. It calls
urgently for:

a) a shift from centralized planning to de-
    centralized and participatory planning;

b) a shift from structures of education con-
    cerned largely with the formal school system
    to structures in which all types of educa-
    tion, formal and non-formal, for children,
    youth and adults, have a recognized place;

c) a shift from adult education programmes
    designed as merely remedial to programmes
    explicitly designed to raise the conscious-
    ness of the adult learner, release his or
    her creative potential and instil into him

> a confidence in his own capacity to con-
> tribute to changing his environment — to
> render him self-reliant but not isolated
> from society.

> Finally, this Conference, comprising adult edu-
> cators, planners and administrators from many
> nations, met in amity to forward the tasks of
> development calls for the development of inter-
> national co-operation and mutual aid in support
> of national efforts to promote adult education
> for development, in a spirit of equality among
> individuals, communities and nations and of
> true self-reliance.

In his closing statement the Conference President, Malcolm
Adiseshiah, spoke of the far-reaching implications of these
agreements, nothing less than the transformation of education:

> We have agreed on a rather radical but construc-
> tive critique concerning the strategies that we
> have been pursuing in Development and Education.
> These strategies have resulted in inefficient,
> unproductive and inequitable — in effect inhuman
> — fruits of both Development and Education. A
> particular insight which emerged is that the
> line is not accidental between the technocratic
> growth oriented models that we have been pur-
> suing and our almost exclusive concentration on
> formal education institutions, whose function
> is to orient and mould its clients, that is,
> school children and university students, to
> safeguard and perpetuate the elite dominated
> status quo, resulting in the absolute neglect
> of Adult Education, which by its content, mes-
> sage and techniques, is and can be subversive
> of the status quo. A second idea that we carry
> back with us is that Adult Education is not
> politically neutral, that, if it is effective,
> its crucial and decisive test is how far it is
> part of the processes of changing our political
> networks, the upsetting of our socio-economic
> decision making centres which are a function of
> our property and assets ownerships, and the
> transformation of our educational and cultural
> techniques which will make the total educational

> process — particularly our formal systems of
> learning — a change agent. A third conclusion
> is that Adult Education, like Development, is
> holistic in its scope; it is the liberation
> of man, and so is "for Man, by Man and of Man".

However, "agreement to seek agreement" did not prevent or inhibit
searching, probing, testing many profound differences in belief
and ideology, questing for better understanding and more useful
concepts that would serve as better guides to action.

Julius Nyerere had set the tone by articulating what development
was not — a series of isolated fragmenting activities and events
— as well as what it is, an integrated and integrating process:

> Adult education is not something which can deal
> with just "agriculture" or "health" or "literacy"
> or "mechanical skill", etc. All these separate
> branches of education are related to the total
> life a man is living, and to the man he is and
> will become. Learning how best to grow soy-beans
> is of little use to a man if it is not combined
> with learning about nutrition and/or the exis-
> tence of a market for the beans. This means that
> adult education will promote changes in men and
> in society. And it means that adult education
> should promote change, at the same time as it
> assists men to control both the change which
> they induce, and that which is forced upon them
> by the decisions of other men or the cataclysms
> of nature. Further it means that adult educa-
> tion encompasses the whole of life, and must
> build upon what already exists.

Honourable Ben Mady Cissé, Minister of State for Senegal,
brought a touch of lucidity to the debate and his own deep concern with the human condition:

> Development is a result of man's action on
> nature. It is man's attempt to transform nature
> in order to improve his own condition. Develop-
> ment cannot be exclusviely economic as it affects
> all dimensions of human existence.
>
> So that man can best resolve the conflict which
> inevitably arises between "having the most" and
> "being the most", he must develop in a society

which is adapted to his needs and over which
he has lasting control. National growth,
therefore, must become more humane. Beyond
its lifeless statistical dimension, national
growth must be "development" as in the definition of François Peroux: "the transition from
a less human to a more human situation".

When Cissé chose to illustrate how development can be fostered,
he presents an African innovation, *animation sociale*:

> It is up to the State to devise this educational
> approach and then execute it. For this purpose,
> Senegal has created a unique organization:
> *Animation*, which is responsible for turning
> over the realization of development to the basic
> communities, and along with it all the conse-
> quences that this participation implies.
>
> *Animation* has many roles. It is a State organ-
> ization. It is, even more, a network: a net-
> work of group leaders (men and women) freely
> chosen by their basic communities, a network in
> which group leaders become the seeds of progress
> without changing their status. If this network
> is effective and is really an integral part of
> the people, it should be able to initiate and
> support a direct dialogue between the unanimous,
> organized communities on one hand, and State
> and institutional authorities on the other.

Per Stensland, from his field experience in many countries, and
his study of the work of his former teacher, Gunnar Myrdal,
offered parallel definitions of adult education and development:

Education: - purposeful and organized lear-
            ning — standpoint of the lear-
            ners;

            - deliberate, systematic and sus-
            tained effort to transmit and
            evoke knowledge, attitudes,
            values, skills and sensibilities
            — standpoint of the educator.

Development: - purposeful and organized change
            — standpoint of the individual;

> - deliberate and continuing
> attempt to accelerate the role
> of economic and social process
> and to alter institutional
> arrangements which are consi-
> dered to block attainment of
> this goal — standpoint of
> "developer" or planner.

But Stensland's interest is not so much in defining but in
achieving an integration of theory and practice, with the participation of multi-disciplines and practitioners:

> Development needs have created needs for new
> education agents ... the doctor, the nurse, the
> skilled worker, the farm leader, the journalist,
> the lawyer, the sanitation inspector, the bridge
> construction engineer, the irrigation expert,
> the policeman ... Training is needed for the
> actors involved, regardless of their previous
> preparation, professional or not. The action
> agents will become the education core of dev-
> elopment, their own actions the core of educ-
> ation.

Ana Krajnc, in a preface to her case study of the Workers Universities of Yugoslavia, says that the goals of adult education
for development encompass both individual and social imperatives:

> We see individual development as dialectically
> connected or inter-related with social spheres,
> where individual interests are coordinate with
> progressive social goals and at the same time
> social progress ... Through adult education in
> Yugoslavia we do not tend only to provide "self-
> actualization" ... but efforts are also made for
> "actualization" on an individual level of what
> is recognized as progressive and anticipated as
> a general goal of our society.

About some notions there was no debate. One is that both development and adult education require and lead to participation.
No disagreement was voiced about the need to cultivate and build
an indigenous art and culture. Conscientization, the concept of
Paulo Freire which has stirred enthusiasm and also evoked resistance over a decade, seemed to be accepted and approved, although

those who struggled in different accents to pronounce the concept may have used it with quite different understanding.

The participants seemed to be more exhilarated than depressed over ideological differences, did not draw back from complex and critical problems, nor were the frightening gargantuan obstacles to progress ignored. Tanzania is not a lotus land, and easy abstractions and facile solutions could not be asserted: the first time they were uttered they were tested in the real situation in which the delegates lived. The voices of several theme speakers were sombre. Majid Rahnema of Iran was determined that no one would continue to count on magical formulations or easy solutions:

> Until quite recently, the process of development has been regarded not only as a means of increasing the resources available to society, but also as a way of assuring their more equitable distribution among claimants. These resources include wealth, in all its forms, as well as the social services which the state provides in increasing proportions and the opportunities which derive from access to them.
>
> If we judge the situation by the legislation which has been placed upon the statute books or even the growing number of social service institutions which have been created, we may find considerable support for this optimistic view of development. If, however, we look behind the laws and into the institutions we have created, the facts do not tend to confirm so optimistic a view.
>
> Between the abstract legal right and the actual possibility to exercise that right looms an enormous and expanding gap. It is a bitter but hard fact that the usual consequences of economic growth have been the exacerbation rather than the amelioration of inequality in health care. The expansion of school has served not to narrow but to widen the gap between the rich and the poor. While governments have preached equality, the observable consequence of development has been the production of inequality. If our "developers" were to choose a slogan describing the outcomes of their actions rather than

the sometimes noble intentions which inspire
them, they might wish to consider the prophecy
of the New Testament: "unto those who have it
shall be given".

There are three major trends in education, particularly evident in the developing nations:

1) Regardless of the widely recognized crisis
    which confronts educational systems the
    trend towards linear expansion of the formal
    system persists. Formal schooling continues
    to consume the bulk of all resources allo-
    cated to education and a growing percentage
    of national wealth.

2) Despite efforts intended to make the formal
    education system more relevant to individual
    and collective needs, it remains largely
    indifferent — if not indeed hostile — to the
    objectives of a truly democratic, man-centred
    and humanizing society.

3) On the whole, there is little evidence that
    efforts aimed at improving education through
    the introduction of non-formal and similar
    programmes have succeeded in making it more
    relevant to the overall needs of peoples
    and societies. Nor have they brought about
    a more equitable distribution of educational
    and other social resources.

Rahnema goes on to ask the reasons for failure:

Is the lack of success due to circumstance which
may be discovered through a critical examination
of past experiences and overcome through the
application of a new educational strategy, or is
the problem, as I believe it to be, more pervasive and profound?

The Finance Minister of Tanzania, A. H. Jamal, provided an
economic analysis that offered no panaceas, no growth except
through hard work and international cooperation:

Both the developing and the developed countries
will have to recognize that they will have to
work together so as to disengage the world from

its present collision course and to move it
towards less acquisitiveness on the part of
the rich and less envy on the part of the poor.

By definition the process will have to be both
simultaneous and parallel. The developing countries will have to undertake their own revolution.

Essentially, developing countries have to restructure their entire educational system as a
matter of priority. This means re-training and
re-tooling a whole society, taking into account
the specialized needs of particular sectors and
the overall needs of the country as a whole.

Internationally, the parallel process of reforming global institutions and the global framework of trade and exchange must begin in earnest
without delay.

No voice was more blunt or more forceful than that of Lucille
Mair, Jamaica's representative at the United Nations. Dr. Mair
spoke directly to the countries of greater development, making
a clear case for a New Economic Order as a necessity for development:

The disparity in the levels of living between
the peoples of one region and the next widens
dangerously, in full international view. Un-
checked consumption continued to characterize
the life-style of a select world minority, while
hunger eliminates millions of the depressed
majority; western science and technology break
through new boundaries daily, while the villages
and towns of the Third World attempt survival
without water, light, housing, health care or
employment.

Faced with the evidence of the appalling lives
which the vast majority of men and women lead
in the three southern continents, despite two
decades of "development", national and international planners now attempt to ensure that
the real target of development becomes the human
being, who will remain central to all redefinitions and to all revised strategies.

The urgent need for developmental models which

can be effective in meeting the basic needs of
men and women has accelerated the search for a
new economic world order. The international
community is at present investing much energy
and expertise in negotiating that order throughout a network of United Nations and other bodies,
regional and international, all of which carry
fundamental implications for a restructuring of
the world system. But there is also the real
possibility that the technical nature of the
negotiations and decision making involved may
lead to a repetition of past deficiencies in
perception. It is not improbable that these
assemblies, inevitably oriented towards trade
and finance, may lose sight of those persons
who will be affected by the economic processes
under debate.

Her remarks concerned peoples in all developing countries but
she also made specific references to the role of the "largest
minority" of all, the role of girls and women in development:

There is already evidence to suggest that at
least one vital segment of a population, viz.
women, respond readily to non-authoritarian informal situations of group interaction in which
past experience is explored, related to future
needs, and thus stimulates a progression towards
creative solutions.

Many basic assumptions of developmental experts,
as is well known, missed their targets, in the
case of women, their stereotypes of female
occupations being often at odds with reality.
A tendency to under-rate the real contribution
of women to the domestic economy led to the
neglect of their potential for participation
in a modern economy; as a consequence few of
the tools of development went their way.

There should be no more need to state the case
for women as agents than for women as targets
of development. Nevertheless, recent and striking manifestations of their part in the dynamics
of national progress deserve mention.

The past two decades or so have witnessed the
remarkable mobilization of large sectors of the

female population in the liberation movements
of Africa, Asia and Latin America. In these
people's wars, where no one is a civilian,
women, fully understanding the political forces
at work, performed strategic functions as educator, communicator, informer and active combatant, quickly learning new skills needed for
the people's victory, and transmitting as they
learnt. Thereby they maximized the resources
available for the challenge, not only of national
liberation, but also of national reconstruction.

After hearing such statements no one could come away in a mood
of facile optimism. Yet none of the speakers was despondent or
was counselling retreat. The problems are not only real; they
are to be faced.

In some ways the case studies provided not just illumination
but an antidote to any gloom associated with the theme statements.
None of the case studies is less honest or relevant, or gives a
varnished, deodorized picture. But the sight of real people
facing real situations and struggling, failing, trying, succeed-
ing, always restores some balance of confidence.

Many of the case studies were from individual countries: Mozambique, Guinea Bissau, Senegal, Hungary. There was keen interest
in all of these; also in Vietnam, from which country one still
hopes to receive a case study of the Peoples Popular Education
movement that pre-dated the revolution and nourished intellec-
tually and spiritually the Vietnamese people through 30 years
of struggle. Close attention was also given to the case study
of Tanzania itself, particularly because the delegates were able
to visit first hand institutions such as Kivukoni College and
some Ujamaa villages.

Interest was also aroused in a case study of the Arab Educational,
Cultural and Scientific Organization (ALESCO), which along with
the Arab Literacy and Adult Education Organization (ARLO) and
the Regional Centre for Functional Literacy in Rural Areas for
the Arab States (ASFEC) is the chief vehicle for non-formal and
adult education in Arab countries.

The case studies led to discussion of more specific problems and
factors of development, including traditional ways of dealing
with needs in various countries. Daniel Mbunda provided some
glimpses of the way people in Tanzania had coped with develop-

ment needs in the past:

> In my village, there was an epidemic. Many
> people died for no apparent reasons. Some
> measure had to be taken. It was a public con-
> cern involving a number of scattered villages.
> The issue had to be discussed, solutions had to
> be sought, and implemented. The problem must
> be communicated to the various groups, who would
> discuss and see what alternatives would be open
> to them. They would opt for the most probable
> approach and devise an implementation plan within
> the set time and frame of reference. The point
> was that it was a matter of general concern;
> basic knowledge about it had to be transmitted
> as raw material for subsequent discussions;
> this would lead to joint action to satisfy the
> need of the community.

> We had no radio transistors. But we had drums
> and horns. A certain blow of the horn or beat
> of the drum meant some one had an important mes-
> sage to tell the community. Through the evening
> still air the beat of the drum rent the air —
> all ears prick! Then came the message — the
> announcer standing on top of "kisanja" — an
> elevated platform used usually for drying maize —
> cassava would cry out the essential message to
> be passed on to all sides by his friends to the
> neighbouring villagers. The message would run
> like this: "Our village is faced with deaths,
> which the local doctors have not been able to
> account for. It is a general concern. We need
> to find out what is wrong and how we can save
> our lives. Our neighbours in village X seem to
> have found a doctor who seems to have a solution.
> Please find out what we can do and let us meet
> tomorrow morning ...".

Problems of languages media of communication and the significance
of indigenous arts in development were studied in small groups
and debated in plenary sessions. Melvin Fox of the Ford Foundation described some of the problems where multi-languages are
fostered in what he calls the "language thicket":

> To the extent one starts at the bottom to try to
> be responsive to local interests, and to engage

community support and participation in educational innovation, reliance on local or regional
languages becomes indispensable. Neither the
subject matter priorities, nor the strategies
for effectively delivering them, can in most
localities be achieved except through the languages that are accessible and appropriate for
particular groups. In Nigeria, for example,
one language is used for official governmental
purposes at the national level (English); other
languages are used for Federal Government notices
and posters distributed regionally, and for radio
broadcasts by the Government (Hausa and Yoruba);
still other languages are used for these purposes
at the State level (e.g. Efik in the southeast,
Fula or Kanuri in the north. In Africa, to be
responsive to and to effectively reach local
communities, one would have to develop basic
education with and through many languages — as
would also be the case in trying to deal with
formally uneducated masses in India, the Philippines, Indonesia, Mexico, or the Andean countries of South America.

The most lengthy document of all has been distilled from all
of these, as well as scores of work groups and assemblies. It
is a Design for Action, a sober inventory and recapitulation of
the many recommendations that were advanced and given assent
during the Conference. The language of the Design is restrained
but the scope of the Design is bold. Shorn of all rhetoric, it
deals plainly with the organizational plans, information services, training and research, the resources, attitudes, behaviours,
that are required if adult education is to be effective in development. The Design is about infrastructure, about priorities,
about cooperation; it is an agenda to stimulate action all over
the world.

In his closing remarks, Malcolm Adiseshiah referred to the
resources of human spirit that are required:

> I call on each of us to commit himself and her-
> self to action to make adult education an effec-
> tive integral instrument for the kind of dev-
> elopment, the liberation of Man, to which we
> have pledged ourselves for the balance of the
> Second Development Decade. The springs that

will nourish this pledge are our own will, and
behind the individual will that each of us brings
to the task, is the community of adult education
to which all of us belong. That community is
the community of the liberated, unquenchable
human spirit that binds us together in an invin-
cible bond that will support and cherish us in
our moments of frustration, days of despair,
and periods of weariness, and which will never
ever let us feel let down, lonely or lost. It
is to that brave brotherhood of the human spirit
that I say, on behalf of all of us, adieu, au
revoir, and bon chance.

It is because these qualities were present at Dar es Salaam and
can be counted on that the pages that follow constitute not so
much a report of one human encounter that took place in the
summer of 1976 but the guidelines and script for a theatre of
action that moved from one city, Dar es Salaam, to communities
everywhere, and for the balance of the Second Development Decade.

Restructuring Adult Education

INTRODUCTION

The only real victory is one in which all
are equally victorious and there is defeat
for no one.

Buddha

The term development means different things to different people
and any conference about development could turn into an exercise resembling some forms of modern dancing, with everyone
moving into his own inner rhythms and communing only with himself. The study of development needs some focus and the papers
prepared for study in advance of the meetings at Dar es Salaam
staked out the themes and topics for study. The issues chosen
are those that deeply affect the present and will continue to
be central at least over the next decade, issues like the need
for and implications of a new economic order. While no attempt
was made to achieve agreement in point of view or in ideology,
and authors were chosen for their differences in experience as
well as quality of experience, they seem to have shared a number of assumptions — for example, that people can affect the
decisions that affect their lives and therefore ways of achieving fuller participation are crucial, that it is possible for
people in different cultures to share and learn from each other,
that education is rarely if ever "neutral" and that in many
senses is infused with political goals and processes.

The style of the papers is provocative. The writers were
urged to express themselves forcefully knowing that each paper
would be subjected to general discussion. The papers appear
substantially as they were first written and while the discussion of them is not appended much of it has been used in the
Design for Action which deals with implications for adult education.

President Nyerere's inaugural address was adopted, with permission, as the Conference's basic statement on the objectives
and strategies for adult education and development, and to be
known as The Declaration of Dar es Salaam.

25

"Development is for Man, by Man, and of Man": The Declaration of Dar es Salaam

Julius K. Nyerere

We in this country have no special qualifications to host a conference on Adult Education — although we are very happy to do so!
Many countries have had longer experience than ourselves in this
work; many can point to greater success. There is only one
thing we in Tanzania can claim, and that is that we are fully
aware of the fundamental importance of education as a means of
development and as a part of development.

For development has a purpose; that purpose is the liberation
of Man. It is true that in the Third World we talk a great deal
about economic development — about expanding the number of goods
and services, and the capacity to produce them. But the goods
are needed to serve men; services are required to make the lives
of men more easeful as well as more fruitful. Political, social
and economic organization is needed to enlarge the freedom and
dignity of men. Always we come back to Man — to Liberated Man
— as the purpose of activity, the purpose of development.

But Man can only liberate himself or develop himself. He cannot
be liberated or developed by another. For Man makes himself.
It is his ability to act deliberately, for a self-determined
purpose, which distinguishes him from the other animals. The
expansion of his own consciousness, and therefore of his power
over himself, his environment, and his society, must therefore
ultimately be what we mean by development.

So development is for Man, by Man, and of Man. The same is
true of education. Its purpose is the liberation of Man from
the restraints and limitations of ignorance and dependency.
Education has to increase men's physical and mental freedom —
to increase their control over themselves, their own lives, and

27

158231

the environment in which they live. The ideas imparted by
education, or released in the mind through education, should
therefore be liberating ideas; the skills acquired by education
should be liberating skills. Nothing else can properly be
called education. Teaching which induces a slave mentality or
a sense of impotence is not education at all — it is attack on
the minds of men.

This means that adult education has to be directed at helping
men to develop themselves. It has to contribute to an enlargement of Man's ability in every way. In particular it has to
help men to decide for themselves — in cooperation — what development is. It must help men to think clearly; it must enable
them to examine the possible alternative courses of action; to
make a choice between those alternatives in keeping with their
own purposes; and it must equip them with the ability to translate their decisions into reality.

The personal and physical aspects of development cannot be separated. It is in the process of deciding for himself what is
development, and deciding in what direction it should take his
society, and in implementing those decisions, that Man develops
himself. For man does not develop himself in a vacuum, in isolation from his society and his environment; and he certainly
cannot be developed by others. Man's consciousness is developed
in the process of thinking, and deciding and of acting. His
capacity is developed in the process of doing things.

But doing things means cooperating with others, for in isolation
Man is virtually helpless physically, and stultified mentally.
Education for liberation is therefore also education for cooperation among men, because it is in cooperation with others
that Man liberates himself from the constraints of nature, and
also those imposed upon him by his fellow-men. Education is
thus intensely personal in the sense that it has to be a personal experience — no one can have his consciousness developed
by proxy. But it is also an activity of great social significance, because the man whom education liberates is a man in
society, and his society will be affected by the change which
education creates in him.

There is another aspect to this. A Man learns because he wants
to do something. And once he has started along this road of
developing his capacity he also learns because he wants to be;
to be a more conscious and understanding person. Learning has
not liberated a man if all he learns to want is a certificate

on his wall, and the reputation of being a 'learned person' —
a possessor of knowledge. For such a desire is merely another
aspect of the disease of the acquisitive society — the accumulation of goods for the sake of accumulating them. The accumulation of knowledge or, worse still, the accumulation of pieces
of paper which represent a kind of legal tender for such knowledge, has nothing to do with development.

So if adult education is to contribute to development, it must
be a part of life — integrated with life and inseparable from
it. It is not something which can be put into a box and taken
out for certain periods of the day or week — or certain periods
of a life. And it cannot be imposed: every learner is ultimately a volunteer, because, however much teaching he is given,
only he can learn.

Further, adult education is not something which can deal with
just "agriculture", or "health", or "literacy", or "mechanical
skill", etc. All these separate branches of education are related to the total life a man is living, and to the man he is
and will become. Learning how best to grow soy-beans is of
little use to a man if it is not combined with learning about
nutrition and/or the existence of a market for the beans. This
means that adult education will promote changes in men, and in
society. And it means that adult education should promote
change, at the same time as it assists men to control both the
change which they induce, and that which is forced upon them by
the decisions of other men or the cataclysms of nature. Further,
it means that adult education encompasses the whole of life,
and must build upon what already exists.

Changes and Adult Education

In that case, the first function of adult education is to inspire
both a desire for change, and an understanding that change is
possible. For a belief that poverty of suffering is "the will
of God" and that man's only task is to endure, is the most fundamental of all the enemies of freedom. Yet dissatisfaction
with what is must be combined with a conviction that it can be
changed: otherwise it is simply destructive. Men living in
poverty or sickness or under tyranny or exploitation must be
enabled to recognize both that the life they lead is miserable,
and that they can change it by their own action, either individually or in cooperation with others.

Work of this kind is not often called "adult education" and it
is not usually regarded as a function of adult education associations or departments. But neither is teaching a child to
walk, or to speak, usually regarded as "education"! It is only
when a child does not learn these primary functions as it grows
out of infancy that organized education takes over the task of
teaching them in "special schools" for the deaf or the otherwise handicapped. Similarly, whether or not institutions of
adult education ought to be doing this fundamental work of
arousing consciousness about the need for, and the possibility
of, change, will depend upon the circumstances in which they
are operating. In Third World countries such work often has to
be done by someone, or some organization. It will simply be a
matter of organization and efficiency whether it is done by
people called "community development workers", or "political
education officers", or "adult teachers". What is important is
that it is done, and that all should recognize it as a necessary
basis for all other developmental and educational activities.

The same thing is true of what I would call the second stage of
adult education. That is, helping people to work out what kind
of change they want, and how to create it. For example, it is
not enough that the people in a village should come to recognize
that something can be done about their endemic malaria — that
it is not an evil which has to be endured. They also have to
learn that malaria can be treated with drugs, or prevented by
controlling mosquitoes, or that malaria can be dealt with by a
combination of curative and preventive action. And all this
must be followed up with action. Thus we have a whole series
of educational activities all of which involve a learning process — an expansion of consciousness. The combination of them
all is required if the development — of men and the environment
— is to be life-enhancing. And all of them can be assisted by
the activities of an educator.

The Scope of Adult Education

Adult education thus incorporates anything which enlarges men's
understanding, activates them, helps them to make their own
decisions, and to implement those decisions for themselves. It
includes training, but it is much more than training. It includes what is generally called "agitation" but it is much more
than that. It includes organization and mobilization, but it
goes beyond them to make them purposeful.

Thinking of adult education from the point of view of the educators, therefore, one can say that they are of two types — each
of whom needs the other. The first are what one might call the
"generalists". They are the political activists and educators
— whether or not they are members of, and organized by, a political party or whether they are community development workers
or religious teachers. Such people are not politically neutral;
by the nature of what they are doing they cannot be. For what
they are doing will affect how men look at the society in which
they live, and how they seek to use it or change it. Making the
people of a village aware that their malaria can be avoided, for
example, will cause them to make demands upon the larger community in which they live. At least they will demand drugs, or
insect spray, or teachers; they will no longer be passive
beings who simply accept the life they know. And if people who
have been aroused cannot get the change they want, or a substi-
tute for it which is acceptable to them, they will become dis-
contented — if not hostile — towards whatever authority they
regard as responsible for the failure. Adult education is thus
a highly political activity Politicians are sometimes more
aware of this fact than educators, and therefore they do not
always welcome real adult education.

The work of these "generalists" is fundamental to adult education. It is after their work has been done — that is after a
demand has been generated and a problem identified — that what
might be called the "specialists" can become effective. If you
go into a village and explain how to spray stagnant water, and
with what, you may be listened to with politeness; but your
effort has been wasted, and nothing will happen after you have
left unless the villagers first understand what the spraying
will do, and why it is important. Of course, it is possible
for the "health educator" to give this explanation himself —
he should certainly be capable of doing so, and prepared to do
so. But his specialized knowledge can be more effective — and
can be spread among a larger number of villages — if the people
have already discussed and absorbed the reasons for anti-mosquito
spraying, and developed a desire to learn how to do it for themselves.

It is at the level of this "specialist" adult education that the
division into health, agriculture, child care, management, literacy, and other kinds of education, can make sense. But none
of these branches can be self-contained; their work must be
coordinated and linked. The work of the agricultural specialist
must be linked with that of the nutritionist and that of the

people who train villagers to be more effective in selling or
buying;   and he may himself find the need to call upon — or
lead the villagers towards — the person who can teach literacy.
Adult education in fact must be like a spider's web, the different strands of which knit together, each strengthening the
other, and each connected to the others to make a coherent
whole.

But in saying that I do not wish to imply that adult education
has a beginning and an end, or that it is necessary for a particular community or individual to travel along all the various
branches of learning at a fairly simple level. The point I am
trying to make is that mass adult education — which is what most
of us are concerned with in our working lives — must not be
thought of as being in self-contained compartments, nor must it
be organized into them. If the people's felt need is improved
health, the health specialist must lead them into an awareness
of the need for improved agricultural techniques as he teaches
the elements of preventive medicine, or helps them to lay the
foundations of curative health service. And the health specialist must have organizational links with the agriculture
teacher, so that this new interest can be met as it is aroused
— and so on.

But certain individuals or communities will wish to pursue particular interest further. The mass education must be of a kind
as to show that this can be done, and to provide the tools with
which it can be done. For example, it must lead to literacy
(if it does not start with that);   and it must incorporate
access to books of different levels, even if it cannot include
provision for more formal teaching. The mass education should
also show people how to learn from the use of resources which
are locally available — like a nearby dispensary, a good farmer,
local school teachers, and so on.

For mass adult education must be seen as a beginning — a foundation course on which people can build their own structures
according to their own interests and own desires. And the adult
educator must demonstrate this function in his own activities —
that is, by continuing to expand his personal knowledge through
reading, listening to the radio, informal discussions, participation in physical development activities, and attendance at
such other organized education courses as may be available.

The Methods of Adult Education

For all these are methods of adult education, and must be understood as such. Which one, or which combination, is appropriate at a particular time will depend upon many things. But one fundamental fact must underlie the choice made. A mother does not "give" walking or talking to her child; walking and talking are not things which has "has" and of which she gives a portion to the child. Rather, the mother helps the child to develop its own potential ability to walk and talk. And the adult educator is in the same position. He is not giving to another something which he possesses. He is helping the learner to develop his own potential and his own capacity.

What all this means in practice is that the adult educator must involve the learners in their own education, and in practice, from the very beginning. Only activities which involve them in doing something for themselves will provide an on-going sense of achievement and mean that some new piece of knowledge is actually grasped — that it has become something of "theirs". It doesn't matter what form this involvement takes; it may be a contribution to a discussion, reading out loud, or writing, or making a furrow of the required depth and width. What is important is that the adult learner should be learning by doing, just as — to go back to my earlier example — a child learns to walk by walking.

There is a second very fundamental determinant of adult education method. It is that every adult knows something about the subject he is interested in, even if he is not aware that he knows it. He may indeed know something which his teacher does not know. For example, the villagers will know what time of the year malaria is worse and what group of people — by age or residence or work place — are most badly affected. It is on the basis of this knowledge that greater understanding must be built, and be seen to be built. For by drawing out the things the learner already knows, and showing their relevance to the new thing which has to be learnt, the teacher has done three things. He has built up the self-confidence of the man who wants to learn, by showing him that he is capable of contributing. He has demonstrated the relevance of experience and observation as a method of learning when combined with thought and analysis. And he has shown what I might call the "mutuality" of learning — that is, that by sharing our knowledge we extend the totality of our understanding and our control over our lives.

For this is very important. The teacher of adults is a leader,
a guide along a path which all will travel together. The organizers and teachers in an adult education programme can be no more
than that; to be effective therefore they have consciously to
identify themselves with those who are participating in it primarily as learners. Only on this basis of equality, and of sharing a task which is of mutual benefit, is it possible to make
full use of the existing human resources in the development of
a community, a village, or a nation. It is within this context
of sharing knowledge that all the different techniques of teaching can be used.

The most appropriate techniques in a particular case will depend
upon the circumstances, and the resources, of the learning community and of the nation in which it lives. For it is no good
spending time and money on elaborate visual aids which need
skilled operators and electricity, if either the skilled operator
or the electricity is lacking in the village which wants to
learn! It is no use relying upon techniques which need imported
materials if you are working in a country which has a permanent
balance of payments problem. And in a poor country the techniques
used must be of very low cost, and preferably capable of being
constructed out of local materials, at the place where the teaching will be done, and by the people who will teach and learn.
Self-reliance is a very good educational technique as well as
being an indispensable basis for further development!

The Organization of Adult Education

This need to become increasingly self-reliant in adult education,
as in other aspects of development, will have to be reflected in
the organization of adult education activities. Obviously there
is no "ideal" adult education organization pattern to which all
nations could, or should, aspire. The type of organization has
to reflect the needs, and the resources, of each country, as
well as its culture and its political commitment.

The one unavoidable thing is that resources have to be allocated
to adult education. It will not happen without them! There is
a regrettable tendency in times of economic stringency — which
for poor countries is all the time — for governments to economize
on money for adult education. And there is a tendency also, when
trained people are in short supply, to decide that adult education must wait — or to pull out its best practitioners and give
then more prestigious jobs and administration.

It would certainly be a mistake to try to duplicate for adults
the kind of educational establishment we have for children —
either in staff or buildings. The most appropriate adult teachers are often those who are also engaged in another job — who
are practitioners of what they will be teaching. But it is
necessary to have some people whose full-time work is teaching
adults, or organizing the different kinds of adult education.
And these people have to be paid wages and given the equipment,
and facilities, which are needed to be effective. How many of
them there should be, and whether they should be in one educational hierarchy or under different specialized Ministries or
Departments, will depend upon local factors, and will probably
vary from time to time. Certainly we in Tanzania have not solved
this kind of organizational problem to our satisfaction.

All this means that adult education has to be given a priority
within the overall development and recurrent revenue allocations
of governments or other institutions. And what priority it ob-
tains is perhaps one of the most political decisions a government
will take. For if adult education is properly carried out, and
therefore effective, it is the most potent force there can be
for developing a free people who will insist upon determining
their own future.

Education arouses curiosity and provokes questioning — the chal-
lenging of old assumptions and established practices. An educated *ujamaa* village, for example, will neither allow nor tolerate dishonesty among its accountants, or authoritarianism among
its leaders. An educated population will challenge the actions
of its elected representatives — including its President. Maybe
this is why adult education is generally the Cinderella of government departments, or why its function is captured by newspaper, cinema, and television owners and editors with a personal
axe to grind! And do not let me pretend that Tanzania is an
exception to any of this. Our policy commitment to adult education is clear. But our practice, and our practitioners, are
— to put it mildly — not above criticism!

But of course, even if a top priority is given to adult education, there are priorities within that priority still to be
determined. Resources are always limited. In poor and backward
countries they are laughably small in relation to the need. So
choices have to be made between such things as generalized education, different kinds of specialized mass education, the radio,
mass circulation of subsidized literature, residential education,
the training of the educators and an increase in teachers un-

trained in techniques — and so on.

Once again, there is no "best" choice or balance among all these
necessary activities. What is appropriate will depend upon the
existing level of knowledge and understanding in different fields,
and upon the existing resources in men, materials and equipment.
In Tanzania, for example, we have now broken through the stage
where miserable conditions were regarded as "the will of God".
Our present task is therefore primarily that of helping people
to acquire the tools of development — the literacy, the knowledge
of health needs, the need for improved production, the need to
improve dwelling places, and the basic skills necessary to meet
all these needs.

We are finding that the organization of this second stage is
much more difficult, with our limited resources, to ensure that
when people have learned a skill, the ploughs and the carpentry
equipment and the survey levels, etc. are also where they are
wanted and at an accessible price level!

But there is a saying that nothing which is easy is worth doing,
and it could never be said that adult education is not worth
doing! For it is the key to the development of free men and
free societies. Its function is to help men to think for themselves, to make their own decisions, and to execute those decisions for themselves.

Expanded Concepts of Development for Action

Lucille Mair

The concept of international development which has been current since the end of the Second World War has proved inapplicable to the world of the 1970s, which is a world undergoing radical transformation. Explicit in that concept was the emphasis on economic growth based on the experience of industrialized free enterprize nations. Their developmental style and strategy appeared to have served them well and it seemed feasible to the architects of the First and Second Development decades that non-industrialized nations should follow similar paths to success.

Indeed, parts of the "underdeveloped" world of Asia, Africa and Latin America and the Caribbean did make economic advances during the past two decades which can be measured by indices such as those of incomes per capita, national incomes, industrial output, and others: and such criteria are consistent with the canons laid down in the International Development Strategies. Few of these indices, however, whether showing negative or positive results, say much that is meaningful about the condition of the largest segments of the World's inhabitants; that condition of desperate poverty is well-known and the context in which we look on today's poverty is one of high visibility. For the mass communication media of today ensures that the privileged of the world knows more about the under-privileged than ever before in history, certainly more than they did 20 years ago. The converse is also true.

The disparity in the levels of living between the peoples of one region and the next widens dangerously in full international view. Faced with the evidence of the appalling lives which the vast majority of men and women lead in the three southern continents, despite two decades of "development", national and international planners now attempt to ensure that the real target of development becomes the human being who will remain central to all redefinitions and to all revised strategies. But this is not easy to achieve: for it is impossible to be confident that in critical decision-making areas there exists a commitment to development commensurate with the global scale of human deprivation. The processes in the United Nations in this regard are significant.

Search for New Development Models

The urgent need for development models which can be effective
in meeting the basic needs of men and women has accelerated the
search for a new economic world order which has been articulated
by various assemblies and organs of the United Nations. The
international community is investing much energy and expertise
in negotiating that order throughout a network of United Nations
and other bodies, regional and international. But the present
global crisis has been so inextricably linked with the energy
crisis, and other specific monetary and economic phenomena —
such as recession, inflation, and trade imbalances — that these
issues have taken centre stage. International discussions focus
on commodities, trade barriers, international debt, indexation,
price fluctuations, technology transfer, among other issues —
all of which carry fundamental implications for a restructuring
of the world system; such a restructuring will make resources
available for development. But these assemblies, inevitably
oriented towards trade and finance, could quite conceivably lose
sight of those persons who will be affected by the economic
issues under debate. These are the persons who will be either
the victims or the beneficiaries of the economic and technical
decisions taken, depending on the intensity of the human concern
which infuses these decisions. For what is really being nego-
tiated is the present and future existence of the millions of
men, women and children of the developing world.

There is a real crisis in sensitivity. One is aware, for instance, of the extent to which the energy crisis shattered the
customary political and economic self-assurance of the western
industrial democracies. While it dramatized the inter-depen-
dence of the contemporary world, it also served to drive some
of these nations into retreat on the issue of their responsibilities in relation to international development. Their commitment was always qualified in some instances; it now shows signs
of receding, while in a number of regional and international
forums the issue of protecting their own societies and economies from future shock seems the major concern. The uncertain
outcome of UNCTAD IV should make us question whether indeed the
human component of development is recognized to a degree that
can be translated into political decision-making.

As the human component of developmental planning assumes greater
significance so does the political. For if the quality of human
life determines the goals, it is the political process which
will define the means, and set the pace for development. Both

the release, as well as the acquisition of the resources needed
demands the explicit exercise of political options. Here the
crisis is one of sovereignty. It is both national and international. It touches all elements in the world community, including those which have in the past exercised extensive extra-
territorial sovereignty and those which have only recently come
into their own. Control of a major portion of the resources
required for development still rests with those who do not always
seem to grasp fully the extent of the needs of the less developed
world. Control also rests to a disturbing extent with those who
retain a vested interest in under-development. Yet the surrender
of those resources is a *sine qua non* of development.

Sovereignty and Self-reliance

Those most concerned with development — newly independent nations
— have still to come to terms fully with their own sovereignty.
Both the distinguished President of this Conference's host country, Hon. Julius Nyerere, and the Prime Minister of my own country of Jamaica, Hon. Michael Manley, have spoken and written,
with brilliant insights, about the "dependency syndrome", which
is a legacy of colonialism, which is a corollary of under-development, and an enemy of sovereignty. This syndrome is a clear
constraint on the capacity of developing nations, as independent
states, and as the world's largest group, to question in really
fundamental terms the principle of the open world economy which
they now attempt to reform, to exercise their sovereign will in
dealing nationally and internationally with the crucial problem
of distribution of resources, to design radically new structures
for development. Much of the developing world has yet to make
a radical breakthrough in conceptualization.

The historical experience of many Caribbean territories has made
them peculiarly vulnerable to this constraint on action. Their
original *raison d'être* arose out of the Western European capitalist demands for New World plantations organized towards export
monoculture and serviced by imported forced labour. Not even
the political independence achieved by the ex-British colonies
during the past decade or so served at first to modify in any
significant way the inherently dependent and external orientation
of these societies. They underwent, as a consequence, the classic application of western developmental models during the 1960s
in terms of, for example, industrialization and capital impor-
tation. They also witnessed the classic indices of the failure
of these models to enhance the lives of the region's people;

unemployment, for example, reaching nearly 25 percent in some
territories by 1972. To reverse the direction of such policies
clearly calls for a break with the past. An essential departure
point, for instance, would be a fresh assessment of agriculture
which remained the neglected area of the sixties and which
throughout the Caribbean declined in relative terms and in some
places in absolute terms.

The search for new means and targets implies drawing on the
capabilities of sovereign states to unhinge themselves from
existing international economic arrangements at the same time
that they construct their own on a foundation of collective
self-reliance. Dependency complexes still inhibit some developing countries from advancing determinedly on this path:
there is the residue of fear that to do this is to grant grat-
uitous relief to the developed countries from their global responsibilities. Certainly the task of creating regional and
international institutions virtually from scratch which reflect
an emerging Third World sense of resourcefulness, is a major
undertaking. It is no less so at the national level. But here
the potential for action is perhaps more easily identified. At
the national level effective mechanisms of change receive their
energy from a population mobilized to see itself in positive
terms as both agent and client of development. The process of
mobilization is a main function of the political process by
which authority and responsibility are exercised, resources
allocated and decisions taken. Political power which provides
the dynamic for this mobilization must be seen by all not as an
independent force but as the collective drive behind the realization of human needs. The political will must be seen to have
one justification and that a moral one.

The question then is how does a society proceed to infuse its
people with the expertise, confidence, and dynamism required for
exercising its political rights, for seizing and converting its
resources into the national good?

The function of education becomes a critical one; education in
its widest meaning implying clearly, as we have heard before in
this conference, an educational process which cannot be neutral.
It can certainly be no less neutral than pre-independence educational systems of the Third World have been. The goals of such
systems have been in the past unmistakably, if at times subtly,
directed towards sustaining the colonial establishment. Newly
independent states have usually inherited these objectives,
accepting them as supplements to the economic developmental

models in use. Their implications are vast. A network of formal educational structures together with formal and non-formal institutions of communication and information constitute what one might term the mind industry, one of the most pervasive of the supra-national enterprises, not always clearly defined as such, and perhaps, for that reason, capable of greater influence.

A recent example of the operations of this industry comes close to home. A financial journal of international prestige and influence a few months ago attacked in scathing terms economic measures adopted by a Caribbean government as part of its policy for dealing with the persistent poverty of large sectors of its population. The journal's critique was labelled, "Dismantling an Island Paradise". The title begged the question which the article (based as it was on many inaccuracies and unwarranted conclusions) left unasked and unanswered. Few persons in the Caribbean need to be informed that one man's paradise can be another man's inferno. But we know of the capacity of this "consciousness corporation" (whose local subsidiaries are often the school systems of the Third World) to turn the truth on its head. It has served to reinforce neo-colonialism, elitism, economic individualism and its resulting socio-economic imbalances, not to mention its eroding effect on indigenous cultures. This educational infrastructure — like the developmental models it supports — has to be re-shaped once its essentially political character and purpose are identified and fully understood.

Educational Reconstruction

The greatest challenge to be faced in the task of educational re-organization is unquestionably that presented by adult populations who are already conditioned, wholly or partially, towards values, skills and non-skills, many of which are irrelevant, if not dysfunctional. The process of unlearning, and re-learning is always complex.

This Conference is fortunate to be sited in a country whose leader conceived its national goals in such original and profound ways, and stated its philosophy of education for independence so comprehensively. President Nyerere's concept of "Education for Self-Reliance" has been acknowledged throughout this Conference as the creation of a man who is both visionary and pragmatist; as a consequence he produced what is both a dream and a blueprint of far-ranging application. The particular national infrastructure which may incorporate that dream and blueprint

is not the issue. What is important in the Tanzanian philosophy
is that the goal of the common national good replaces the un-
restrained right of the individual to operate within a free
market system guided by the law of maximum profit. This economic individualism is the hard core of western liberal beliefs
which evolved at another time in another place and whose validity for a Third World in convulsion must be seriously questioned.

Above all it must be questioned by those masses of men and women
who have, by western standards, few, if any technical or intellectual accomplishments but who will nevertheless provide the
momentum and the material for national reconstruction; who will
re-shape and be themselves re-shaped by a relevant educational
structure rooted in a relevant philosophy of development. The
institutional forms must therefore facilitate their multiple
function of nationalist, builder, producer, and student.

The scope of this paper allows only a few general remarks on
the subject of institutional reconstruction which is seen as an
essentially participatory experience. People in all segments
of a society, including the least articulate, have their own
views of how to organize their lives. Their perception may well
be limited by environment and opportunity. But it is a reality
which, if ignored, could be a serious counter-productive factor;
if respected and utilized it can enlarge the pool of resources
available for the learning process. The critical appraisal of
the UNESCO/UNDP Experimental World Literacy Programme has some
lessons to offer. The evaluation of the progress made in teaching young adults in a number of developing countries indicates
that authoritarian forms of teaching produced less positive
results than those which "gave explicit recognition to adult's
experience and insights as a valid starting point for learning".

The myth of the stubborn conservatism of "the little people" —
in particular those of the countryside — dies hard. Such persons, it is sometimes said, react reluctantly to innovation.
But this assumption underestimates the increasing sensitivity
of the masses of rural and urban poor to the true quality of
their lives: the corollary to this is their increasing willing-
ness to be part of an experience which offers alternatives to a
grim status quo. A greater obstacle than popular conservatism
may well be that of an entrenched bureaucracy which needs to
see itself in a changing relationship with people and with institutions, to understand the priority of the one over the
other, to develop the fexibility which permits structures to
grow out of a community's stated needs, and to accept the val-

idity of many indigenous structures which have evolved out of just such a process.

The Third World is rich in authentic cultural forms which express a people's resourceful response to the challenges they face daily, whether in the field of religious, agricultural, financial, or domestic organization. To salvage and to maximize traditional values and systems is not to step backwards in time but rather to ensure that revised developmental policies are humane, rational, and truly dynamic as they use the secure base of the old and familiar to launch into the new and unknown. "We are moving", writes Martha Stuart, a communications pathfinder who has made imaginative use of videotape, "from a world of authority and control to one of information and choice". And out of this concept emerged programmes which employ today's media technology in innovative ways not to alienate people from their traditional societies or themselves but to put them more fully in touch with themselves, with each other, and with the options which tomorrow offers.

Women as Agents of Development

There is already evidence to suggest that at least one vital segment of a population — women — respond readily to such non-authoritarian, informal situations of group interaction and experience sharing which is related to future needs and sets in motion a progression towards creative solutions. This is significant for any expanded concept of development. For it will be impossible to move towards the innovative policies demanded for the remainder of this century without taking into full account what that process will require of women, who constitute the majority of the adult population of the developing world and who have been the classic non-participants in development. In their condition is found both a rationale and a catalyst for change. For some of the most compelling evidence of the failure of western models to solve the human problems of the 1960s and 1970s related to women; and this fact alone, if no other, constitutes reason enough for re-evaluation and redirection of these models.

Many basic assumptions of developmental experts missed their targets; in the case of women, their stereotypes of female occupations being often at odds with reality. A tendency to under-rate the real contribution of women to the domestic economy in so many underdeveloped countries led to the neglect of

their potential for participation in a modern economy;   as a
consequence few of the tools of development went their way.
One consequence was to confound the optimistic thesis of "inevitable improvement" which the planners of the 1950s popularized.
The reverse became true of women the majority of whom — in the
words of the economist Dr. Irene Tinker — "are playing more res-
trictive economic roles today than in the pre-developed economy".
The capital intensive projects which accompanies "bootstrap"
programmes of Latin America and other developing regions made
women's customary economic skills obsolete without offering alternative openings. The overall Gross National Product of many
such countries did indeed often rise but at the expense of large
groups of the population, including conspicuously, women.

Today some of the most critical indicators of under-development
relating to health, education and economic opportunity apply
preponderantly to the women of the developing world. The appalling incidence of infant mortality and malnutrition throughout
the Third World says as much about the condition of women as
about the condition of infants. Women constitute the largest
percentage of those persons who cannot read or write. Their
rate of unemployment is the highest in many regions. In the
Caribbean, for example, an alarming national rate of unemployment of 23 percent or 25 percent conceals an even more alarming
statistic — the level of female unemployment which is over 30
percent, approximately twice that of male. It is still more
disturbing that few developmental strategies, either national
or international, have really come to terms with the significance
of that female bulge in the phenomenon of under-development.
It is perhaps true to say that conceptually it is acknowledged;
implementation, however, lags behind. The condition of women
has still to be made an integral component of any analysis and
appraisal of developmental policies. Even the United Nations,
which played a dominant role in alerting the world to the dimensions of women's under-development, is only now moving slowly in
the direction of making it an explicit index in the review of
international development strategies.

A clear implication for any expanded concept of development
which replaces quantitative by qualitative criterion is that
women must unequivocally be targets of development. There
should perhaps be no need to state the case for women as agents
of development. And especially so in the field of adult education where women represent large proportions of those who teach
as well as those who are taught. In the Caribbean women constitute the majority of adult educators. I doubt that this is

unique to that region, but it is a fact which has not been conspicuously reflected in the presentations of this Conference or the composition of its main speakers. It appears that the case does need re-statement. And in that context recent and striking manifestations of women's part in the dynamics of national progress deserve mention.

The past two decades or so have witnessed the remarkable mobilization of large sectors of the female population in the liberation movements of Africa, Asia and Latin America, in particular the countries of Vietnam, Cuba, Angola, Mozambique, Guinea Bissau. In these people's wars, where no one is a civilian, women, fully understanding the political forces at work, have performed strategic functions as educator, communicator, informer and active combatant; they have quickly learned some of the new skills needed for the people's victory and they have transmitted as they have learned. In the process they have also enlarged their own horizons as women. Thereby they have maximized the resources available for the challenge, not only of national liberation, but also of national reconstruction.

To harness that latent dynamism in women could open up vast possibilities for expanding developmental concepts and goals as indeed for adult education as well.

Implications of a New International Economic Order

Amir H. Jamal

Such commitments as have been made by the international community to build a new economic order would not have been possible without the solidarity and singleness of purpose on the part of developing countries with their demand for a just and equitable economic order in the world.

Indeed, the *raison d'être* for a new economic order is a global development process, interdependent but deliberately weighed in favour of the poor developing countries. Thus, it is just not possible to conceive of a new economic order without making "development" its central purpose; development not of the few but of the many, which means the development of the poor on this earth.

The task now facing the international community is that of ensuring that the world's resources will be immediately and increasingly directed towards meeting the very reasonable demands of the historically disfranchised majority of the world's population.

Both the developed and the developing countries need to apply themselves to the performance of this task, separately as well as together. The development of the under-developed must be the core of public policy of all countries, rich as well as poor.

This will only happen when there is adequate and timely realization of certain facts.

Facts to be Recognized by Industrialized Countries

In the first place, the rich industrialized countries of the world must recognize that there is a law of accelerating capital formation which leads to accumulation of capital in the hands of the technologically advanced societies. Put in clear terms, it is that the more dynamic the actual empirical process of technological development, the more will it lead to accumulation of capital. And since so much new capital is formed globally in any given period of time in the context of international trade and exchange, the greater accumulation of capital in some soc-

47

ieties is inevitably at the expense of the others.

Another fact which the industrialized rich countries must recognize is that the values which permeate their total economic activity directed at developing new technology, inexorably make capital formation their central purpose almost by definition. Thus industrialized societies are caught between multiplying the modes as well as material contents of consumption and producing even more "efficiently" through developing new technology. In the process, the essential humanity of man is being surrendered in favour of almost mindless production and consumption. This poses a threat to humanity.

Another fact which the industrialized countries must recognize is that the parallel accretion of poverty in other parts of the world, as a direct consequence of the interplay of economic forces weighed in favour of accelerating technology, also poses a threat to the survival of humanity, because humanity to be meaningful has to be synonymous with human dignity. And poverty and human dignity cannot co-exist indefinitely, much less on a deteriorating gradient.

Facts Developing Countries Must Recognize

The developing countries, on their part, must also recognize certain facts.

They must realize that the more adverse the environment surrounding them in the form of spiralling technological development, the more resolutely they will have to sustain themselves through their own efforts on the basis of collective self-reliance. They must recognize that imitating the consumption and thus production practices and modes of the developed industrialized countries is no answer to their problems. The historical imperative which they have to impart to the world is the rejection of the values underlying production and consumption in the rich countries and replacing them with the construction of mutually reinforcing co-operative societies fully in control of the machines they have created.

The developing countries must realize that imitating the consumption modes of the industrialized countries is to ensure alienation from their own reality with all its attendant consequences.

The developing countries must see in the present vertically growing global industrial process, a challenge and an opportunity to depart from this process by directing their aspirations towards the achievement of dignity through co-operative production and consumption in accordance with all essential human needs, both material and cultural.

Developing countries must recognize that even if they did not feel compelled to question the values prevailing in the industrialized countries, the sheer arithmetic of an average global per capita income figure of the same magnitude as obtaining in the industrialized countries does not provide any valid basis at all. If striving to get as rich as the rich was to be their single purpose, only interminable human strife and conflict is bound to be the world's heritage. The developing countries would have added no new original chapters to the unfolding of human history, only more pages of war and turmoil, with different *dramatis personnae* acting out their parts.

Simultaneous and Parallel Process

Both the developing and the developed countries will have to recognize that they must work together so as to disengage the world from its present collision course and to move it towards less acquisitiveness on the part of the rich and less envy on the part of the poor.

By definition the process will have to be both simultaneous and parallel. The developing countries will have to undertake their own revolution. Only Tanzanians can bring about the much needed change in their own society. To do this, they have accepted that they should build only one society in which the alien tendencies of class division give way to a society where all work co-operatively in total mutual dependence. Unless their own total development strategy is deliberately conceived to make this possible, Tanzanians will not be able to make any significant contribution to the process of global development aimed at achieving similar objectives internationally.

Essentially, developing countries have to restructure their entire educational system as a matter of priority. This means re-training and re-tooling a whole society, taking into account the specialized needs of particular sectors and the overall needs of the country as a whole. And for countries such as Tanzania, where 90 per cent of the people live rural lives, it

is quite obvious that the entire thrust of educational effort
has to reflect, without delay, the realities of our villages
even as the villages themselves discover their own entity,
through self-management. It is only when the villages produce
their basic needs, or exchange their specialized products with
the products of other villages, when they develop their own cultural pursuits, and develop a continuous relationship with the
administrative and technical capability of the state on the
basis of equality, that we will be able to claim that the Tanzanian revolution has fulfilled its historical task of establishing dynamic balance between production and consumption to
meet the needs of all and not just a few.

Internationally, the parallel process of reforming global institutions and the global framework of trade and exchange must begin in earnest without delay. Because the efforts of poor countries to re-train and re-tool themselves, so as to free themselves from the inherited colonial premises in the direction of
self-fulfilment, will be surely frustrated in the absence of
fundamental reforms of international development and finance
institutions and of the policies of the industrialized countries.

If the developing countries continue to bear the burden of the
unjust terms of trade reflected in the exchange of raw materials
and commodities with the products of capital intensive technology, of shipping freight rates weighed so much in favour of the
rich countries (shipping freight from London to the Seychelles
and Dar es Salaam to the Seychelles is identical), of the trans-
fer-price practices of the transnationals operating globally,
and a multitude of similar injustices, what hope is there for
capital accumulation within our own borders, so essential for
re-investing in productive efforts?

Identifying the New Economic Order

So, those who dare speak about a new international economic
order must accept that only the convergence of the efforts of
the rich through reform of their own as well as of international
institutions and of the poor through their efforts to re-train
and re-tool themselves in accordance with their total needs,
will lead to the emergence of a new order.

An economic order is certainly not a static concept. A just
and equitable order will be all the more dynamic to be itself.
Indeed, only by clearly building into it a process which moves

inexorably towards ceaseless lessening of injustice and inequity
will it be possible to identify it as the new economic order.

The poor countries are not immediately going to be all equally
less poor or immediately reduce their poverty in equal proportion. The process will be long and tortuous because despite
deliberate structures, mechanisms and policies aimed at increasing their capability for self-development, some will develop
more rapidly and spread the benefits more widely than others.
The economic order will not be any less just or equitable for
that.

Questions to be Answered

The real criteria will be: Is the process deliberately conceived
both by the rich and the poor? Has it arrested and reversed
the automatic accumulation of capital in the hands of the already
rich? Has it created irreversible conditions for accumulating
capability in the hands of the poor, for meeting their essential
needs unimpeded by the powerful combination of technology and
financial resources? Has it created a certainty in the minds
and hearts of the poor that as long as they put in a good day's
work, they can look forward in their life time to getting water
for all, to educating their children without exception, to con-
structing reasonable shelter in accordance with their climatic
needs, to producing adequate food for their needs, and above
all to achieving all this in a framework of co-operation rather
than conflict or competition?

If what I have said so far makes any sense at all, the international community will have to co-operate in rapidly developing
appropriate means to meet these ends.

Today science and technology serve for the most part the purpose
of capital accumulation in the hands of the few. Instead science
and technology must now move into the rural areas and the slums
of the world, and make a frontal attack there in the service of
healthy human development. It is a colossal waste of global resources for the rich to continue to direct science and technology to increase their own capacity for still higher consumption
as well as towards arming themselves more efficiently so as to
defend the process of their accelerating consumption, when the
same effort aimed at the villages and slums of the poor countries
would benefit ten times more people, and by doing so provide a
more lasting basis for security than all arms piled up together.

At present the world is threatened with multiplicity of institutions ostensibly intended to promote co-operative effort.
The picture is somewhat frightening. It looks as if an enormous
global bureaucracy is pursuing Parkinson's law on a global scale.

Science and Technology: A Service of All

Even those who are loudest in protesting against this process
are, in fact, contributing to the same process with their efforts
to either dominate or neutralize such institutions in accordance
with their political and economic motivations. In doing so, they
devise new means which all add up to make the world a pyramid of
functionaries to serve functionaries truly gigantic. The burden
of carrying this weight is adding to the other burdens of the
poor countries.

If science and technology truly are to serve global objectives
of development, then the world has to embark quickly on the task
of re-tooling the world's institutions to meet these ends. Time
must be made an ally, not an enemy, to achieve it.

Clearly a new economic order must embody a technique for development as much as providing the minimum essential resource conditions to enable the technique to work. And since means condition ends, a just and equitable order must imply co-operative
effort for global self-development. Only such co-operation can
hope to lead to a just and equitable economic order.

The People's Involvement in Development
Ben Mady Cissé

Development is a result of man's action on nature. It is man's attempt to transform nature in order to improve his own condition. Development cannot be exclusively economic because it affects all dimensions of human existence. This is especially true in the framework of a group carrying out development in response to the challenge of its environment — an environment which has become more complex as a result of the rapid changes characteristic of the 20th century.

As traditional institutions become obsolete they can no longer meet the requirements of a modern world. Concise guidelines are needed to assert the status of our independence and to allow for our full-fledged entry into the family of nations. At the same time, we must have an image of man which fosters the development of new values and the rethinking of old ones in an effort to bring them up to date. The pace at which we are forced to develop today is much different from that of the past, and our goals far surpass the concerns of our ancestors.

So that man can best resolve the conflicts which inevitably arise between "having the most" and "being the most", he must develop in a society which is adapted to his needs and over which he has lasting control. National growth, therefore, must become more humane. Beyond its lifeless statistical dimension, national growth must be "development" as in the definition of François Peroux: "the transition from a less human to a more human situation".

While still giving priority to economic goals, such an approach to development also includes all the sociological, health, social, cultural and even political factors which, in turn, motivate man and condition his behaviour. The complexity of the problems of development impose decisions on governments — not only for reasons of effectiveness but also for reasons of human development.

Although development does, in fact, require capital and technical expertise, it implies, as a vital prerequisite, a national will and an internal effort in each country. A nation can

progress successfully only through internal development and
reliance on its own human resources. In such a way, all classes
are involved and first experience development on a personal
level. The nation must encourage and motivate each individual
to enable him to freely and willingly take part in the development of his country.

To fulfil this prerequisite takes time and requires plans, programmes and projects which should not be imposed. On the contrary, they should be derived from a concerted effort on the
part of everyone, and should aim for the true involvement of
the people at all stages from design to implementation.

Therefore, the idea is not only to disseminate new techniques.
Vague psychological measures are not enough either. On a deeper
level, there must be a realization by each social group of its
responsibilities and a subsequent deepening of the realization
as the group — through increased knowledge and training enabling
group action on an informal basis — progressively commits itself.

The diversity of our countries and our resources, of our aptitudes and potential and the fine differences in political options
are such that one could not expect the existence of a unified
concept of development. But, with our technological backwardness in mind, "a minimum of agreement leaving the future open"
should lead us towards the same goal. This goal is to define a
national development policy directed by people who are capable
of developing it into a dynamic and well adapted framework and
who are, at the same time, capable of promoting unity in our
fight against deterioration in the conditions of trade.

The undertaking will be successful only when all participatory
structures are involved in a multi-purpose organization for
development. These structures — the outgrowth of training and
animation methods — are concerned with the people. Assuming
the economic functions which condition the growth of productivity, these participatory structures give rise to organizations
at the grass roots level, organizations which are, in their
turn, participatory. Conceived as points of action for both
government and the work of *animation*, these local institutions
also extend their commitment to economic tasks, assessment of
needs and their evaluation, collective bargaining, distribution
and management of marketing structures.

This double progression makes participation structures viable
entities that unite and co-ordinate the various means and goals

of development. Thus, the local organizations are basic units
where goals are adapted and carried out by the people. In order
that local units so formed may be factors of progress, they must
be true communities represented by responsible leaders who are
truly chosen by the group and who willingly share their knowledge and training with the members of their group.

This requirement implies that any action to increase the people's
participation cannot be limited to strictly technical or sec-
torial dimensions. Such action must, on the contrary and in
response to those participating in development, induce various
activities in accordance with the realities of existing conditions in their full human dimensions. If the approach taken to
achieve productivity or other economic goals is to have any
lasting effectiveness, it must allow for all aspects of the
people and their communities — their problems, their needs and
their aspirations.

Within this concept of development the role of catalyst belongs
to the State. It must fulfil, at the outset, very different
tasks which relate to the developing nation. As actual communities become capable of assuming responsibilities directly, decentralization is called for. The State's basic approach will
be one of education, training, teaching and group activities;
this approach is to enable the communities to organize with the
necessary competence to take over development operations.

Such is the concept that the Senegalese people have of their
society. It is this ideology, which is the basis of work in
animation, that has led to the creation of an Office for
Human Development. This office is the focus of the entire policy of participatory development undertaken by the State.
According to this ideology the central element of education for
development is the dialogue initiated between local institutions,
which are the people, and the institutions of the State.

From the earliest days of its independence, Senegal has opted
for:

        — development arising from a national awareness of the
need to take responsibility and from active involvement on the
part of all citizens;

        — development that integrates all dimensions of man and
which is not restricted to mere economical growth, though the
latter is a basic condition of national existence;

—development which is based on our own reality, on our
values and on our structures, and which, through a process of
adaptation, permits that reality and those values and structures
to contribute to the overall national development effort.

It is within this context that education has necessarily been
reconsidered so that everyone — literate and illiterate, adults
and children, men and women — could see this nation-wide project
in their own social and cultural context, could contribute to it
in a determined and effective manner and could receive, in return, the information and training they need. It was necessary
to devise a new approach based on dialogue and on active, collective and progressive educational principles.

The foremost authority in charge of development is the State
which serves the interests of all the people. It is up to the
State to devise this educational approach and then execute it.
For this purpose, Senegal has created a unique organization
called *animation*. It is responsible for turning over the
realization of development to the basic communities and all the
consequences that this participation implies.

Animation has many roles. It is a State organ   It is, even
more, a network: a network of group leaders (men and women)
freely chosen by their basic communities; a network in which
group leaders become the seeds of progress without changing
their status. If this network is effective, and is really an
integral part of the people, it should be able to initiate and
support a direct dialogue between organized communities and
State and institutional authorities.

This dialogue implies a tremendous effort from the people as
well as from the authorities; an education effort to bring both
sides to accept each other, to come together, to listen to each
other and to search together for solutions to everyday, tangible
problems. If both communities and authorities fulfil their
mutual responsibilities, this implies that they must organize
accordingly and work out a new kind of relationship that is more
open and more dynamic. This is the purpose of administrative
decentralization which was established at the time of independence. While bringing the authorities closer to the people,
these policies, at the same time, lead the people to take over
all the functions from the State that their abilities qualify
them to fulfil.

The development structures established at different levels

throughout the nation and their purposes are:

— seminars for middle-level staff which bring together
cadres within an area to discuss specific topics of relevance
to the activities. These seminars cover several weeks. Through
first-hand contact with the people in their villages, participants study development projects of interest. When these projects have been studied and drawn up they are organized into a
programme which is carried out on a contract basis with the
State;

— district "field days" which enable rural councillors,
who are delegates of the people, to better understand their role
in administration of the budget, in land distribution and, in
rural community organizations;

— the National School of Applied Economics (ENEA), where
middle-level cadres receive the kind of training that enables
them, upon graduation, to assume responsibilities in national
planning;

— the Centre for Basic and Advanced Administrative Training (CFPA), which offers dynamic training to middle-level cadres
of all sectors of the administration, so that they are true
agents of development;

— the Centre for Polyvalent Studies for Adults (CEPA)
provides continuous training through refresher courses and
appropriate training for all cadres so as to enhance the value
of their life experiences;

— the Standing Committee for *Animation* in Government
Agencies (CPAAP), a meeting ground for all sectors of the Government where officials can re-think their problems in order to
better co-ordinate them with national development.

Animation, as a moral guide to development, prepares the coming of a civilization in which people who are aware of their
own problems organize to solve them in freedom and justice.

Therefore, Senegal's first step as an independent nation was to
turn its attention to the rural sector. This sector not only
includes 80 per cent of the population but is also the basis of
the economy and of the social life of the nation. From colonial
times, farmers had been the most exploited class of the population, but also the least colonized. Even today, only they can
grow the crops that free us from dependency on the outside world.
Because they can provide the most solid foundation to our economy they constitute our most genuine cultural assets.

Far from stifling traditional values, development is genuine
only if it is rooted in those values which are still alive among
the people and if it can adjust these values to present realities. Development will be genuine only by taking shape within
our local institutions, by helping institutions grow in accordance with today's socio-economic life to become the foundation
of the society we are building. That is why *animation* is
equally concerned with listening to the people and with educating them. *Animation* helps people to express themselves and
to make themselves heard by constantly transmitting grass-roots
reactions to higher levels. One of its goals is to encourage
people to examine the structures in which they live in an effort
to find structures which are more adequate to development activities.

Development does not take place without a certain amount of
challenge. At each new step, new problems appear. Therefore,
we must constantly go back to the fundamental options which
serve as the basis of all *animation* work and which must be
the guiding principles of all forms of action. They are:

        a) involvement of all the constituents of the develop-
ing nation on a personal, motivated and determined basis;

        b) a global outlook which integrates all the social,
economic, cultural and political spheres;

        c) respect for traditions and for local institutions
in which all development must have its roots;

        d) adjustment of the state administration to the re-
quirements of development which are based mainly upon a national
effort and on the strength of the masses.

Animation is all-embracing. Since all dimensions of the individual are involved, the basic correlation should make it possible for him to receive a thorough education. Another aspect
of *animation* is a process of consciousness-raising which helps
the individual define himself and at the same time make the
necessary tools available to him to reaffirm his determination.
The different aims of the Office for Human Development respond
to this need. By having the individual deliberately transcend
the limitations of his own environment, the Rural and Urban
Animation Administration appeals to the consciousness of each
citizen to lead him in the direction of the road to progress.
Rural Vocational Training gives the individual the necessary
technology to become a member of a modern world which he can
control through his ability to write. Young people, respectful

of their past but mobilized by a functional education, carry on
the civilization of their people. This reliance on our own
values conditions our consideration of contributions from the
outside world and purifies these so that they can become our
own. It is through this effort, and by building on their knowledge, that our societies de-alienate themselves and create our
own modern society.

In such a context, the role of education and that of the social
educator take on considerable importance. Information must be
selected and transformed by contact with existing reality into
original, but adapted, knowledge which can be accepted by the
group as its own. Before being transmitted, the message to be
received must, therefore, undergo a kind of metabolim which
brings it into the dimensions of those for whom it is intended.

The social educator must avoid facile attitudes through which
the masses can invent their development ideology without giving
it any specific design. Between a mindless wait-and-see attitude and one of dictatorial control, the educator must create
the conditions which are necessary to enable the masses to play
an active role in organizing their development.

Such a process implies practice in the analysis of reality on
the part of the individual himself. This analysis points out
relationships between the different sectors of development as
well as solutions to the challenges of the environment and the
consequences of one's actions. Awareness of these close relationships between material actions and the legitimate ideal,
between economic activities and traditional techniques, makes
it possible to define a new social project which gives satisfaction to the group and urges its members to willingly recognize its structures and to choose a way of life that is better
adapted to their own spirit. Any response to problems of the
environment gives meaning to the group decision.

In this way, the social educator becomes a true agent of development as a vehicle of progress. This progress is pragmatic
and respects the environment, its structures and the people
living therein. As such, the educator is aware that economic
changes alone cannot bring about development. It is also true
that any development without economic growth is an empty prom-
ise. The educator cannot work in isolation. His action is
valid only if it is carried out in collaboration with other
development workers. Since he is better prepared to understand
the universal social character of the group than are technical

cadres, he can and must lead them to reconsider their action
in the light of this universal nature, to analyze the values
they hold and to evaluate them in the light of their ability to
help the individuals they are working with to master reality.

Can we draw conclusions? In the developing world, more than
anywhere else, any conclusion is temporary. Successive changes
constantly modify the context of the problem, and each change
requires an appropriate solution. The thrust of any kind of
education which aims at participation is towards making an
adjustment which is in the profound interests of the societies
concerned. At the same time the thrust should mobilize societies so that the outcome of a comparison between even the recent
past and the present becomes their own, so that they can see a
promising future.

Elsewhere, the problem has been to determine whether progress
should be condemned. But our technological backwardness forces
us to seek progress wholeheartedly, although we must be selec-
tive. Let us say that between the question of the existence of
progress and that of its importance, we would seek the latter
and begin with it in order to make, at each stage, a better
choice of the quantities of progress.

This situation, which applies particularly to our young independent states, should make us unite more fully to face the threat
of apocalypse brought upon us by the "malaise" among the great
nations and by the deterioration in the conditions of trade.
This urgent political task should be the most important goal of
the Organization of African Unity if we are to "appeal to the
conscience and the foresight of the advanced nations" concerning
our vital needs — the needs that we ourselves will have defined,
and not those suggested to us. In the context of this search
for a plan of action which would liberate us, planning would
enable us to compare our strategies, to know our needs and to
determine the stages of our progress. But above all, it would
make us understand that if the people are receiving the necessary training and knowledge, their concerted involvement will
considerably accelerate the development of our countries.

Education and Equality: A Vision Unfulfilled
Majid Rahnema

Until quite recently, it was assumed that the process of development would not only increase the economic resources available
to society but at the same time ensure their more equitable distribution. Greater expenditures on education, health care and
other public services were expected to improve the well-being
of all and, particularly, that of the under-privileged elements
of society.

If we consider the amount of legislation that has been placed
upon the statute books, or even the growing number of new social
service institutions, we apparently find ample support for this
optimistic view. If, however, we search behind these legal and
institutional facades and examine the underlying power relationships which are the source of inequalities, our assessment of
the situation will be less sanguine. Between the abstract legal
right and the actual ability to exercise that right looms an
enormous and expanding gap.

It is a hard and bitter fact that the usual outcome of economic
growth has been the exacerbation rather than the alleviation of
inequality. The expansion of education and health services,
increased public employment opportunities and other measures
and products of development have served not to narrow but to
widen the gap between rich and poor. While the rhetoric of
development has stressed equality, its observable consequence
has been the production of inequality.

THE EDUCATION CRISIS: THREE MAJOR TRENDS

Three major trends are particularly evident in the developing
nations and also appear in more subtle forms in the developed
nations. The first two are hastening the educational crisis
while the third attempts to avert it by introducing reforms.

1)   The expansion of formal schooling.
     Regardless of the widely-recognized, almost universal,
     crisis confronting education systems, as expenditures on
     formal schooling consume an increasing proportion of nat-

ional revenues, the trend towards linear expansion of the
formal system persists. Formal schooling continues to
appropriate the bulk of all resources allocated to education and a growing percentage of national wealth.

2)   The irrelevance of the educational systems to genuine dev-
      elopment.
      Despite attempts to make the formal system more relevant
      to individual and collective needs, it remains largely in-
      different — if not positively hostile — to the objectives
      of a truly democratic, man-centred and humanizing society.
      Most of the existing systems spawn the alienated and alien-
      ating elites who, while themselves failing to foster dev-
      elopment, actively discourage the emergence of endogenous
      development patterns founded upon the creativity and self-
      reliance of individuals and groups, particularly among the
      rural masses. So-called "reforms" of educational curricula
      and structures, while ostensibly designed to adapt these to
      the needs of a nation and its citizens, have, in fact,
      frequently served only the needs of an internationally-
      constituted power structure and the prevailing international
      division of labour upon which it is based.

3)   The growth of non-formal education.
      The concepts of life-long, non-formal and adult education
      have recently received considerable attention. Almost
      everywhere lip-service is paid to them. Educational plan-
      ners appear, at last, to be showing a serious interest in
      these forms of education as offering a "parallel track"
      to the formal system and, more generally, a means of adap-
      ting education to labour and production needs. Non-formal
      education is now popularly perceived as a miraculous "beast
      of burden", whose small appetite will not deplete the
      economic feeding trough and whose strong back can "deliver
      the goods" to areas inaccessible to the formal system.

Many well-meaning people sincerely believe that the education
crisis may be overcome by applying the concepts of life-long,
non-formal and adult education. However, there is little evidence that the introduction of non-formal programmes has succeeded in making education more relevant to the overall needs
of individuals and societies. Nor has it resulted in a more
equitable distribution of educational and other social services.

Why have such potentially promising methods failed? Is the lack
of success due to mistakes that can be identified by critically

examining past experiments and then corrected by applying a
new educational strategy, or does it stem from the fact that
the underlying problems are, as I believe them to be, more in-
sidious and deeply rooted?

EDUCATIONAL REFORM AND SOCIAL CHANGE

Attempts to reform education without changing the structure of
society or — even more ambitiously — to transform society through
educational action alone are, I contend, founded upon a basic
misunderstanding of the part-whole relationship of education
and society. Such attempts vastly over-estimate the role of
education, ascribing to it an importance in the shaping of society that it simply does not possess.

A glance at the educational situation of the past decades rev-
eals the close interdependence of education and the wider socio-
economic structures of which it is a part. In most countries,
economic growth and increased productivity have not led to
greater economic equality. Similarly, educational growth has
not led to greater educational equality or to more democratic
access to education.

Schooling and Inequality

The school system may still claim to give a fair and equal chance
to all and, in so doing, to play an important role in the demo-
cratization of society. This may be true in principle, but in
practice only a minute percentage of the less privileged classes
actually reach the top. Further more, the system has little or
no effect on the power structure and the inequalities upon which
it is based. It merely integrates a few successful members of
the disadvantaged classes into the ruling elite, thereby strengthening the very structures that constitute the basis of existing inequalities. Educational reform cannot transform the
social structures that breed inequality. Such reform will remain a marginal activity in constant danger of erosion or per-
verse distortion if the structure of society is not itself
transformed in a manner capable of sustaining and supporting
the movement toward equality.

LIBERATION EDUCATION: ITS ROLE AND LIMITATIONS

One must beware of concluding from the foregoing remarks that
nothing can be done. In fact, a liberating and "conscientizing"
type of education could conceivably be a catalyst in the process
of accomplishing the needed social transformations. The problem
is that changes are either not tolerated in societies based on
class or elite domination or, at best, constitute exceptions to
the rule. In any event, they can hardly lead to meaningful
structural alteration unless they are part of a wider political
action.

The Political Role of Education

The educator must always act simultaneously as an authentic
teacher and an active agent of social change. His role should
be not only technocratic and purely pedagogical or professional
in nature but also political, in the widest sense of that term.
This aspect is of crucial importance in measuring the true dimensions of educational action under different socio-political
conditions.

A truly liberating educator will use dialogue as a political
instrument to increase people's awareness and assist them to
accept their responsibility as the primary agent of their liberation. Rather than offering them ready-made solutions, the
educator's mission is to initiate learners into the art of posing questions, to develop their ability to see the world clearly
and to help them find their own way in full solidarity with
their fellow-men. Education can thus become an integral part
of a much wider effort to achieve social and economic liberation, to mobilize human and other resources and to develop the
inner potentialities of communities with a view to their collective promotion.

The Limitations of Educational Reform

Unfortunately, this type of education is not always possible.
In most cases, the masses are either insufficiently prepared or
flatly denied the right to bring about the basic societal
changes needed to create an educational process designed to liberate men. Under these circumstances, prospects for significant
and effective action are indeed very dim, yet it may still be
possible to initiate reforms on a restricted scale. Educational

planners should, however, be clearly aware of the institutional
limits to their actions.

Despite the many obstacles to necessary social change, a more
rational and equitable allocation of resources to educational
activities may constitute a first step in the right direction.
It is essential, however, not to confuse symptoms with causes.
The actions that planners are empowered to initiate may, although
needed, be insufficient to overcome the forces producing inequality. Well-intentioned changes — under certain conditions — may
actually aggravate the underlying problems or cause them to
manifest themselves in new ways.

Non-formal or adult education is a case in point. The inefficiency of formal education systems, modelled on those of the
West, has been so evident that non-formal education, in whatever
form and under whatever conditions it has been introduced, has
proved its relative superiority. In terms of both educational
efficiency and cost effectiveness, non-formal and adult education activities have yielded much more satisfactory results than
those produced by the formal school system. This is especially
true of functional literacy programmes and other similar non-
formal activities aimed at applying need-oriented and problem-
related approaches.

It would, however, be a mistake to over-estimate the potential
of such activities. While non-formal education may prove successful in achieving narrowly-defined objectives — such as skill
training — it does not appear to have removed the socio-economic
barriers which prevent the under-privileged from applying the
learning resources of society to the betterment of their lives.
Let us not be deceived into believing that these ventures point
the way toward wider reforms of the structure of society. If
motivated solely by the objectives of greater productivity,
better processing and modernization, non-formal education will
have very limited impact indeed. It may possibly be more
effective in reaching manpower training targets. It may even
provide a temporary solution to the problems of employment, particularly in the case of people rejected by the school system.
It may actually help certain disadvantaged groups to acquire
greater cognitive or vocational skills, to improve their lot
slightly and to gain better individual chances of social achievement.

Yet, precisely because such improvements increase the efficiency
of the sub-system, their ultimate contribution to equality will

be negligible — indeed, it may be negative. The non-formal
system, far from generating reform, may become a prop supporting
the power structures responsible for the inequality it is designed to combat. In any event, it is barely conceivable that
better allocation of educational resources alone is capable of
re-structuring non-formal or even formal education in such a
way as to play a major part in changing the "rules of the game"
governing the organization of society.

STRATEGIES FOR EDUCATIONAL REFORM

The Ultimate Solution

Given the basic interdependence of the educational sub-system
and the greater societal system, it seems clear to me that ultimately the only logical and effective solution is to plan educational actions as an integral part of the overall re-structuring of society. It is naive to believe that a liberating,
human-centred, equality-oriented education system can operate
or succeed within a society geared to different and conflicting
objectives. It is equally naive to suppose that an elite-ruled,
technocratic and modernizing society will for long tolerate an
education system which threatens to become a powerful instrument
of internal subversion.

Education is meaningful only where and when it helps people in
their daily efforts to create a better and more congenial life,
to humanize the world and to enrich their *praxis*. Only thus
can education be liberating; and a liberating education can
only take place and develop in a society deeply committed to
human liberation at all levels.

However, few countries are prepared to adopt such a revolutionary and "radical" position, even if it provides the only ultimate solution to the problem. They favour an alternative and
evolutionary approach, calling for a re-definition of educational
priorities and a re-allocation of resources designed to ensure
a more equitable distribution of income and social services.

Makeshift Solutions

The available alternatives are: a) to increase allocations to
non-formal or adult education while continuing to promote the
linear expansion of the formal schooling system; b) to init-

iate a series of reforms leading to the re-structuring of the education system as a whole, taking into account the wider objectives of development and the lessons already learned from non-formal and adult education programmes in different parts of the world.

The easier alternative. The first solution is the simpler and more familiar of the two. Yet, it is the less effective for three main reasons: <u>Firstly</u>, it tends to turn non-formal or adult education into a second-best or "bargain basement" solution geared to the disadvantaged and the drop-outs. <u>Secondly</u>, it creates the illusion that non-formal education activities are being promoted. In fact, what happens almost inevitably is that the formal education system continues, as a result of public pressure, to receive the lion's share of available resources and the minute budget allotted to non-formal activities is reduced whenever Governments are in difficulty. <u>Thirdly</u>, by maintaining and widening the gap between the two types of education, it minimizes the chances of their ultimate integration within a single system.

The better alternative. It is to the second solution, i.e. the integration of all education programmes, formal and non-formal, within a totally re-structured system, that one must turn for more comprehensive and imaginative action. The problem of the re-distribution of resources will no longer be presented as a rigid choice between two opposing and on-going types of activity, but will be based upon criteria established after re-definition of the overall needs and aims of education, taking into account all dimensions of development.

The first requirement is a systematic approach to educational needs as related to all other aspects of development. It necessitates constant reference to the re-defined goals and objectives of society.

Principles and priorities. Priorities should be established with respect to the overall needs and objectives of society, rather than to those of the educational sub-system alone. Thus, a wide spectrum of factors should be taken into account, including:

    a) the country's stage of development and its human and material resources;

    b) the needs of the people "at the bottom";

    c) the priorities imposed by a human-centred, endogenous and self-reliant development policy;

d) the types of activities and competencies required
    to meet the needs of the most disadvantaged;

e) the most efficient way of sub-dividing the
    required general competencies into specific tasks
    and skills;

f) innovative approaches to the effective training
    of the new categories of personnel required,
    giving particular attention to the services and
    competencies most urgently needed at the base
    of the social pyramid.

To this end, a principle to be constantly borne in mind is
Gunnar Myrdal's harmonious "movement upward of the entire system".
This principle is of major importance in societies characterized, on the one hand, by discrimination, dependence and inequality of all kinds and, on the other, by the interests of the
classes or elites in power and the activities initiated by them
at national or international levels. Growth cannot otherwise
be founded on a sound, democratic and truly autonomous basis.
This "movement upward" must have an essentially endogenous character in order to make communities as self-reliant as possible
and to end their dependence on external power structures and
centres of decision over which they have no control.

The human and economic resources needed for education, as well
as for other aspects of an endogenous and self-reliant development must, therefore, be drawn primarily from the communities
and regions concerned. Experiments with community-based development projects in the past decades have convincingly demonstrated that the bulk of the resources needed for both developmental and teaching/training purposes can easily be found and
mobilized at the local level. The creative and effective utilization of these resources is not only a basic objective of an
authentic and participatory development, but is essential for
economic and financial reasons.

IMPLICATIONS FOR EDUCATIONAL PLANNING

If our objective is the provision of both relevant and liberating education, we must, as planners, re-order our educational
priorities, devise new methods for mobilizing and allocating
resources and engage in fresh thinking about the forms and content appropriate to our new educational goals. It is not pos-

sible in this paper to give detailed proposals concerning various possible new forms of education. Instead, I shall limit myself to examining the concept and content of basic education.

Basic Education: Concept and Content

The two major components of basic education might be defined as "general conscientization activities" and skill instruction. In view of the limited resources available and the right of every citizen to <u>some</u> degree of general education, each country should define the essential educational needs which it is able to satisfy. The identification of needs and objectives will be governed by many factors, in particular by the availability of resources. The aim of basic education should be to equip <u>all</u> citizens, and particularly the least privileged, with the basic knowledge and skills they require in order to understand and cope with their milieu and to participate consciously and effectively in the process of their own liberation. As this type of education is usually radically different from the primary or secondary schools, its implementation calls for extremely bold and imaginative reforms and necessitates the re-structuring both of the present formal schooling system and of adult non-formal education programmes. But the reform of these must be only a beginning. To achieve lasting success, the milieu as a whole must be transformed in such a manner that living and learning, studying and doing become inseparable aspects of man's being.

In planning education, urgent attention must be given to the provision of training in the basic skills required for individual and community development. In most Third World countries, particular emphasis should be laid on the training of front-line workers or "animators" needed at the grassroot level to perform basic functions in the fields of production, agriculture, community development, health, education, literacy teaching, cottage and small industry, etc. A major shift of resources to the training of these vital cadres should be a priority, as well as the provision of more advanced training for individuals supplying support services to the front line workers.

The Organization of Learning

The main reason for the failure of the formal system is that, instead of serving the learning objectives for which it was originally created, it has turned into a processing machine

serving certain sectors of the economy and providing a minority
of its clients with the social status, income and privileges
that accompany employment in elite occupations. Yet the place
and importance of formal schooling in the power structure have
become so great that it absorbs nearly all the resources available for education. Instead of serving the purposes of development, it is, paradoxically, becoming an instrument of under-
development. In particular, it constitutes a threat to the
growth of non-formal, problem-related and other relevant forms
of education and skill training. Few will deny the urgent need
to test new approaches that place the resources of society at
the service of all instead of in the hands of a privileged few.

The objectives of educational reform and social progress cannot
be achieved by the creation of any single institution. What is
needed is an environment or milieu conducive to authentic education and endogenous development. Such an environment is, at
once, a pre-condition for development and a means of mobilizing
resources to achieve the legitimate aspirations of society.
There is no reason to invest a single institution with an educational monopoly whereby the common resources of society are
allocated to a small minority. It is the milieu which needs to
be reorganized. Society must become the "school" and the expression "living is learning" a reality as well as an aphorism. Only
in this way can one meet the complex needs of a truly developing
community which has decided to master its destiny through *praxis*:
i.e. through the combination of knowledge and action, theory and
practice.

Alternative Institutions

The Ujamaa cooperative villages in Tanzania, the Nucleos Educa-
tivos Comunales of Peru and the Schools for Collective Promotion
in a few French-speaking African countries are interesting examples of this type of integrated activity. Their merit is that
(a) they tend to create new relationships between the school and
its socio-economic, cultural and natural environment; (b) they
aim at the collective promotion of the milieu rather than the
individual advancement of those attending them; (c) they are
based on the principle of friendly co-operation and solidarity
rather than on competition; (d) their objective is to contribute to the socio-economic and cultural development of the whole
community rather than to impart knowledge to a few; (e) they
aim to serve the process of creative learning rather than to
prepare students for acquiring diplomas.

A careful evaluation of the impact of such programmes upon development, and particularly their effectiveness in reducing economic and educational disparities, is urgently required. There is a pressing and evident need for innovative strategies aimed at finding, mobilizing and re-allocating educational and other resources so as to ensure a more equitable distribution of opportunities.

Structures and Development

Malcolm Adiseshiah

INTERNATIONAL STRUCTURES

In the 1950s in the Third World, real output increased at between 4.1 and 5.2 per cent averaging 3 per cent per capita (1).
In the 1960s its growth rate declined to 4.5 per cent averaging
2.5 per cent per capita (2). Up to the mid 1970s the mid-point
of the current Second Development Decade, the per capita growth
rate of the low income countries (those below per capita incomes
of $200) declined to 0.5 per cent for 1969-1970, -0.5 per cent
in 1974 and -0.7 per cent in 1975, with the prospect of ending
the decade with 0.2 per cent against the target of 4 per cent (3).

Transnationals

The liquidation of overt imperialism and colonialism in the
Third World has been accomplished by declining levels of development. During the past three decades 80 countries in the Third
World have emerged as independent countries but have discovered,
to their dismay, that national development is more than a national flag or a national anthem. In 1933, Keynes forecast that
the protection of a country's existing foreign interests, the
capture of new markets, and the progress of economic imperialism
are a scarcely avoidable part of a scheme of things which aims
at the maximum of international specialization and the maximum
geographical diffusion of capital, whatever its seat of ownership (4). These prophetic words find their expression in the
transnational enterprises whose value added was 20 per cent of
world GNP in 1971. Each of the top 10 firms had a value added
larger than the GNP of more than 80 Third World countries and
accounted for one-third of world foreign investment in these
countries through 4,000 subsidiaries and controlled 60 per cent
of manufactured trade in one part of the Third World, Latin
America (5).

One reaction to this situation during the last decade and a
half has been the takeover of 845 foreign enterprises by 62
Third World countries, mainly in mining, petroleum, agriculture
(37 per cent), banking and insurance (30 per cent) and manufac-

turers (16 per cent)(6). The structural changes now developing
in the Third World to meet the obstacles to their policy of
self-reliance include (excluding foreign investment in certain
sectors) establishing ceilings on remittances of foreign firms'
profits, imposing control of transfer pricing and royalty payments between subsidiaries and parents, ensuring scrutiny and
filtering of collaboration agreements with their in-built res-
trictive business practices and preparing revised patent laws.

But the basic structural change needed is the almost Gandhian
solution of self-reliant development propounded by Keynes when
he declared in 1933:

> I sympathize, therefore, with those who would
> minimize rather than with those who would maxi-
> mize economic entanglements among nations.
> Ideas, knowledge, science, hospitality, travel
> —these are the things which of their nature
> should be international. But let the goods be
> home spun whenever it is reasonably and con-
> veniently possible and, above all, let finance
> be primarily national.

Trade

The structure of international economic relations is such that
both the quantum and the terms of trade (on which the development of the Third World depends for its foreign exchange resources) act as a constraint and a negative factor. The initial
constraint is that the international trade structure results in
three-fourths of the world's people, who comprise the Third
World, participating to the extent of only 18 per cent of the
total quantum of world trade. This quantum can be increased if
UNCTAD decisions are carried out by the industrialized countries
and if there develops greater intra-Third World trade and an
expanding production base in those countries.

A second constraint is the trade in food. From being net ex-
porters up to the early 1950s, the Third World has become net
importers of food to the extent of 51 million tons in 1973.
Ninety per cent of these imports are from one developed region,
North America, and this has given rise to discussion of food as
a weapon in America's diplomatic armoury. Meanwhile, 500 million out of a total 2 billion people living in the Third World
are on the hunger line. Whereas in 1970 food stocks were 150

million tons, in 1975 the stocks were (and for the rest of the
decade will be) 90 million, which is 25 days of food supply.
It is against this background the World Food Conference in Rome
decided to set up the International Fund for Agricultural Development to promote food production in the Third World, to increase world food security by a system of reserve stocks both
to ensure adequate food supplies and reasonable prices and double
food aid to 10 million tons a year (8).

A third issue is the terms of trade which are skewed against the
Third World oil consuming countries, due to discriminatory tariff
and non-tariff barriers against their imports, inflation and
more recently recession and stagnation in the industrialized
world. World Bank studies show that if the affluent countries
dismantled even partially their trade restrictions against Third
World agricultural imports, the latter's export earnings will
increase by at least $4 billion (9). As for the uneven impact
of world inflation, in 1974 the prices of Third World imports
rose by 40 per cent and in 1975 by 46 per cent while their export prices rose only by 27 per cent in 1974 and 20 per cent in
1975. This results in growing deficits in their balance of
payments estimated at $50-55 billion in 1975, and the worsening
of the terms of trade of the low income Third World countries by
2.2 per cent per annum between 1952-1972 and by over 20 per cent
by the end of the decade (from 100 in 1970 to 95 in 1973 and a
projected 77 in 1980). The structural way out from this situation is for the affluent countries to adhere to the generalized
system of preferences (GSP) and remove non-tariff barriers recommended by UNCTAD over 12 years ago; to execute the UNCTAD
plan for creating international buffer stocks in 11 commodities
at a capital cost of $10,700 million; and some kind of indexa-
tion of Third World exports to provide a modicum of stabiliza-
tion in their export earnings (10).

One result would be a more rational, effective and efficient
division of labour between the affluent and Third World countries, under which the rich countries will no longer, under
cover of high tariff walls, continue to produce goods and services which can more efficiently and at lower cost be produced
by the Third World. The relatively abundant capital and limited
labour supply of the affluent world can move into the more sophisticated industries in which those countries have a comparative
cost advantage, and which will, as a consequence, raise further
living levels of its labour force as it moved into higher producing industries. In turn, such an international division of
labour will increase by 300 per cent the employment opportuni-

in the Third World in the labour intensive occupations (11).
This might also help in changing the world industrial structure
under which 70 per cent of world population living in the Third
World produces 7 per cent of the world's industrial output and
move towards their goal of a 25 per cent share by 2000. Such
a development might balance the uncertainties of the current
heavy reliance on export led growth of the Third World.

Money, Debt and Aid

The international monetary structure in which international
liquidity and decisions thereon have been the exclusive privilege of the affluent world has over the past three years broken
down and is now in question. Part of the fight for structural
reforms on which the development of the Third World depends
include: the struggle against the allocation of higher quotas
and greater management power in the system to the oil producing
Third World countries; the continued resistance to the link
between the SDRs and development assistance; the prolonged
delay in renewing and operating the International Monetary Fund's
compensatory financing facility; and the deadlock over IMF gold
sales and the establishment of the Trust Fund.

Meanwhile, the international debt burden of the Third World has
increased to $80 billion, with annual debt servicing amounting
to $7 billion. One effect of this passing of their limit for
debt replayment and servicing has been the contraction of $4.5
billion Euro currently credits by the low income Third World
countries in the first six months of 1975. Debt rescheduling
and moratoria which are now ad hoc and forward exercises have
to be built into the international economic structure as an
integral component (12).

The gap is widening between living levels of the low income
Third World countries whose GNP per capita, according to the
World Bank estimates, will increase from $105 in 1970 to $108
in 1980 and that of member countries of the Organization for
Economic Cooperation and Development, which will accelerate from
$3,100 in 1970 to $4,000 in 1980. While the OPEC countries are
providing official development assistance (ODA) in 1974 and 1975
of around $10 billion which is 3 per cent of their GNP, the ODA
provided to the Third World by the OECD countries in 1975 is
less than half of their pledged target, 0.33 of their combined
GNP against the target of 0.7 per cent. The widening of the
gap could be slowed down if the 0.7 target is attained for the

balance of the Second Development Decade, which the World Bank
points out would be just 2 per cent of the incremental wealth
of the affluent countries during this period 1975-1980 (13).
It could also act as a balance for those countries who are not
able to use international trade as their major instrument of
growth.

NATIONAL STRUCTURES

Some 50 per cent of people in the Third World countries are
living below the poverty line, defined as those spending less
than $75 per capita per year, in conditions of hunger, malnut-
rition, illiteracy, low life expectancy and poor housing. If
one assumes minimum needs of food, clothing, housing, safe drin-
king water, education and health standards involving a per capita annual expenditure of $120, about 70 per cent in these coun-
tries live below the minimum needs line. Taking the first
group of the absolute poor, 700 millions live in rural areas and
200 millions in urban areas. National studies also show that
as in inter-countries inequalities, at the national level, the
fruits of such development as has taken place are being unequally
distributed, so that the rich within the country are growing
richer and the poor poorer. One of the studies in India shows
that the rural poor increased from 38.03 per cent of all rural
people to 53.02 per cent during the decade 1960-61 to 1970-71
(14). The largest number of the poor live in Asia, particularly
India, Bangladesh, Indonesia and Pakistan, followed by Africa
and Latin America, where the problem of skewed distribution is
more the distorting factor than absolute poverty. These tragic
facts have been amply documented (15).

Rural Poverty

Attempts to deal with rural and urban poverty through special
programmes are necessary but not sufficient. In the rural areas
special programmes have been and should be devised to help the
small farmer, the marginal farmer and the drought-prone farm
holdings through promoting production activities which, with
their abundant labour and limited land they can develop, and
through inducing such institutions as rural banks, co-operatives,
farmers service societies, etc. to take part. It has been suggested that the creation of large and medium size farms on which
small farmers can be employed should be facilitated, accepting
the proletarianization of agriculture as a historical necessity.

Short of such a dialogical development, the land base of small
farmers can be strengthened through the provision of suitable
technologies and organizational structures which will provide
animal husbandry and agro-processing occupations. But the results in lifting the farmer above his poverty level have been
limited because all these programmes function within the existing
rural structures which are biased in favour of what is called
"the progressive farmer" who is the well-endowed farmer. They
are not aimed at removing the basic causes which prevent the participation of the small man in the development process.

Urban Poverty

Similarly, the programmes of employment generation and slum
clearance and improvement to help reduce urban poverty are necessary but not sufficient to eradicate urban poverty. This is
validated by the fact that the extent of urban poverty has deep-
ened during the 1960s from about 50 per cent of people living in
poverty at the start of the decade to around 60 per cent at its
end (16). Contrary to the view that rural-urban migration in
the affluent countries is due to "pull factors" and in the Third
World to "push factors", and on the basis of which even the
World Bank programmes are developed (17), case studies in the
latter countries show that it is not the disadvantaged rural
people but those who are more educated and more advanced who so
migrate. They migrate not to all cities but only to those with
a growing industrial infrastructure. As a result, the migrants
to the cities usually belong to the hereditary well-off groups,
and the homogeneity of members within groups and inequalities
among groups make for social exclusivism which feeds into inequality. Urban poverty and inequalities are at base structural
in nature and causation.

Growth and Equality

The problem of poverty is not traceable simply to the over-
emphasis on the objective of growth as against the objective of
social justice. First, the growth record of the Third World
with which this paper started is such that there can be no serious contention that the countries have really performed well
on this score. In fact, in face of the anti-growth lobby, the
conservationists' fears of depletion of resources, and various
suggestions to limit growth in the affluent countries, (which
however have not prevented their governments and policy makers

heaving a sigh of relief when the GNP curve began rising from
the last quarter of last year), the importance and urgency for
the Third World countries to achieve high rates of growth should
not be in question. The Chinese record over the last two decades is a pointer to all in the Third World: high growth without foreign aid; attainment of this growth in parallel with
improved living standards; a programme of education and self-
reliant industrial, agricultural and infrastructural development
as the basis for future sustained growth (18).

Secondly, it is equally true that growth *per se* need not promote
social equality. GNP is only an aggregation in value terms
(using current prices) of a heterogeneous collection of goods
and services. In the Third World, existing prices reflect existing income distribution and, behind it, the distribution of
ownership of land and industrial assets. The collection of goods
and services will reflect the consequent demand pattern, with
the predominance in the supply of non-essential goods and services for which there is an effective demand, and limited quantities of essential food items, clothing, housing, reflecting
their limited effective demand. So the national output, what
we call GNP at any given point of time, is a function of income
distribution and the demand pattern flowing from it, and are
themselves the reflection of the system of factor ownership.

Structural Change

The eradication of rural and urban poverty in the Third World
countries calls for structural changes. These involve restructuration of the rural society in the form of land ceilings and
distribution of surplus land to the landless; secure and recorded tenancies; abolition of share cropping and various forms
of bonded labour; establishment of minimum wages for landless
labour; consolidation of fragmented holdings in co-operative
or State farms and, in urban and other areas, public ownership
of major industrial and infrastructural assets and control of
the rest. Such a structural change must be accompanied by a
social valuation, instead of the market valuation. This will
ensure that the goods and services needed by the majority poverty sector are produced by that majority. Again such a produc-
tion-cum-distribution pattern will be disaggregated in terms
of worker categories in each locality who, mobilizing all local
resources and available national inputs, can themselves undertake the urgent task of eradicating poverty. That is, or should
be, the essence of development planning by Third World countries.

Such development calls for major national and international
structural changes which are not technical nor educational nor
economic decisions, but first and foremost political decisions.
However, the technical analysis and economic programming will
have to await the prior political decisions. Adult education
and all forms of non-formal education can prepare the ground
within countries and between countries for the hard political
decisions that have to be made as well as act as an instrument
for both humanizing and ensuring the effectiveness of the decisions when they are made.

REFERENCES

1. United Nations, World Economic Survey, 1963, p. 19. New
   York, 1963.

2. Ecosoc Committee for Development Planning, Report on Sixth
   and Seventh Sessions, pp. 22, 24. New York, 1970.

3. McNamara, R.S. Address to the Board of Governors, pp. 6, 7.
   World Bank, Washington D.C., 1975.

4. Keynes, J.M. National Self-Sufficiency, p. 757. Yale, 1933.

5. United Nations, Multinational Corporations in World Development, p. 122. New York, 1973.

6. Economic and Social Council, Permanent Sovereignty over
   National Resources, p. 132. New York, 1974.

7. Keynes, J.M. National Self-Sufficiency, p. 758. Yale, 1933.

8. United Nations Food and Agricultural Organization, Report
   of the World Food Conference, Chapter V. Rome, 1975.

9. UNCTAD, Annual Report, p. 124. Geneva, 1975.

10. McNamara, R.S. Address to the Board of Governors, p. 10.
    World Bank, Washington, D.C., 1975.

11. International Labour Office, Employment Growth and Basic
    Needs, p. 174. Geneva, 1975.

12. Madras Institute of Development Studies. Madras, vol. V,
    No. 10 (1975), p. 531.

McNamara, R.S. Address to the Board of Governors, pp. 10-
11. World Bank, Washington D.C., 1975.

13. McNamara, R.S. Address to the Board of Governors, pp. 6-8.
World Bank, Washington D.C., 1975.

14. Bardhan, P. Green revolution and agricultural labourers,
Economic and Political Weekly, V, 29-31 (1970).

15. World Bank, Annual Reports 1973, 1974 and 1975. Washington.
Myrdal, G. Asian Drama. Parthenon, New York, 1968.
Dandekar & Rath, Poverty in India. Bombay, 1970.
Publication by M. Clifton, D. Thorner, E.J. Mishan and
K. Bould.
Reports of the Economic Commissions for Africa and Latin
America.

16. Dandekar & Rath. Poverty in India, p. 28. Bombay, 1970.

17. International Bank for Reconstruction and Development,
Annual Report 1975. Washington.

18. Hsinhua News Agency, New Leap in China's National Economy.
Peking, January 11, 1972, p. 5.
Eckstein, A. Economic growth and change in China: a twenty
year programme, China Quarterly, April 1973.
Gurley, J. Maoist economics, Monthly Review, 1972.

Case Studies

INTRODUCTION

Everyone sleeps on the side which he finds
comfortable. He who doesn't put his little
pot on the fire, his heart doesn't rejoice.

Arabic

Dans la vie, chacun dépend d'un autre.

Guinea

As any poet or novelist knows, the deepest insights are not
found in generalized recommendations or resolutions but in the
wisdom of the hearth and market place and folk-memory. At each
international meeting on adult education, participants learn
afresh how much they share, how great is the concensus that is
emerging. Yet what is often most profound is what is unique in
the experience of individual nations or cultures. Issues, and
the papers that analyze and examine these issues from a large,
sometimes a global perspective, have been included, but of
equal value are the experiences recorded within a single country. In the tapestry of international development, the warp is
composed of filaments spun from singular experiences within a
country. Unfortunately we have no room for a recital from each
of the 82 nations represented; there has been room only for
some examples, chosen to illustrate variety of experience and
ideology.

Member States of the Arab League

M. E. D. Saber

The states of the Arab League represent an integrated community
with a long history of common experiences and aspirations. In
1972, Arab countries had a total population of about 134 million
people which is approximately four per cent of the world's population. The Arab homeland is fifth among world population
groups next to China, India, the Soviet Union and the United
States. The Arab States in Africa make up about 70 per cent of
the total Arab area and of the total population; in Asia they
represent about 30 per cent of the area and of the population.

In terms of economic and social structure, the Arab countries
belong to the developing world and as such are undergoing a difficult transitional phase in absorbing modernization and change.
On the positive side, the countries have a historical, linguistic and cultural unity that plays an important part in the educational and scientific heritage of the past and in their similar systems of education. Nevertheless, the capacity of such
systems to bring about cultural change — that is, development —
remains an essential question. The problem common to Arab, and
to developing, countries is that the educational system has
failed to be relevant to and rooted in the social and cultural
environment. It is this problem that Arab countries are working
to overcome.

Battle Against Illiteracy

One of the most crucial problems in adult education is illiteracy. Statistics from the period 1966 to 1971 show that the
average ratio of illiteracy in about 14 Arab States was 62 per
cent among those ten years old and more; among men it was over
50 per cent; among women it ranged from 27 per cent to 91 per
cent with an average of 75 per cent. Thus, adult education in
the broad sense has alphabetical literacy as its basic phase,
followed by cultural illiteracy. Arab governments have concentrated their efforts on illiteracy and these take the form of
two general trends:

1) The first trend is to deal with illiteracy at the source —

158231

the young — through legislation for compulsory primary education.
Fourteen Arab States now have compulsory systems of education
for both sexes at the age of six (age seven in Sudan). But the
attempt to absorb all children into the school system is a difficult one. Some 34 children out of every 100 miss the opportunity for education each year. Through research and remedial
methods of education attempts are being made to narrow the number of dropouts from primary education and to eliminate the
causes.

2) The second trend concentrates on facing the overall problem
itself. Literacy activity in Arab countries has been strongly
linked with the long struggle against imperialism over more than
50 years. The awareness of the close connection between freedom
and learning has resulted in various forms of popular education
in which the scope of literacy has been broadened. In all countries official departments and central organizations have been
established. In some countries literacy has not been confined
to official activities but has involved the people both in the
planning and implementation of the program. Most Arab States
have issued legislation to organize action and responsibility
for literacy work and to lay down incentives. The principle of
planning for literacy and adult education and to relate this
to national development plans is beginning to spread so that
curricula and programmes are being established within the specific time periods. Greater attention is now being paid to technical training programmes for a wide range of people including
technicians, administrators and organizers.

It should be pointed out, however, that these growing efforts
have not made any tangible impact on the battle against illiteracy. Statistics from 1971 to 1973 indicate that the rate of
those enrolled in literacy classes (in proportion to all illiterates) is 19 in 1000 on the average; out of these illiterates,
six per 1000 succeed. These figures show why an overall strategy to combat illiteracy is now being planned for and carried
out in major experiments.

Three Types of Experiments

One type of experiment is characterized by voluntary participation of the people and organizations side by side with government support. The national mass campaign in Somalia in 1973
affected the urbanization of Bedouins and the development of
agricultural resources; large numbers of rural people were

given literacy training; hostile customs and traditions were
exposed. The mass awareness that the campaign created resulted
in the opening of many schools, through voluntary community
effort, and the setting up of training and rehabilitation centres
for adults and of cooperative societies.

In 1976, the Democratic People's Republic of Yemen launched a
mass programme to identify the number of illiterates within the
context of a previously designed plan for a national campaign.

The second type of experiment relies completely on government
financing. Such experiments are taking place in the Kingdom of
Saudi Arabia and the Gulf States to increase primary school education and to link literacy activities for adults with general
education in a kind of "enlightened educational integration".
Adults who complete these studies have the incentive of social
and material advancement because of the demand for their new
skills in many development projects. These experiments also
witness a great demand by women to join literacy centres and
classes.

In the third set of experiments governments provide the major
financing with participation from the people. Iraq is launching
an overall campaign for the eradication of illiteracy over three
phases of five, seven and nine years. An interesting approach
to young illiterates has been devised in Egypt for remote villages through "one-class" schools which comprise different age
groups at different levels with special curricula. Schooling
lasts for two to three years. The plan is to set up 1000 such
classes each year. In addition, public organizations, factories,
government departments, the army and police are committed by law
to undertake the literacy training of their personnel. This is
taking place side by side with the expansion of primary education which is expected to include all children by 1985.

Adult Education Activities

A number of experimental projects are underway for adult education that follows the literacy phase. These efforts take the
form of extending formal education through literacy classes as
in Saudi Arabia and the Gulf States. Sometimes it takes the
form of technical and vocational training carried out in a variety of ways such as through public service programmes in local
communities by educational institutions. In other cases adult
education provides classes for people to improve their educa-

tional and vocational qualifications.

In addition to the efforts of governments and popular bodies, Arab and international organizations play a significant role in adult education.

International Organizations

The first international work in the Arab area was in 1952 when UNESCO, in conjunction with Egypt, set up the Regional Centre for Functional Literacy in Rural Areas for the Arab States (ASFEC). The Centre has been a pioneer in a variety of situations such as the training of leaders, research and development of methods and materials for adults. It works closely with Arab organizations.

The United Nations Children's Fund plays an important role through centres that include literacy lessons and cultural and professional education for people who have not been able to continue their education. UNICEF has also been involved with the training of teachers in a number of countries such as Sudan and Jordan.

Arab Organizations

The Arab League Educational, Cultural and Scientific Organization (ALESCO) aims at fulfilling the same objectives of its international counterpart, UNESCO. In 1966 a specialized body was set up for adult education by the Arab League under the name of the Arab Regional Literacy Organization (ARLO). It became part of ALESCO in 1970 when its function and name changed to the Arab Literacy and Adult Education Organization. Some of its programmes and projects throughout the Arab world include:

— Research to acquire information about conditions of work; analytical study of data and reports; research on adult education within the context of lifelong learning.

— Experimental projects in three communities representing social change in labour, agriculture and nomadic life.

— A pilot experiment on simplification of the Arabic script which will be of direct benefit for literacy learning.

— A program for libraries for neo-literate adults
  that will emphasize technology and natural sciences
  and thus link new learners with contemporary life.

— Planning, surveys, field researches and studies
  for an Arab strategy for adult education, which
  became the working papers for a major policy conference in Baghdad in December 1976.

— A technical assistance programme to provide Arab
  States with expertise in such illiteracy problems
  as research, planning, organization, preparation
  of curricula, the use of modern techniques.

— Cooperation and information exchange between ARLO
  and other Arab and foreign regional and international organizations on developments in literacy and adult education.

Guinea Bissau

M. Cabral

During the pre-industrial period, as everywhere in the world, there were few schools. Pre-colonial Africa was no exception. However, the non-existence of schools did not mean lack of education. Every child was trained by the adults in socially rewarding work. While learning to work the child was also learning the social rules and traditional legends and myths. In a way, this kind of education was limited because it did not introduce great alteration in the local social structure, but on the other hand, it had the great advantage of being perfectly identified with the socio-economic basis and prepared the necessary working hands for the development of the society.

The Colonial System

The Portuguese colonial education system reflected a more advanced phase of human development because it had been introduced at the beginning of this century. It was based on what was known about progress and science until that date. However, it was not anything more than a codified education system to transmit as much as possible in the shortest possible time. The few who graduated would then move ahead to other institutions to continue their studies.

The colonial education was born in an old-fashioned classist European society and reflected these characteristics. The schools created in our country could be a way to progress for a few, but this raised many difficulties for the development of our people. The system had the following characteristics:

a) Selectivity: only a few of our people could attend school.

b) Inadaptation: the subjects in the programme were far from the socio-cultural reality of our people.

c) Discrimination: the values "sold" in that "shop" praised the white occidental supremacy in order to impress in the mind and conscience of those who were learning a feeling of inferiority, incapacity, submission and lack of initiative.

Besides these main characteristics, common to all colonial education systems, there was the necessity for anyone who wanted
to go to school to give up all the cultural values, to adopt
Portuguese citizenship and a Christian name. This means, to use
a very significant word, that we became "assimilated". While in
French-speaking and English-speaking colonies there had been an
effort to integrate some values of the colonized people into
school programmes for the advancement of the purposes of the
colonizers, in the Portuguese system the government philosophy
expressed in Salazar's maxim "proudly alone" meant that deaf
ears were turned to all innovations taking place elsewhere.

Above all, the colonial education purposes were to "dis-african-
ize". With such a system we knew everything about the Portuguese
and other European countries' geography, economy, history, and
nothing at all about our own land, Africa, or the Third World's
contribution to human development and progress. Until 1960, the
colonial education system did not in any way reduce the illiteracy in so-called Portuguese Guinea. At the beginning of our
glorious armed revolt towards national independence in 1960,
99.7% of our people were illiterate.

Basic Education

The Portuguese system, based on the absurd principle that "only
the sons of the civilized had the right to instruction", plainly
denied access to almost all the people. In earlier years there
had been a difference between the government education and rudimentary education as organized in government schools and rudimentary schools. Government schools had licensed teachers and
were under the direct administration of the Education Department. Rudimentary schools were under the administration of the
Catholic Missions that accepted non-licensed teachers, most of
them with only elementary standards of education. Later, the
colonial system adopted a distinction between government education, para-government education, and private education. The
schools of the Catholic Missions were included in para-government education. During the last few years, pressed by the national liberation fight, the Portuguese tried desperately to
create new schools, built and maintained by the colonial army.

Preliminary Education

What is called preliminary education began in Bissau during the

school year 1967-68 and was identical with that in Portugal.
It extended compulsory basic education from four to six years
and replaced the first and second forms of high school education.

Secondary Education

Secondary education became official only in March 1958 when the
colonial government decided to establish, as Honorio Barreto
High School, the Honorio Barreto Institute which had been founded in 1949 under the name of Bissau College High School.   In
October 1974, the Commissioners' Council of Guinea-Bissau re-
named it Kwame Nkrumah High School in honour of that great son
of Africa and defender of African unity. This was the first
education institution to be named after independence. At present there are four high schools in the country. One is a national high school (Kwame Nkrumah) and three are local ones
(Huj1 Ya Henda High School in Bafata; Ho Chi Minh High School
in Cantchungo; José Marti High School in Bolama).

The former policy meant that only a few selected pupils could
attend high school. In 1966 there were only 400 pupils and 60
per cent were Europeans. By 1961, only 14 indigenous people (of
whom 11 were still alive) had attained a university degree.

Technical Education

In 1960, a technical school was founded. The program was almost
all academic, the system was similar to the high school teaching,
and the programme lasted for three years. Some technical subjects were added to the high school programmes but without much
success. At the end of 1975, technical education was divided
into basic courses in commerce, electricity, mechanics, agriculture and an education training course for girls.

After independence we began to introduce some changes in order
to adapt the training of technicians to the needs of the country.
As we begin to enlarge our education system the lack of school
buildings is one of our greatest problems. We have managed to
convert all possible buildings into schools; for example, the
quarters used by the army has been adapted to a technical school,
and similar adaptations have been made for other education centres.

Today, we are getting together the necessary equipment so that

our education system will be technical and skill-training in
character. Formerly, the technical school programme was academic
rather than practical and students who graduated wanted to continue studying in the high school because they knew they were
not prepared for technical training. Now, the technical school
is being changed into a technical institute for the training of
technicians who come to it after the ninth form.

The Actual Education System at the Time of Liberation

The fall of fascism in Portugal assisted the total liberation of
our country with all the consequences that this entailed. We
had organized political and administrative life in all the liberated zones but independence raised many new problems. Guinea-
Bissau was a country without a strong economy; with an annual
income that did not cover more than one third of the expenses;
and without an experienced national government. The people were
completely non-politicized; they had lived under colonialism;
and they suffered from the lack of morality common to all
people under war-time conditions. Alcoholism, prostitution,
thievery and drug abuse were some of the problems we inherited.
The Party had to face all these problems and to find solutions
for them.

Where to Begin?

How could we fight all these vices and create a new social and
economic relationship? A huge task was assigned to education:
to transform the mentality of the opportunists, to end the spirit of submission and dependence of students in areas formerly
under Portuguese control, and to create conditions for a new
man — the one dreamed of by Amilcar Cabral and his Party. Education cannot rebuild "the old man" — even less build "the new
man" — if it is not deeply in touch with the national problems
and the perspectives of development for and by progressive
people. The absurdity of the colonial system was that it was
completely divorced from the reality of the people.

This meant we had to modify the education programme from the
very foundation. No rosy solution was possible. It was necessary to analyze the entire education structure and consider
seriously some basic questions such as:

Education or Why?
             For what?
             How to organize it?
             For what purpose?
             For whom?

We could not count very much on our own nationals to initiate
and coordinate such an undertaking because after five centuries
of colonialization and ten years of massive demagogy the Portuguese had left fewer than five graduated teachers. We had none
of those experts who are full of miraculous solutions to be put
into practice before "feeling the voice of the land" or trying
to understand the situation or the ideas and wisdom of the
people. It is by following the basic philosophy of Amilcar
Cabral and learning from the life and experience of the people
that we are building the basis for the reformation and innovation of the educational structures and programmes in order to
attain our social objectives.

What Has Been Done

1) Training of teachers. One of the biggest drawbacks to any
innovation in educational reform is the lack of qualified teachers. About 35 per cent of the teachers in our secondary
school (5th to 11th form) are foreigners and this percentage
increases in the higher forms. We had no more than one per cent
of qualified national teachers. Most teachers of the 5th and
6th forms are themselves students in the sense that they are
just a little ahead of those they are teaching. In basic education the situation is not much better because 65 per cent of
the teachers only have 4th form education. How could we face
a structural change with this kind of teaching staff?

Knowing that the lack of trained national teachers was the main
barrier to change, one of our first decisions was to intensify
the training of teachers. This was developed in three phases:

    a) regular training in school;
    b) continuous training through annual develop-
       ment programmes and programmes of contin-
       uing education for teachers;
    c) guided and self-guided learning.

Until liberation there was only one school for the training of
teachers. We decided to create, first of all, a school for the
training of teachers who had been in the army. Later, we

created a model school for teachers who would do supervision
monitoring in order to reinforce the technical and professional
competency of the qualified staff.

2) Content of School Curriculum. The objective of education
in any socio-political structure is to change and improve local
social conditions. Since Portuguese society was oriented to a
capitalistic and reactionary ideology, the school system had
the same characteristics in its programme and in its relationship between the school and the community. In terms of our
philosophy and convictions, the task of educational reform had
meant bringing about a major change so that not only the educated but all the people have a say in making decisions. Since
we had an urgent need to attack and banish the basic problems
of the colonial education system, some modifications in content
have been made, particularly in social and humanistic subjects
where ideology is strongest, such as language, history, geography, and also scientific subjects.

We have tried to adjust work and learning to the realities of
local conditions. Our objective is to look at education as a
school for life. Thus the content of education and the selection of students must reflect the relationship between work and
production in each region of the country. The basic education
schools have mainly an agricultural orientation and some of the
lower secondary schools could also be oriented to agriculture
or industry. Schools at the higher levels would mainly support
the political organizations in that their work is to organize,
direct, and bring civic and political consciousness to the
people. All schools now pay attention to their relevant possibilities and to the concrete needs of the community. We believe
that we can fight the divorce between manual and intellectual
work as well as the divorce between school and life.

3) Building and Equipping Schools. Our ideal is that the school
is not just a building where classes are given; it involves the
relationship between teacher and students living in the bio-
ecological structure. However, we cannot forget that education
requires a building, didactic and pedagogical materials, and
that it generates a dynamic that connects all the above-mentioned
principles. We need many schools and so we mobilize pupils,
teachers, parents and all the population to build them.

The Portuguese had left nothing in the way of schools. If they
had not been obliged to build headquarters to defend themselves
from our revolutionary armed forces we would not even have buil-

dings for our boarding schools. Amilcar Cabral said one day,
when watching a boy rowing a boat under great difficulties,
that if culture was to know how to live in one's own environment,
then our people are exceptionally cultured. But we also need
to be receptive to the universal culture.

4) Organizational Structure. No organizational structure existed during the colonial period. To profit from the experience
gained in boarding schools as well as in the *tabanca* schools,
we created — especially in secondary schools — an organization
to give impetus to the teaching/learning process for all types
of schools. The concentration of our attention and action is
on the basic point that we must have education for the entire
population that is based on need and on the economic possibilities of the country.

Thus, the integration of productive work within the school curriculum is to achieve two objectives:

a) Pedagogy based on the idea that school is a main part of
    the society. The teaching/education system is one of the
    socio-cultural factors of development and it will not affect
    the training of the young if it ignores production and
    relationships to local production.

b) Economy is the principle that without the minimum structural
    basis for encouraging development, education would continue
    to be for an elite if it continued to be divorced from work.
    An education with poor support of and in society is gener-
    ally poor in quality. The fact that our education system is
    for all the people does not mean it will not be based on
    quality.

Our system is based on "the collective direction" and personal
responsibility. This collective direction concentrates on every
social group: teachers, pupils, employees and, in the near
future, on the popular organizations of the country. This process is developing well even if it cannot be put into practice
in the advanced education levels at the moment due to the socio-
political development stage of the society. The participation
of popular-based committees in the schools is highly praised
and we are preparing the foundations of school councils to include teachers, pupils, parents and, when necessary, socio-
economic organizations.

5) Adult Education. Under the colonial policy adult education
was ignored. The only evidence of something called "adult edu-

cation" was the fact that a few adults attended evening courses
in city schools and learned the same subjects and took the same
programme as children. Some evening classes had been created
to give army officials the chance to earn a few more escudos to
compensate for "the sacrifice they made to help the people of
Guinea".

There was no campaign for literacy; not a single effort to
fight against illiteracy; absolutely nothing.

During the Revolution we tried to put into practice a few literacy programmes in the liberated zones but our method was not a
good one. After the complete liberation we made the first serious attempts. We still do not have very much experience but
we have a very clear idea of our possibilities and of the difficulties we face to carry out a literacy campaign. Since September 1975 we have been able to count on the technical support of
the Institute of Cultural Action and the Office of Education of
the World Council of Churches as well as the rich experience of
Paulo Freire. For literacy work we count on the Institute's
technical support and financial support from the Service Univer-
sitaire Canadien Outre-mer.

The World Council of Churches has also sent some audio-visual
support and equipment. At the moment, this is the only help we
receive from abroad to fight illiteracy.

Achievements

The colonial system left us with 80 per cent of our people illiterate. Our task is a big one. To accomplish it we have created the National Committee for Literacy under the control of a
National Committee headed by the President of the State Council
and composed of representatives of the Ministry of Education,
the Revolutionary Popular Armed Forces, the Ministries of Agriculture, Information, Health, Home Office, Industry and Public
Works and representatives of the Party, women's organizations,
trade unions and youth.

We know that literacy programmes must be connected with and be
part of the socio-cultural and economic development of the
people. Priorities have been defined for the relation between
formal and non-formal education because the broad objectives
are the same: to work for the achievement of a modern society
in which the citizens themselves shall bring about the transformation.

Due to the fight for liberation, our people are more and more
using Creole as the national language. However, it cannot yet
be used as the official language because it has not been stan-
dardized. Thus, Portuguese has been chosen as the official language. In our literacy work we have to face this problem;
since we are dealing with adults who do not speak Portuguese it
is not possible to use this language. Our compromise has been
to use Portuguese for literacy instruction but to speak in
Creole. However, this decision will be changed as the local
conditions change.

At the moment, literacy takes place in two areas: the Revolutionary Popular Armed Forces and the popular civil field. For
the first group the work is easy because those who participated
in the liberation struggle know that education is the continua-
tion of the revolution. They understand that by fighting illiteracy — one of the main weapons used by colonialism against our
people — they can still take part in the transformation of our
society. Today, more than 80 per cent of the armed forces can
read and write after one year of intensive work.

It is in the area of the civilian population that the work is
more difficult. It is not easy to find teacher-monitors, to
motivate the illiterate population, and to organize literacy
programmes. There are many reasons for this situation:

1) The political consciousness of the urban population is low.
    However, the political work of the Party will improve this
    situation.

2) Literacy work has not been related to socio-economic devel-
    opment projects. Many illiterates want to learn in order
    to improve their jobs and are using literacy programmes as
    formal education.

3) Lack of monitors and teachers.

4) Lack of understanding about the relationship of literacy
    objectives and formal education.

5) Lack of experience of the coordination teams.

6) Insufficient propaganda to promote literacy and to motivate
    monitors and teachers.

All of these limitations have not prevented the training of
monitors in zones where we are planning to develop literacy.
Many volunteers have begun to appear in the different zones to
take part in our first National Literacy Campaign.

The large number of illiterates and the small number of educated persons shows us that it will take many years to reduce illiteracy. However, the experience accumulated through the new situations that will appear during the campaign will help us to develop a strategy to fight illiteracy as a part of a political process, as part of a number of socio-economic development projects, and as part of our ability to recruit and motivate teachers. With this experience we know we can succeed.

6) <u>Project for the Reform of the National Education System</u>. Education is invariably one answer to the development needs of society. Just as a man knows he can dominate and profit from nature by hard work, we are defining the educational system according to the social situation that exists in the country. Our objective is to transform the content and objectives of education in agreement with the political philosophy of our Party and Government at the same time as a new social structure is being established.

a) <u>Basic education</u> will be for six years and be divided into two parts — four years and two years. In the first stage, the pupil will receive knowledge that relates to the forming of his personality; acquire basic education; and begin scientific training. In the second stage, he will learn more about science so that even if his education stops here he will have all the necessary elements to help the future development of his life. The state intends to provide these first two stages free to everyone.

b) <u>General multivalent education</u> is for three years. During this time, in addition to deepening his knowledge of general subjects, the pupil is directed in learning how he can use his education in productive ways if he continues to higher education or if he works in the community. It is at this level that training prepares people to be teachers of basic education, nurses, agriculture technicians and skilled industrial workers.

c) <u>Third level training</u> will be divided into two branches:
   i) pre-university education for candidates to university;
   ii) secondary polytechnic education for the training of agriculture technicians, nurses, teachers and industrial technicians.

The objective is to train at the secondary polytechnic level most, if not all, of our young people. Only those who show a

particular skill and understanding of the production process
will continue into university courses.

This plan is for formal education and we must yet establish a
plan for the transition into new programmes and new objectives.
Non-formal education is an important part of this transition so
that it will be coordinated and enriched by the formal system.
Both systems will be similar, not separate or contradictory.
The participation of the people is a vital part of this plan so
that we can create structures for such participation in the work
of the Ministry of Education and in the staff training connected with development. If this condition is not met education
will simply be a factory turning out unemployable people, as
President Iniz Cabral has said.

All of these directions show us the necessity to plan the
educational system in full consultation with the social development of the people, bearing in mind their national potentialities and their role in the regional context of West Africa and
in the world.

Hungary

The basic feature of the formal adult education system in Hungary is workers' schools that are equivalent to each level and type of the formal school system (primary, secondary and tertiary). This means that adults who study while they work can earn scholastic qualifications equal in value to those obtained by students in regular day schools. It also means that the school system is completely open and that everyone has the possibility of earning qualifications up to and including university degrees.

The eight-year primary schools are free of charge and compulsory up to the age of 16.

There are three types of secondary schools:

— Trade training schools to train skilled workers for industry, commerce, transport and agriculture in a three-year period. These schools are not equivalent in value to the other secondary schools and graduating students are not qualified to continue their studies at university or higher college level.

— Specialized secondary schools train skilled workers for trades requiring a high level of theoretical knowledge. Students sit for matriculation examination at the end of four years. These are full secondary schools and students are qualified for entrance to university or higher college level.

— Grammar schools specialize in the humanities. Their main function is to prepare students for university and higher college studies. Graduation is after four years.

Tertiary education (five years; six for doctors) is given in universities and in higher education colleges (three to four years).

Workers' Schools

Workers' schools have become one of the means for the high
degree of social mobility which has marked Hungary in the past
quarter of a century. They have made an important contribution
to new leadership, to satisfying the growing demands of industry
for skilled workers, to urbanization, and to providing training
for the modernization of agriculture. During this time almost
one million have reached matriculation; and over 100,000 have
earned university or higher college diplomas. The fact that
the population of Hungary is only just over ten million people
indicates the significance of these figures.

More and more the workers' schools are responding to demands for
further training and for lifelong education. They also carry
out certain rehabilitation tasks and ensure the possibility for
new careers. Curricula and textbooks are different from those
used in the regular schools and study materials take into account
the adults' experience of life, knowledge gained on the job and
their special interests. In this regard, experiments have been
launched to link both the content and organizational form of
trade training and general education. This is done at the primary level through combining study with the provision of skilled
training, and the secondary level through specialized secondary
schools for workers.

For both primary and secondary schooling there are two forms
of workers' schools: night schools which workers attend three
evenings a week, and correspondence schools which workers
attend once a week along with individual home study. A new
form of primary schools for workers was introduced a few years
ago. It links further vocational training with compressed
courses of five months that cover study materials for one year
and that closely link the trade training to the general education material. A new form of secondary school, also introduced
recently, is for workers with skilled training. Only general
education subjects are taught; the material is covered in three
scholastic years; and successful students can continue training
for qualification as technicians or enrol in higher educational
institutes.

In the early 1950s the principal task of higher education for
those in employment was to enable those who were from the working class to take leading positions in the economy, public
administration, politics, cultural life, the army, and to gain
higher qualifications. Higher education for those in employment

thus played a major role in creating the new intelligentsia for
our socialist society. To an increasing extent its main task
is becoming that of postgraduate training. The chief motivation
comes from demands being made by the economy and by social needs.

Recent Developments in Further Training

The government has set up a new institute to direct training and
further training for workers: the National Workers' Further
Training and Research Institute. Training covers a wide field
in objectives, content and type: refresher courses and training
to update knowledge; special training; preparation for new
jobs; training for the guidance of groups of workers.

A special development in the past three years is the system of
courses to prepare young skilled workers for university and
higher college studies. The preparation covers 12 months: nine
months of correspondence study and three months of intensive
training when the workers live in a hostel. Those who pass the
examination are admitted to the day course they have selected
in the university or higher college (of technology, economics
or law). Skilled workers admitted in this way to higher education can earn their regular salary throughout the study period.
Important political considerations led to this system: after
completing higher education studies these young factory workers
are selected for top positions in production and in public administration.

A new system of trade training and further training has been an
achievement of recent years. Under a government regulation,
trade training for workers is provided in the evening in correspondence branches of the schools that train skilled workers.
Another regulation stipulates that workers must be given further
vocational training every five to eight years. This further
training covers improvement of workers' general education, expansion of their vocational knowledge, and their political education. Another government regulation provides for the further
training of middle-level specialists, the training of master
skilled workers, and of foremen.

Extra-Curricular Education

The objective of the extra-curricular branch of the adult education system is to bring an awareness of the progressive and

spiritual values of our people, of mankind and of socialist
cultural works; to contribute to increased activity in public
life; and to assist in the creation of the intellectual framework for the extension of socialist democracy. An extensive
network of public education institutes serves these objectives.

— The institutes involved with artistic and scholastic creations
   have a network of theatres, cinemas, exhibition and concert
   halls, museums, galleries, artistic workshops, etc., that
   contribute to satisfying people's demands for education and
   entertainment and to developing visual and musical culture.

— Television is assuming a leading role in public education
   work as a whole. It is active in spreading and transmitting
   education and also has an influence in organizing education
   such as folk song circles, talent contests, contests of
   occupational skills, poetry recital contests, etc. Television and radio are especially important in spreading education in places where the public education institutes are inadequate.

— In the past decades great efforts have been made to develop
   the network of cultural centres. There are now 2,825 cultural
   centres in the country. The public libraries play an important part in developing a literate culture and in ensuring
   the possibility for continuous education. There are around
   8,700 public libraries with a total of 27 million books,
   2.3 million readers and 57.7 million books borrowed each year.

— The amateur arts movements (acting and poetry recital circles,
   orchestras, dance groups, photography and fine arts circles,
   etc.) offer an opportunity for active education, for community
   experiences and for contacts with artists. Over 200,000
   people from different age groups, and particularly young
   people, take part. There are also numerous scientific,
   technical, civics and local history circles.

— Adult education in science is coordinated by the Society for
   the Dissemination of Scientific Education. It has a membership of some 20,000 qualified experts and carries out a complex task relating to the development of workers' general
   and professional education and improvement of their political
   education. The Society's network of language schools has
   become the most comprehensive extra-curricular form of language teaching. It also publishes eleven adult education
   publications.

— Social and mass organizations also operate adult education
   institutes and have resources for public education. This
   participation of other organizations increases the number of
   people taking part in public and adult education and expres-
   ses the interests and needs of different sectors and cultural
   groups within the society. Trade unions in particular play
   an outstanding role.

Active Role of Trade Unions

The trade unions organize adult education in the workplaces and
among workers in general in cooperation with the company, factory
and economic managers. They take the initiative for the organization of separate factory schools and special branches and
classes and for setting up special interest circles such as for
technology, innovation, natural sciences, literature, arts,
languages. While training and further training of a professional
nature is organized by the economic departments of the company
or factory, the trade unions also have an important role in encouraging and mobilizing workers.

Adult education in the workplace is planned so that companies
must carry out a survey among the workers every five years, in
connection with the State five-year plan, to determine the types
of adult education in which workers intend to gain further
training. The companies provide specialists to give advice on
career direction and to carry out the adult education plan.
Joint committees set up by the management and trade union committee ensure that development of the workers' political, general, technical and professional education is carried out as an
integrated whole and that this activity is in accord with plans
for production, technology and manpower management.

The Constitution ensures the right to education for adults as
well as for children. The State ensures the necessary conditions
for this to take place and gives moral and material support to
workers continuing their studies. The system of benefits is
defined and guaranteed by law and includes the following provisions:

— Workers continuing their studies may not be employed in jobs
   and at times which would prevent them from studying; they
   are entitled to one hour off work on days when they attend
   classes.

— Workers continuing their studies are entitled to six to 24
    days of study leave each scholastic year, depending on the
    type of school. They are entitled to this leave in addition
    to their normal annual leave.

— Travel expenses are refunded for workers studying in an insti-
    tute at some distance from their home.

— There are different possibilities for encouraging and rewar-
    ding workers who continue their studies while also working
    well such as ensuring classification equivalent to the quali-
    fications gained, awards, holidays, cash bonuses.

Future Directions

Adult education in Hungary has now reached a new stage. While
previously the main function of adult education was to make up
for missed schooling, the demands of the scientific and technical revolution, the extension of democracy, urbanization, the
transformation of the contents and structure of education and
the demand for personal development means that adult education
is playing an increasingly important role in lifelong education.
The policies for public education, formal education, science,
and the arts together form the State's educational policy. This
means further efforts in the future to ensure that the process
of social and individual education is carried out through the
planned cooperation and interaction of these areas.

New types of institutes are needed to carry out the new tasks
of adult education. These include institutes that are capable
of carrying out the functions of adult education in a differen-
tiated way, that combine the methods of formal and adult education and that rely to a greater extent on voluntary activity by
adults. Being set up for these purposes are workers' cultural
centres, centres of further training and special workers' schools
provided with modern equipment. Television is offering wide
possibilities for adult education. From the autumn of 1976,
radio and television will be broadcasting the study material for
the workers' primary schools under the title of "Everyone's
School". Consultation centres will also be set up to enable
even more workers' groups to sit for school examinations.

Hungarian adult education specialists consider that the social
and economic development of the next 10 to 15 years will make
it necessary to set up an independent "remote teaching" system

of study that relates to the living and working conditions of
adults and that ensures a uniform nationwide level of services
for those who are far from cultural centres. The effectiveness
of "remote teaching" in comparison to the traditional systems
lies in its ability to apply new ideas of teaching and learning
theory and to use a multi-media system for communication, com-
prehension and consolidation.

Indonesia

D. Sanjoto

Adult education has always been a deep concern of the Indonesian
government. Adult education activities are carried out not only
by the Department of Education and Culture, but also by other
ministerial departments. These activities comprise mainly non-
formal education, the main objective of which is to impart to
the people more knowledge and to improve their skills in the
performance of their jobs so that they may be more productive
and become more effective participants in the development process as outlined in the Indonesian Five-year Development Plan.
In this plan also attention is given to adult education, not
only in the matter of vocational training, but also with regard
to attitudes and behaviour, in particular those affecting the
rural community.

ADULT EDUCATION BY THE DEPARTMENT OF EDUCATION AND CULTURE

1) The Directorate for Community Education

Activities of adult education of this department are carried out
through the Directorate for Community Education, established in
1950. Prior to that date there was already a section in the
department in charge of adult education, notably for the eradication of illiteracy, but the revolutionary situation in Indonesia was not too favourable for such activities. Only after
1949 when the situation became normal again could full attention
be given to this very important matter.

Since then new institutions have been created called Community
Education Inspectorates, established in each of Indonesia's 26
provinces. Sub-inspectorates were established in the sub-prov-
inces, divided into regions called kacjamatan. Each kacjamatan
has a Community Education Supervisor, to whom is given the task
of organizing the supervising adult education activities in the
villages.

To guide the activities in adult education the Department of
Education and Culture outlined a system, called the Panca Marga.

2) The Panca Marga

The Panca Marga, or Five Ways, focusses on the following activities:

a) Fundamental or elementary education
b) Community libraries
c) Leadership training centres
d) Information and guidance to women with regard to their
       role in family welfare and family planning
e) Volunteer youth activities.

Fundamental or elementary education, in which were also included activities for the eradication of illiteracy, was given top
priority because of the very high percentage of people without
formal schooling and illiterate people. Campaigns to wipe out
illiteracy were therefore one of the first steps to be taken.

The next step was the establishment of community libraries to
stimulate reading habits and to provide people with a meeting
place for community discussions about various subjects relating
to community development.

With regard to community leadership, it was customary for certain people to be accepted by the members as their community
leaders; they are looked upon with high respect and people are
ready to follow them. Unfortunately, however, most of these
leaders have been lagging behind somewhat in attitudes and knowledge. Training opportunities for these leaders are therefore
essential.

In development and nation building, attention should also be
given to the important role of women in our society. Our society consists of families; the welfare of the society should
not be at the expense of, but rather based on, the welfare of
the families. Family planning nowadays is a necessity, and in
all such matters the success of the undertaking for the greater
part depends on the extent of participation of the women.
Again, in every development activity the youth should be given
the opportunity to participate as fully as possible so that
through involvement in community activities the young people
will obtain deeper insight and will be more aware of the needs
of the community.

In the Five Year Development Plan the emphasis given to the
development of the rural area is based on the following consid-

erations:

a) More than 85 per cent of Indonesian society consists of village communities.

b) The backbone of Indonesian society is the rural community where 70 per cent of the national labour force is available.

c) Rural development will help to check urbanization.

Perhaps this partly explains why in Indonesia the board for adult education is called the Directorate for Community Education.

All this does not mean that adult education in urban communities is neglected; it is mostly carried out by municipalities through special institutions. The methods or system applied by municipalities may be slightly different, but the objectives are pretty much the same, e.g. to impart to the people knowledge about their jobs and related matters and to improve their skills in order to make them more productive participants in development.

ADULT EDUCATION BY OTHER DEPARTMENTS

The activities of the various departments can be grouped into the following categories:

  1) Pre-service training
  2) In-service training.

1) Pre-service training

Pre-service training is organized with the aim of obtaining the best qualified and most capable personnel. Eligible for this training are those who pass a qualification test. Candidates can be recruited from high school or college graduates, but quite often priority is given to department personnel with excellent service records although they may not have a strong background of formal education. This provides a chance for outstanding personnel to climb to higher positions, which, otherwise, would be beyond their reach.

The training varies from three months to one year, depending on intensity.

2) In-service training

The aim of this training is to increase knowledge in matters
related to jobs, to improve performance, and to instruct personnel in additional strategic approaches.

a) Basic courses. Open to junior personnel after three or four
   years of satisfactory service. In many cases people have to
   complete this training successfully to be eligible for promotion to a higher rank or position.

b) Advanced courses. These courses are open to middle rank
   personnel. Seniorship can be obtained after approximately
   ten years of satisfactory service.

c) Senior courses. These courses are open to senior officials
   after approximately 15 years of satisfactory service. They
   are meant mainly for government executives with the rank of
   directors and directors general, or minister-counsellors up
   to ambassadors for diplomatic personnel.

In addition, each ministerial department has its own institutions
for adult education, which will be illustrated with several examples.

1) Department of Information

The Central Information Service is located in Jakarta, while the
District Information Services are located in the provinces.
The main function of these institutions is to convey to the
masses all necessary information. The scope is very broad; it
includes administrative procedures, economic and cultural affairs, government political approaches in certain matters, etc.
In brief it covers the entire spectrum of life. *Radio dan Tele-
visi Indonesia* belongs to this department. Since all the other
departments are making use of these radio and television broadcasts, there are close relations between the Department of Information and other departments, notably the Department of Agriculture.

2) Department of Agriculture

In co-operation with the Department of Information, this Department has regular radio broadcasts for farmers. On such occas-

ions farmers in the villages gather around the radio receiver,
which will be a transistor radio in the absence of electricity.
These broadcasts contain useful instruction for farmers, such
as how to till the land, how to select the best seeds and the
right fertilizers. Occasionally some kind of an intermezzo in
the form of musical or other forms of entertainment is presented
during the programme to make the broadcasts more attractive.

3) Department of Health

This Department operates through Community Health Education
Centres and a National Training Centre in Jakarta. In this
centre departmental officials receive regular training for better job performance. The training of senior officials to become Health Educators is also carried out in this centre. The
department intends to have at least one Health Educator in each
province and sub-region. The Health Educator is expected to
recruit and train assistants to help him in the performance of
health services such as the supervision of hygiene regulations,
environmental sanitation programmes, etc. His assistance is
also sought in family planning campaigns, activities in preven-
ting and combatting communicable diseases, etc.

4) Department of Manpower

In the Department of Manpower are several programmes of adult
education:

- — Workers Education Programme which aims at in-
    creasing the knowledge and skills of the members
    of trade unions;

- — Vocational Training Centres for agriculture,
    industry and management which train adults in
    certain skills, such as carpentry, wielding and
    also managerial skills;

- — Mobile Training Units which visit rural areas
    and train the young adults in certain skills.

In addition to these schemes the Department has two institutions
involved in adult education:

a) BUTSI

This body was established in 1968 as in inter-departmental

institution under the chairmanship of the Minister for Manpower. The following ministerial departments are involved:
Foreign Affairs, Health, Social Affairs, the Interior, Information, Industry, Education and Culture, Public Works
and Electric Power, Agriculture, Transmigration and Co-
operatives, Relgious Affairs, and the National Development
Planning Board. The activities of BUTSI are three-fold:

— To organize and administer volunteer programmes in
Indonesia.

— To co-operate with the volunteer organizations of
foreign countries in making arrangements for volunteer programmes in Indonesia.

— In the future, to send volunteers abroad.

When BUTSI started operating in 1968 it was able to send
only 30 university graduates to villages, as generalist
workers with the objectives of helping the people in the
villages in all kinds of daily activities. In 1970 BUTSI
was able to send 48 volunteers, now entrusted with the
additional responsibility of carrying out UNICEF's Applied
Nutrition Programme. In 1971 BUTSI was incorporated into
the Indonesia Five Year Development Plan and the third
volunteer group in 1971 consisted of 270 young pioneers
sent to remote villages at the request of provincial governors to help people in all kinds of development activities.

b) <u>Labour Intensive Programme</u>

This is a system in which available unemployed or under-
employed labour is recruited for the implementation of certain development projects, such as the construction or improvement of roads, bridges, dams, irrigation systems, etc.
as well as the erection of community buildings such as
mosques, schools, etc. The system has a pattern:

— The planning, implementation and supervision of
the project should be the responsibility of the
government.

— The work should be done by unemployed and under-
employed people, using their own tools.

— The project should be decided by the community,
according to need.

The need for such a system is deeply felt in Indonesia where

a high precentage of unemployment is to be found. And the
high rate of population growth, estimated at 2.3 - 2.8 per
cent annually makes it even more urgent. It has been estimated that each year job opportunities for not less than
1.3 million people have to be found.

5) Department of Social Affairs

.This Department has many institutions engaged in adult education
activities, the aim of which is not merely to impart to the
people more knowledge and improve their skills, but above all to
educate the people in such a way that they become deeply aware
of their own needs and then by themselves try to find ways and
means to solve them.

One of the institutions initiated by this Department was the
village Social Welfare Committee (LSD) established in 1952.
The main objective of this organization is to accelerate the
growth of the village towards progress and development by using
social work and community development methods towards social
action. This means that the LSD does not only provide social
assistance proper such as the care of orphans, the handicapped,
victims of natural disasters, drug addicts, etc., but also, and
above all, to make the people socially conscious, which means
to make them aware that social changes are necessary for development. Activities for the implementation of these ideas or
specific development projects, can then eventually be carried
out with the assistance of other appropriate ministerial departments. Irrigation, for example, could be carried out with the
help of the Department of Agriculture and new roads could be
constructed with the help of the Department of Communications.

Social work methods are used in the attempt to discover common
needs and how to meet them, while community development methods
consist of eliciting and stimulating the participation of the
village people in helping themselves.

 — Village development, carried out by the adults in
   the villages.

 — Family development by way of integrating families
   into the village development process.

 — Youth participation in village development.

As was mentioned earlier, LSD is an independent non-governmental
organization, independent in its financial support and expenditure.

Examples of significant adult education can be found in several
other Ministries, such as Department of Religious Affairs and
the Department of the Interior.

ADULT EDUCATION AND NATION BUILDING

While there are many disparities between countries, the main
objectives of adult education are almost the same everywhere,
directed to the fulfillment and enlargement of human beings and
to the development needs of nations and peoples.

In addition to these objectives, adult education in Indonesia
is also directed towards nation building and national resilience.

What is Nation Building?

Nation building could not be carried out when the people were
not independent. Prior to 1945, what the Indonesian national
leaders tried to achieve through adult education was the awakening of national consciousness. In this they were very successful. People became aware of their own indigenous cultural values
and that they were by no means inferior to other peoples.

After Indonesia proclaimed its independence on the 17th of
August 1945, all activities, including adult education, were
directed towards one national aim: the defence of the new
Republic.

Most of the adults were trained in combat fighting and guerilla
warfare, without neglecting necessary educational activities.
In spite of the many difficulties, literacy programmes were
carried out, although on a limited scale. Courses in politics
for adults, especially relating to the Five Principles of the
Indonesian State Philosophy, the national freedom movement, and
national political history were also offered. By the end of
1949 Indonesian sovereignty was established under an Indonesian
National Government and the first stage in nation building was
successfully accomplished.

National Resilience

National resilience is an attitude of self-preservation and is
therefore indivisible from nation-building. Indonesia must

strengthen itself physically, economically, politically, socially and culturally, if it wants to survive and preserve its
identity in the turmoils and upheavals of the present. The
idea of national resilience will have little meaning, however,
if it is not in harmony with the neighbouring countries. In
global politics it is a harsh fact that countries must maintain
themselves against the powerful nations. That is why Indonesia
has joined fully with the other ASEAN member countries and is
advocating a regional resilience, based on education, mutual
respect, interdependence and co-operation.

Mozambique

Mozambique is one of the young countries in Africa born of a
ten-year people's war against Portuguese colonial fascism.
Consequently, our experience with literacy and adult education
is somewhat limited. Nevertheless we consider it important and
valid.

The Constitution of the People's Republic of Mozambique contains
the following provisions:

Fundamental rights and duties of citizens:

In the People's Republic of Mozambique work and education constitute rights and duties of every citizen. Fighting the backwardness created by colonialism, the State promotes the necessary conditions so that these rights may be extended to all
citizens.

General principles:

The people's Republic of Mozambique undertakes an energetic
fight against illiteracy and obscurantism and promotes the development of national culture and personality. The State acts
to promote internationally an awareness of Mozambican culture
and to enable the Mozambican people to benefit from it.

Education in Mozambique

Up to the time of the Portuguese colonialist invasion, Mozambique
was essentially dominated, as were various African countries in
the sixteenth century, by a feudal regime. During the colonial
period two kinds of education existed that reflected forms of
social organization: traditional education and colonial education.

The first, which corresponds to traditional society, was characterized by superstition, by the oral transmission of tradition elevated into dogma, and by the fight against new ideas.
This resulted from a superficial knowledge of nature and from
a traditional society based on subsistence agriculture. The

second was aimed at perpetuating the domination of the colonial
bourgeousie through foreign cultural values and contempt for
our culture. Individualism, elitism and social and racial discrimination were fostered since they maintained the colonial
system.

A consciousness of national unity led to the organization, on
June 25, 1962, of a resistance movement through the formation
of a vanguard that embodied the aspirations of our people — the
Mozambique Liberation Front (FRELIMO). In September 1964, the
people, under the FRELIMO leadership, launched the armed national
liberation struggle. A struggle within FRELIMO between a revolutionary line and a reactionary line clarified that the struggle
for the creation of a new society and new structures would fail
without the creation of a New Man with a new mentality capable
of taking on the revolutionary fight.

The triumphant revolutionary line and the gradual deepening of
the political processes of the war itself demanded a new definition of education as placed at the service of the people. Thus,
the two articles of the constitution quoted above, synthesize a
permanent and continuous preoccupation that FRELIMO has expressed
since its foundation: to provide everyone with access to an
education geared principally, at that time, to the formation of
cadres for the tasks of political and armed action and for the
tasks of national reconstruction, particularly in agricultural
production. It is within this context that there was born a
new type of revolutional education to raise the political,
scientific and technical knowledge of the people so that they
can participate effectively in the creation of the New Man and
in the construction of a new society.

The fundamental objectives of this new kind of education were
expressed by the President of FRELIMO and of the People's Republic of Mozambique, Samora Moise Machel, in a speech in September 1970:

> "... In order to implement the bases of a pros-
> perous and advanced economy, science must con-
> quer superstition. To unite all Mozambicans
> above diverse languages and traditions requires
> that in our consciousness the tribe dies so
> that the Nation may be born."

This means that education is not merely to teach reading and
writing, nor is it the means of creating an elite group with no
direct relationship to our objectives. We do not want science

to serve the enrichment of a minority, the oppression of man
or the denial of the creative initiative of the masses.

In teaching, each one of us must assume his revolutionary responsibilities; to see study as an instrument at the service of
the masses and as a revolutionary task that must be combined
with the revolutionary tasks of production and combat. He who
has studied must be the match that comes to light the flame
that is the people. The principle task of education — in teaching, in textbooks and in programmes — is to inculcate in each
of us a scientific, objective and collective ideology that permits us to further the revolutionary process.

Education must prepare us to develop the new society and meet
its demands. Education must give us a personality which, without being subservient, knows how to assimilate critically the
ideas and experiences of other people. We must acquire a scientific open attitude free from all superstition and traditional
dogma. We must make everyone assume the necessity of serving
the people, of participating in production, of respecting manual
work, of freeing individual initiatives, of developing a sense
of responsibility. That is, we want a revolutionary mentality
that uses science to serve the people.

Pre-Independence Literacy Activities

With FRELIMO, the literacy process arose as a response to the
immediate problem of the war and national reconstruction. As
a result of the obscurantist policy developed by colonialism,
98 per cent of the population were illiterate.

From the beginning it was clear that this rate of illiteracy
constituted an enormous obstacle to the rapid development of
the armed struggle and national reconstruction. To wage a modern war that demanded the execution of advanced plans and the
handling of modern weapons, and to build a new society, it became necessary for the agents of this process to possess political, scientific and technical knowledge. This knowledge could
only be acquired if people knew how to read and write.

The development of the armed struggle brought the liberation
of a large part of our territory and population. The need to
administer the liberated areas made even more clear that illiteracy was a brake on the implementation of national reconstruction tasks. By teaching reading and writing we are enabling

every Mozambican to increase his technical and scientific knowledge. This will permit him to better understand society and
the world in order to be able to act in a creative manner. It
has been necessary, at first, to use Portuguese as the language
of literacy and as an instrument of unity since a variety of
languages are spoken throughout the country.

Two Literacy Seminars, the first during the armed national liberation struggle and the second during the transitional government in April 1974, contributed towards the definition of the
fundamental objectives of literacy and adult education. These
can be summarized as follows:

Adult education is a means of freeing the creative initiative
of the people, of helping them to use their own energies and
means to find adequate methods for their complete independence
and national reconstruction. The objectives are:

a) to engage all the people in the revolution for the creation
    of a new society;

b) to spread the political philosophy of FRELIMO through the
    conscious study of problems in order to create ways for the
    country to advance collectively;

c) to relate popular education to production so as to make the
    school a base for the people to take their power and to lead
    them to understand their role in the transformation of soc-
    iety through the value of manual work and a collective spi-
    rit;

d) to activate the tasks of national reconstruction by turning
    attention to the countryside where the greater part of our
    population live, making them resolve their own problems,
    meet their needs, and transform their cultural and material
    life;

e) to permit the individual to rediscover his positive tradi-
    tions, his personality, and his values through knowledge of
    history, culture, human and economic geography;

f) to learn reading, writing and arithmetic so as to better
    fight against exploitation and obscurantism; to acquire
    scientific knowledge; and to undertake cultural exchange
    with other peoples;

g) to reinforce national unity and develop the awareness of
    the nation as being one people;

h) to develop an internationalist spirit and solidarity with all peoples struggling against colonialism and imperialism.

The liberation of great areas of our country created the need
to develop educational programmes for children and for adults.
(In 1970 there were some 20,000 children at school in the liberated areas.) In the first phase, those already literate dedi-
cated themselves to literacy work. Later, during their holidays,
students from FRELIMO schools taught literacy throughout the
liberated areas. However, the conditions of war limited the
continuity and success of these efforts. The population was
subject to frequent displacement because of the need to transport war materials to zones further in the interior, and because
of enemy movements and bombing raids. There was a shortage of
cadres to serve as teachers; no centralized programme; and a
lack of all support material for literacy activities. Despite
these difficulties, we succeeded in making part of our people
literate and in raising their political and technical level.

A Literacy Seminar held with people from the liberated areas
resulted in a decision to launch a national literacy campaign
because, due to lack of continuity, many adults had lapsed into
illiteracy. It was agreed that a special campaign should
train monitors to work with new literates and who would then
become literacy teachers. Priorities for literacy centres on
comrades engaged in the politico-military and administrative
structures of FRELIMO since they had, and would have, a fundamental role in the new society. The urgencies of war made it
impossible to put the recommendations into immediate practice
but they constituted fundamental guidelines for subsequent activities.

Transitional Phase

When the transitional government took office, the President of
FRELIMO outlined its task. In education, the fight against
illiteracy was a priority to be concentrated principally in
rural areas where schools were practically non-existent.

Since the objectives of the transitional phase were to enable
FRELIMO to assume politico-military control of the country, it
was necessary to create conditions that would extend popular
democratic power through structures capable of consolidating
FRELIMO on a national scale. These structures are *grupos dinamizadores* which are embryonic future party committees and
which include a literacy and adult education section. Through-

out Mozambique, the teaching of adults is based in the *grupos
dinamizadores* who apply directives, mobilize literates to teach
the illiterate, and apply the principle of self-reliance. Literacy emerged as a political task because it communicates knowledge of FRELIMO's philosophy and plans to all the people.

A second Literacy Seminar in 1974 brought together the experience
of the liberated areas and the initiatives of the recently formed
grupos dinamizadores. In some areas illiteracy was so widespread
that it was difficult to find anyone who could teach. Lack of
books and materials, as well as lack of coordinating and supporting structures, continue to plague the programme. Despite
these difficulties, advances have been made in the improvement
of methods that are more suitable to the realities of the people,
in the development of political awareness, and in the communication of scientific knowledge. At this point, it is still difficult to evaluate the results of these efforts.

However, in the country and in the towns, in factories and public offices, in a variety of locations where minimum conditions
for study exist, the initiatives of the people continue to develop, incorporated within the local political structure.

Administration of Literacy Activities

The Ministry of Education and Culture is responsible for the
whole system of literacy and adult education at the national
level. Within this Ministry is the National Directorate of
Literacy and Adult Education (DNAEA) which has a National Adult
Literacy Service to orient and control adult education programmes
and a National Adult Education Service to organize the funcional
training of the recent literates.

Both national services are charged with the training of literacy
and adult education monitors. Under their guidance is the Commission for the Elaboration of Programmes and Texts and the
Commission for the Formation of Cadres. The development of these
programmes demands the contribution of various sectors, particularly those linked to agricultural production, health and
housing. The Ministry of Education recently created literacy
structures at the provincial level to coordinate, plan and
organize activities. In a majority of the districts, Ministry
structures are already active.

Present Tasks

The first task of the National Directorate of Literacy and
Adult Education (DNAEA) was a survey of information, statistics
and material. This makes it possible to undertake effective
planning and to benefit from the rich experience of people in
various parts of the country as well as to study and identify
the best way to support the activities that are already developed. At the same time — based on earlier experiences, particularly those of the liberated areas — a start has been made
on a common literacy method and on common programmes that stem
from the realities of the People's Republic of Mozambique and
that are oriented, in particular, towards workers, peasants,
and elements of the Mozambique People's Liberation Forces.

To achieve the objective of making all people literate, the
DNAEA relies on Party structures that will intensify their ex-
planations of the need for literacy and of the essential political nature of this task. To support this work, mass media
will be used. Moreover, the work of the Party structures,
rooted as they are in the people, will enable the recruitment
of voluntary teacher monitors since a national campaign demands
a large number of monitors and the people's active commitment
to literacy.

The information gathered, and the consolidation of structures
at all levels, will create conditions for a national meeting on
Literacy and Adult Education to study the situation of literacy
and adult education throughout the country, priorities, guidelines for continuity, methods of training monitors and pedagogical techniques. The conclusions of this meeting will permit
the organization of training courses for literacy monitors which
will start at national level and extend to district level. With
this background it will be possible to launch a National Literacy Campaign in 1977. The campaign will give priority to younger people, because they are the productive force of the nation.

One factor which will make an important contribution towards
assuring the continuing practice of reading and writing is the
People's Newspaper (Jornal do Povo) which is organized by
FRELIMO's Department of Information and Propaganda. Displayed
in various locations in town and country, these newspapers
transmit directives from the organization, national and international news, as well as local news and problems. Not only do
these newspapers provide practice in reading, they also offer
practice in writing, through write-ups on local events and con-

cerns.   Special radio programmes support these newspapers as
well as the whole literacy programme.

Literacy and Adult Education in Communal Villages

> "Mozambique is an essentially rural country in
> its social composition, a country that depends
> essentially on agriculture. Despite this, we
> are a country in which agricultural resources,
> land and water, are under-utilized. This means
> we are forced to import agricultural products
> and the overwhelming majority of the peasants
> live in atrocious misery, deprived of the
> principal elements of humanity."

> (The President of FRELIMO and the People's
> Republic of Mozambique, Samora Moise Machel)

During the national liberation struggle FRELIMO understood that
a fight against colonialism would include a struggle to destroy
capitalism, the essence of which is the exploitation of man by
man. Since such exploitation is indissolubly linked to private
property, the "Communal Village" is an instrument of this
struggle, because it is an organized form of collective production.

> "The "Communal Village" will permit the peasants
> — until now dispersed throughout the country-
> side, based in their large majority on subsis-
> tence agriculture — to unite their forces
> through collective production. Integrated into
> FRELIMO structures, they will consolidate wor-
> ker peasant power, through collective study
> and discussions and through the constant prac-
> tice of a collective life. The creation and
> development of "Aldeias Comunais" will certainly
> lead to the construction of towns that we want
> to be free and self-sufficient; towns born of
> the forests, from the means that we possess;
> towns that, corresponding to our needs and the
> level of economic progress, really contribute
> to the free and harmonious development of men
> and Mozambican society.

> (Extract from the Resolution on Communal Vil-
> lages, Eighth Meeting of the FRELIMO Central
> Committee, February 1976).

In the light of the above, literacy is an important support to
the work of mobilizing the peasants into communal villages for
collective production, for fighting against traditional and
colonial-capitalist ideas, for developing self-confidence and
for making everyone feel the importance of his role as a transforming agent of society. The priority for literacy is based
in units of organized production which by their very nature will
guarantee not only a better organization of literacy activities
but will also bring about increased production because of new
attitudes and new knowledge on the part of the literates.

Thus, in a first phase, the teaching of the language and of
reading and writing, will be accompanied by intensive political
and ideological education aimed at changing attitudes with regard to life and work and fostering active engagement in the
social revolution.

In the second phase — to ensure continuity of literacy — scientific and technical information, including an explanation of
natural phenomena, will constitute an important weapon in the
fight for increased productivity. Thus, the preparation of
literacy and adult education teacher-monitors will have a multi-
displinary character which will enable them to be dynamic agents
in the intended transformation not only of their pupils but
also of the whole community in which they are placed.

Vietnam

At the Conference, the representative of
Vietnam, Nguyen Van Luong, explained that at
all stages of the struggle for freedom "the
Vietnamese people's revolution has been fought
not only on the political, military and economic fronts but also on the cultural and educational fronts. It is on the latter fronts
that the elimination of illiteracy and the complementary educational work have supplied us a
whole army of revolutionary intellectuals sprung
from the peasants and we have drawn useful lessons for the formation of a new education."
Because of the general interest in Vietnam, and
the role of the popular education movement
during three decades of political and military
struggle, a "case study" of this work prepared
by Lê Thành Khôi is included.

LITERACY TRAINING AND REVOLUTION: THE VIETNAMESE EXPERIENCE

History has shown that, up to the present, revolutionary regimes
have been the only ones capable of organizing successful mass
literacy campaigns. From the Soviet Union to China, from Vietnam to Cuba, all revolutionary governments have given high priority to the eradication of illiteracy because teaching people
to read and write awakens consciousness and stimulates participation in political action. It is impossible to transform society if the great majority of adults do not turn a critical eye
upon social reality and do not strongly desire to build a better
future and to assume responsibility for their destiny.

Vietnam provides an example of the integration of education into
the movement of national and social liberation, generating acceptance by the people of the necessary efforts and sacrifices and
of the need to eradicate ignorance.

Literacy and National and Social Liberation

Until the beginning of this century, tradiational culture was
based on the *han*, or classical Chinese, despite the romanization
of the Vietnamese language of *quôc ngu* by early missionaries and
its spread by the colonial regime as a means of countering the
influence of the nation's literati who led the resistance. *Quôc
ngu* proved to be so simple and easy to learn that the nation-
alists adopted it and transformed it into a cultural weapon
against foreign domination — a fine example of the dialectic of
history!

The renewal of *quôc ngu* and the eradication of illiteracy were
among the urgent tasks of the Communist Party of Indochina when,
in 1943, it launched its guerilla war against the French occupation. After the victory of the revolution in August 1945, the
Democratic Replublic of Vietnam concentrated on three fundamental tasks: to conquer hunger, the foreign aggressor and ignorance. These tasks were organically linked because a new country
cannot accomplish its political and social revolution without
at the same time promoting a revolution in the economic and
cultural fields.

Following the establishment of the Department of Popular Education in September 1945, Hô Chi Minh called for the eradication
of illiteracy:

> In order to safeguard our independence and to
> make our country strong and prosperous, each
> Vietnamese citizen should know his rights and
> his duties, and he should be capable of contri-
> buting to the work of national construction.
> Above all, everyone should be able to read and
> write *quôc ngu*.
>
> Those who already know how to read and write
> should pass their knowledge on to the others.
> The illiterate should make every effort to
> learn. Husbands would teach their wives;
> older brothers and sisters should teach their
> younger brothers and sisters; children should
> teach their parents; the master of the house
> should teach those living beneath his roof.
> As for women, they should study all the more
> assiduously in order to make up for the count-
> less obstacles that have prevented them from
> obtaining instruction up till now. The hour

has struck for them to catch up with men and
to make themselves worthy to be fully-fledged
citizens.

At that time, 80 to 90 per cent of the population was illiterate.
The percentage was even higher in the mountainous regions inhab-
ited by minorities, many of whom had no written culture.

When the war spread from North to South, the war on illiteracy
was an integral part of the resistance and classes in literacy
merged into political classes. Peasants learned to read practically through political and military directives and discussions.
In 1953, the government launched its agrarian reform with the
objective that power in the countryside would pass into the hands
of the peasants and consolidate the worker-peasant alliance;
that the peasants, once freed and masters of the land they worked,
would raise their output and living standards; and that once
the majority were able to feed and clothe themselves adequately,
they would work to educate themselves with greater enthusiasm.
During this period, literacy training was linked to the class
struggle and the agrarian revolution. The agrarian reform contributed to the victory at Diên-Biên-phu in 1954 which liberated
the country from French occupation.

One year after the restoration of peace, a three-year-plan for
popular education was implemented which led to the virtual elimination of illiteracy in the plains. By the end of 1958, 93.4
per cent of those between age 12 and 50 could read and write.
Thus, literacy training in Vietnam was conceived, first and foremost, as a political task aimed at raising the political consciousness of the masses and, in consequence, their ardour in
the revolutionary struggle and in the process of production.

Ideology alone was not enough. It was backed by a varied and
highly flexible organization.

Organization and Training of Instructors

The organization of literacy training was based on the "mass
line". This means it is essential to make the masses conscious
of the fact that the struggle against ignorance is their struggle
so that they will eventually assume responsibility for it and
find their own ways of overcoming practical obstacles. The
Vietnamese Party does not believe in "revolutionary spontaneity".
Because of the prevailing illiteracy and the country's long his-

tory of exploitation and subjection, the first priority was to
conduct a process of awakening, explanation, mobilization and
organization. The movement was directed and controlled by the
Party and the State with mass organizations of youth, women,
trade unions and peasants acting as transmission belts.

The following is how one leader described the different stages
of the literacy campaign*:

a) Propaganda and mass mobilization
    Books, the press, radio, leaflets and directives are extreme-
    ly important but they are inadequate unless backed up by
    living and attractive "mass" measures such as: slogans and
    tracts; processions and spectacular displays like giant
    model penholders and exercise books; songs, dances and
    plays; the sale of spelling books to illiterates; invit-
    ations to literates to pass beneath the "gateway of honour".
    Towards the end of the last stage of the campaign people
    who encounter difficulty or who lack determination are
    dealt with individually. We try to make them realize the
    disadvantages of remaining illiterate and the benefits of
    being able to read and write. Once a person is convinced,
    he or she becomes a propagandist and the evidence of the
    concrete results they have achieved makes their powers of
    persuasion frequently irresistible.

    At the end of each literacy course, a solemn prizegiving and
    certificate distribution ceremony is organized and onlookers
    are called upon to register for the following literacy course.
    The best pupils receive an honourable mention. Ceremonies
    are organized for the presentation of honours to families,
    villages, districts and provinces that have successfully
    eradicated illiteracy. The government offers a series of
    rewards, including the Order of the Resistance and the Order
    of Labour to villages, districts or provinces.

b) Organization of courses
    Courses are organized to ensure that studies can be under-
    taken outside working hours; that studies become a function
    of working conditions in each region and according to each
    season; and that the studies are appropriate to each cate-
    gory of pupil. Most classes have relatively few pupils since

* Ngo Van Cat, La Liquidation de l'analphabétisme et l'enseignement complémentaire pour adultes, in L'Education en RDV, Etudes
Vietnamiennes No. 5 (Hanoi, 1955), pp. 37-42.

they are organized for each hamlet;   sometimes even for each
family. The greatest difficulty was to organize classes for
fishermen and for those who must travel constantly for their
work. In such cases it is necessary to see that they are
accompanied by a literacy instructor or to ensure that at
least one of their number is capable of teaching the others.

We had to strongly fight the tendency to organize regular
classes along the lines of school; this approach is utterly
unsuited to the conditions under which the people live and
work. We had to fight hardest against this in the latter
years of the war on illiteracy.

c) **The necessary means for studying**

As the movement spread, so the problems of means became more
difficult to resolve, especially during the resistance when
there was a great shortage of books, exercise books, ink,
metal pens, etc. Where ordinary school accommodation proved
inadequate, classes were started in private homes. Masters
and pupils made their own tables and even built classrooms.
Even the most rudimentary methods of printing were used and
pupils taking general schooling willingly copied lessons for
illiterates as dictated by their teachers during spelling
lessons. Paper was scarce and many pupils used banana leaves
for writing on. Some kinds of leaves and fruits provided a
liquid that served as an ink.

d) **Rapid teacher training**

How does one go about teaching hundreds of thousands of literacy instructors a method that can produce maximum results
in the least possible time? Accelerated training courses
were organized and implemented by the regions and the mass
organizations.

In most cases, these courses were no longer than five or
six days. The bulk of the course consists of political and
ideological classes designed to make these trainee-instructors
conscious of their responsibility and to make them love the
task that is about to be entrusted to them. Problems of the
organization of education mainly take the form of discussions
of the personal experiences of those involved. Accounts of
concrete successes already obtained help guide trainee-instructors.

A good many teachers have been granted the accolade "combat-
tant de l'émulation patriotique" (Hero of Labour) or have

received congratulatory diplomas or medals. They have come
up with countless innovations, such as popular songs that
help pupils to memorize more easily or to distinguish more
readily between certain letters that are similar in appear-
ance. Vietnamese writing is not difficult to learn. An
ordinary person, studying one hour a day, can learn to read
and write within three or four months. At the height of the
movement, organized competitions brought the average learning
period down to 72 days.

Complementary Education

Learning to read and write is just the first stage of a long
process. To ensure that the newly literate do not relapse into
their former state, they must have books and newspapers to read,
and effort must be made to broaden their range of useful knowledge. In 1946, Hô Chi Minh recommended that where illiteracy
has already been eliminated, teachers should take a further step
forward by teaching basic elements of hygiene, scientific ideas,
the history and geography of the country, and the rights and
duties of citizens. These recommendations were not always respected. At the end of the resistance period in 1954, a good
many of those taught to read and write had forgotten all they
had learned.

With the advent of peace, the North threw itself into a three-
fold revolution of socialist construction: a revolution in
production, a technical revolution and an ideological and cultural revolution. All three called for a constant process of
raising the cultural, scientific and technical level of workers,
peasants and cadres destined to become the "collective master
of the nation". These classes had to learn how to manage a
cooperative or a factory, how to distribute labour and income,
how to introduce technical or organizational change, etc. The
first Five Year Plan (1961-1965) gave priority to complementary
education for adults in the educational system. The problem
grew even more urgent in 1965 with the American escalation. It
now became necessary to maintain or to increase output under
bombing; and to learn to handle anti-aircraft guns, artillery
and missiles which call for complex calculations. Thanks to
accelerated study courses, it was possible for women and old
peasants to manage cooperatives and thus replace the men who
had left for the war.

As with literacy, complementary education was organized along

flexible lines with content and methods varying according to
the age, profession, sector of activity and level of instruction
of each group. Like general education, it was divided into three
cycles of study* and the equivalent to grade IV was considered
the minimum level for all workers. Since adults already possess
a body of practical knowledge from life, it was decided to base
instruction on this practical knowledge so as to help them understand what they already knew from experience and then to go
on to acquire theoretical knowledge.

Programmes were devised on the basis of the needs of each category of workers, in addition to certain subjects taught univer-
sally, such as language and mathematics. Each subject contained
both fundamental concepts and other concepts that were dealt
with in more detail according to each category of worker. In
the case of physics, for example, the accent was on electricity
in classes intended for electrical workers, and on mechanical
engineering in classes for mechanics. The idea was to enable
those who operate machines to understand the principles behind
these machines; peasants, on the other hand, were taught the
utility of agricultural machinery and of the need to improve
their implements. The two criteria for these programmes were
realism — the relationship with productive work—and conciseness
— concentration on the main points. Similarly, teaching methods
emphasize the relationship between theory and practice so that
adults can make use of their experience in order to assimilate
scientific concepts, and to apply their learning to the solution
of problems arising in their work and thus improve their performance.

The forms of teaching vary greatly, depending upon the availability of workers. In government offices, factories, construction sites, classes are held twice a week. In cooperatives and
on State farms, their frequency varies according to the work
schedule, farming seasons and even the weather. By studying
five or six hours weekly, an adult can complete the 1st Cycle
in three or four years. There are types of school for workers
who temporarily leave their jobs (while continuing to receive
their wages or their share of cooperative income). Some of
these offer advanced vocational training (in which case the
adult subsequently returned to his former job); others enable
young workers or peasant cadres to enter technical secondary
schools or higher education. The Army, too, has its own teach-

---

* General education lasts 10 years and is divided into three
cycles of 4-3-3 for those aged 7-10, 11-13 and 14-16.

ing institutions. Workers' and peasants' clubs play host to
lecturers who give talks on current affairs, on problems of
hygiene, science of technology. Special sessions are organized
for women (child-care, family planning, hygiene, education).

Since 1960, the number of people engaged annually in complementary education has amounted to around 1-1.5 million, not to mention classes arranged by the army*. One problem has been to
recruit sufficient teachers at a time when the number of educated persons was relatively low. The 1960 census showed that
for every 1000 inhabitants, 327 had attained the 1st Cycle, 33
had completed the 2nd Cycle, five the 3rd Cycle, and one person
had completed higher education. As with literacy training, the
mass line was adopted for teacher training. Professional teachers were mobilized, as well as pupils in secondary and technical
schools and in the advanced classes of the complementary education programme, skilled workers, managers of factories, those
on construction sites, cooperatives and State farms, and crafts-
men.

A body of regular teachers, specialized in complementary education, was gradually built up. These numbered over 7,000 by
1970, most of them teaching in the 2nd Cycle. They receive
training and attend refresher courses in special teacher training schools existing at both central and provincial echelons.
In addition, all teacher training colleges, at whatever level,
provide classes in adult psychology and teaching methods so that,
even if young teachers are appointed to teaching posts in the
general education system, they can also play an effective role
in complementary education.

Literacy Training for Minorities

The eradication of illiteracy has taken longer in the mountain
regions than in the plains because the degree of cultural backwardness is greater and because most of these peoples have no
written language. While the most numerous people, the Viêt or
Kinh, live in the plains, the mountain regions, covering two-
thirds of the total area of the country, have close to 70 ethnic
groups, totalling 3.7 million in the North and 1.5 million in
the South. They represent 12 percent of the country's total
population of 45 million.

---

* Hoang To Dong, l'Enseignement complémentaire pour adultes, in
L'Enseignement général en RDVN, Etudes Vietnamiennes, No. 30
(Hanoi, 1971), p. 31.

From the time of its foundation, in 1930, the aim of the Communist Party of Indochina has been to achieve the union of nationalities on the basis of equality and mutual assistance and to recognize their right to self-determination. This policy enabled the DRVN to establish and consolidate its guerilla bases in the High Plateaux Region and to wage its resistance and revolutionary campaigns successfully. The 1959 Constitution explicitly recognizes the equal status of all nationalities, their right to their own language, to develop their national culture and to create autonomous regions (of which there are two at the present time).

To achieve real equality, the minorities must catch up with the rest of the national economically, socially and culturally. Literacy campaigns have been organized along lines similar to those in the plains. In 1946, 80 cadres working in popular education and originating from 24 minorities were trained to serve as the core of the movement. With the restoration of peace in 1954, "shock brigades for the fight against ignorance" were sent into the mountains to

> "live amid the local populations, to share their
> way of life and to take part in production.
> At the same time as holding literacy classes,
> they also played an active part in other social
> activities, notably in prophylactic movements,
> in the fight against superstition and in the
> construction of a new lifestyle. Their example
> spread rapidly and small groups of local volun-
> teer instructors were formed. Among certain
> semi-nomadic peoples living at altitudes up to
> 2000 metres, these groups initiated adult lit-
> eracy classes for five or six families along
> with one or more general education classes for
> children." *

As a result, literacy was virtually wiped out in the mountain regions of the North by 1961.

Attention turned then to complementary education mainly aimed at the peasants in cooperatives and the cadres of communes — those in the party, the local authorities, the people's militia,

---

* Nhat Hung, L'Enseignement au service des minorités nationales, in Régions montagneuses et minorités nationales en RDVN, Etudes Vietnamiennes, No. 15 (Hanoi, 1967), p. 119.

youth, women's organizations. Each year, around 100,000 montag-
nards, aged between 18 to 45, attend these classes. In order
to train cadres more rapidly, complementary education schools
were established to enable adults to come and study for six
months or a year at State expense. Programmes are chiefly designed to enable cadres to learn new techniques in agriculture
and forestry, along with management principles for the agricultural cooperatives. In addition, a number of "Labour Schools"
hold classes in both general and complementary education for
young adults. Each school possesses its own farm; half of the
curriculum is taken up by study, the other half by production.
The pupils put up the school buildings, make the furnitue and
are responsible for running the school. First Degree education,
literacy training and complementary education for adults are
conducted in both the mother tongue and in the national Vietnamese language.

It took eight years (1953-61) to arrive at this result. In 1945,
the Thai alone possessed a written language, derived from Pali,
which is completely different from the *quốc ngu*. Priority was
given to the creation of a script for the Vietnamese-related
languages of Tay, Nung, Meo and Muong and to perfecting the
Thai script. In this way, since 1961, 85 per cent of the minority populations in the North has acquired a script. A similar
policy in the South has developed scripts for other languages.
Special schools are training teachers of the various nationalities.

Conclusion

The following lessons emerge from the Vietnamese experience:

1) The <u>political</u> factor (struggle for independence, for social
   emancipation) is the most powerful driving force in persuad-
   ing populations to accept the necessary sacrifices and
   efforts in order to wipe out ignorance. But the political
   factor alone is not enough. In one year, 2.5 million were
   taught to read and write, which is a remarkable achievement
   (even if the degree of literacy acquired was rather superficial), but it was a long way off the target. Illiteracy
   was not entirely eliminated until 1958. It took 13 years
   to teach the entire population to read and write, although
   the initial rate of illiteracy was high (80 to 90 per cent)
   and the task was carried out in war conditions. (It is
   worth remembering that the eradication of illiteracy in the

Soviet Union took a quarter of a century. The illiteracy
rate, which stood at 75 per cent in 1917, fell to 49 per
cent in 1926 and to 19 per cent in 1939. One reason (among
others) why Cuba was able to eradicate illiteracy within
one year was that the initial illiteracy rate was 23 per
cent.)

2) Ideology must be backed up by suitable <u>organization</u> in accordance with a <u>mass line</u> so that people know it is their job
to implement literacy programmes and that they should do so
by relying on their own material and human resources rather
than on the State. The role of the State or Party intervention comes at the outset of the process in the work of
ideological "conscientization". We are not concerned with
doing things <u>for</u> the masses, but rather with making them
capable of carrying out the work themselves.

3) Apart from the political factor, Vietnam benefited from
such favourable conditions as the existence of a <u>written
language</u> with a long secular tradition of study. The written
Vietnamese language is exactly the same as the spoken one
and is extremely easy to learn because it is a monosyllabic
invariable language. The lack of this favourable factor is
one of the reasons for the failure of certain literacy campaigns where political motivation was nonetheless strong
(as in Algeria in 1963 after independence where literacy
campaigns were conducted either in a foreign language —
French—or in an Arabic that differed from the spoken language).

4) Learning to read and write is merely a first step. There
has been no relapse since 1954 because constant effort has
been made to raise the educational level of the people.
Each year, complementary education mobilizes some 1-1.5
million adults. The dynamism of the <u>environment</u> plays a
major role in helping to imprint knowledge permanently and
to broaden it.

5) A multi-national state such as Vietnam is obliged to pay
close attention to the education and training of <u>minorities</u>.
It is not enough merely to being about political and economic improvements; it is also necessary to raise their cultural level, to create written languages where none existed
before, to fight against feudal traditions and superstitions,
to rapidly train local cadres. Autonomy for minorities and
the improvement of their material and cultural levels —
these are a guarantee of national union and integration.

Nguyen Van Luong in his concluding remarks at the Conference
described plans for the present and future:

a) As far as the improvement of the cultural standards of the
    cadres and the people are concerned we have asserted that
    the common responsibility is shared not only by the various
    educational institutions but also by various other branches,
    the mass organizations at all levels and the leaderships of
    the institutions (villages, factories, construction sites,
    state farms ...); thus, there should be an active and close
    coordination among them. These joint commissions are called
    the Leadership Board for Elimination of Illiteracy and Com-
    plementary Education with a cadre from the Administrative
    or Party Committee as head and representatives of various
    branches as members. The Central Commission for Elimination
    of Illiteracy and Complementary Education of our country
    has been headed by President Tôn Dúc Tháng over the last 20
    years.

b) As the complementary educational work assumes a mass charac-
    ter, launching emulation movements is of special importance.
    We have taken the emulation as the lever to drive forward
    the movements among the teachers, the learners and among
    the branches concerned and emulation movements have started
    in every province, every district, every village, every fac-
    tory and even in every school.

c) Over the last 30 years, under the leadership of the Vietnam
    Workers' Party, we have sought to eliminate illiteracy and
    on this basis, gradually raised the cultural standard of
    the cadres, young folks, workers and peasants. Though we
    have truly recorded a few achievements, we still meet with
    difficulties and commit errors that we should try hard to
    do away with. Our industry and agriculture are embarking
    on the path from a small-scale to a large-scale, socialist
    production. Thus, it is thanks to the strong determination
    on the part of the people and the state that the complemen-
    tary educational work can develop and meet the demands of
    the revolution.

Issues for Development

INTRODUCTION

Art is better than strength.

Spanish Proverb

Sometimes by a jump, sometimes sidling, sometimes crawling, and sometimes on all fours.

Russian saying

It may be true that according to an ancient adult education pre-
cept "ideas have hands and feet" but international development,
on a national or on a world scale, requires much more than the
power of an idea if there is to be distribution, penetration
and impact. Flexible, sustained organization and appropriate
methods are required everywhere. Some present forms of organization have long been outmoded and sterile, they need to be
drastically revised or replaced. Training of all kinds and
levels should be close to where action is taking place, not
only in a remote library in some far-off continent. Research
can be mystifying and alienating and it can be a tool of intellectual colonialism, not a liberating aid to decision-making
and action. It is not only a question of more research but
what kinds of research will hobble or can promote participation.
Much of the preparatory work for the Conference was about organization and methods for development, and plans and experiences
were reviewed by two-score different groups. These constituted
the laboratory where ideas were tested in relation to their
effect, and where proposals for the next five years were formulated.

Agricultural Extension and Development

James De Vries

In attempts to develop their agricultural sectors and rural
populations, many Less Developed Countries (LDCs) have invested
considerable resources in agricultural extension systems. International agencies also stress the need of educating farmers both
as a means towards agricultural development and as an end in
itself. Many aid programmes therefore include extension and
training components. Most of the extension systems in the LDCs
are modelled after those in the USA and Western Europe apparently
in the hope that the latter's success can be duplicated by following its example. Schultz, however, points out that in most
LDCs extension has not lived up to expectations and has therefore come in for a great deal of criticism in recent years.

In part, the disappointment is due to the fact that expectations
regarding the impact of extension have been unrealistic. Many
believed that by merely educating and "motivating" peasants,
major improvements in agricultural production could be realized.
While education is undoubtedly an important factor, they failed
to take into account the complex nature of agricultural development. Agricultural development depends on a large number of
factors such as: good marketing systems, attractive prices,
relevant new technology, favourable and stable government policies, and the availability of credit and agricultural extension.
The success of extension efforts therefore not only depends on
how well the extension system functions, but also on the complex
social, political, economic and physical environment in which
it operates. Agricultural extension alone may therefore have
very little impact. Part of the disappointment with extension
therefore seems because extension has been oversold in many LDCs
to the neglect of some of the above factors which interact with
extension in the promotion of rural development.

Much of the blame can be placed on the extension systems themselves. For a variety of reasons they have failed not only in
their traditional role of bridging the gap between researchers
and farmers but also in their more recently assigned roles of
broadly educating and mobilizing the peasantry. The blame is
often put on such factors as: poorly trained and motivated
staff, lack of planning, ill defined responsibilities, lack of

back up facilities, and poor links to research, with the result
of pleas for more funds, better staff, more vehicles, closer
supervision, etc. However, new training programmes, additional
staff, more demonstration materials and more "expert" advice
seems in many cases to have had little impact on programme success. This leads us to question whether the problem with agricultural extension in LDCs had been conceptualized correctly.

In general, the problems of agricultural extension in LDCs seem
to have been conceptualized within the framework of the conventional western model. This is because most of the "expert" consultants brought in to evaluate extension systems come from the
US and Western Europe or have been trained there. It seems that
this model has been recommended and adopted in LDCs without much
critical thought as to how well it applies to a situation which
is radically different from the one in which the model evolved.
A basic principle of extension organization is that it must be
adapted to the situation in which it is to function. Can a system evolved to meet the needs of large scale, capital intensive
farms be expected to meet those of small scale, largely subsistence oriented farms? The fact that the conventional extension
system has failed, after 75 years, to solve the problems of small,
poor farmers in the US and Western Europe seems to have been ignored by those who advocate its adoption in LDCs. Not only is
the concrete development situation very different, but development objectives and strategies also vary widely. While Western
countries have chosen capitalist, market oriented economies,
many LDCs have adopted socialist, centrally planned economies.
While the West seeks to maintain its dominance of LDCs in order
to continue to exploit them, LDCs seek to liberate themselves
and end this exploitation. Can a system which even in the US
has been much criticised for favouring the status quo really
contribute to this liberation?

The story is told of a visitor to China who after a week of
studying China's agricultural system had dinner with Mao Tse-
tung. Mao asked the visitor what was the primary lesson he had
drawn from his experience. The visitor said he was very impressed
by the Chinese system and urged Mao to make experts available to
advise other countries that were doing less well. At this answer Mao looked very troubled. Asked why, he stated that he was
disturbed by the guest's reply. Mao explained that there are
no easy solutions to problems. The complex Chinese system evolved over many years and had involved a lot of mistakes. It
would be wrong to attempt to duplicate it elsewhere. The only
thing replicable from the Chinese experience was the slow, pain-

ful, dialectical process of experimentation that the Chinese
had pursued in evolving their unique system.

Can the problems of extension in LDCs really be solved within
the framework of the conventional extension model, or is this
model itself part of the problem? A detailed look at the experience of one African country in attempting to follow and adopt
this model to its own needs may offer some tentative answers.

> Professor De Vries uses Tanzania as a case study
> to analyze the results of a traditional extension
> programme applied to a LDC. While the Tanzanian
> programme of developing Ujamaa villages has been
> successful, the author argues that extension has
> tended to reinforce dependency, as opposed to
> self-reliance, to emphasize innovations from the
> outside and "top-down" decision making, to in-
> crease rural differentiation through its work
> with the richer peasants. The full text is
> available from the Internaional Council for
> Adult Education.

In summary it seems fair to say that while Ujamaa villages have
offered new opportunities for extension work, the extension
system has largely failed to convert these opportunities into
reality. Part of the blame for this failure can be attributed
to the fact that while rural development policy and the rural
situation which form the context for extension work have changed
drastically, the extension system has remained basically the
same. This problem was clearly recognized by participants in
a recent workshop on agricultural extension in Ujamaa village
development, and resulted in a wide range of recommendations to
adopt extension to the needs of Ujamaa villages. In our view
for extension to fill the role assigned to it will demand a
complete restructuring to the present system. The key aspect
of this change must be bringing the system much more directly
and effectively under farmer control. Only when the farmers
exercise real control over the system will it serve their interests and thus aid in their self-liberation and development.

One possible way to implement this would be to have agents directly employed by the Ujamaa village with their salary either
coming from the village or controlled by it, thus making them
directly responsible to the Village Development Committee and
Chairperson. Village members could be recruited to be trained
as these village level extension workers and their level of pay

could be linked to their contribution to the village's development similarly to other farmers' income. As such, all village
level extension activities would be closely linked to the production activities and plans of that village and farmers would be
automatically and directly involved in the planning, implementation and evaluation of extension work.

Training of this level of extension worker would be of a short
term nature and could be done in any Ujamaa village which had
relevant experience and expertise. For example, a person to be
trained in poultry production would live and work in a village
where there already exists a successful project and someone with
expertise in this area. Various members of the village would
receive training in different areas so that each village would
eventually have a team of village "experts" performing the functions now filled by government employees. Such village level
teams could then be assisted by a hierarchy of agricultural
specialists employed by Ward, District and Regional Development
Committees. Such a restructuring would facilitate genuine dialogue between agricultural "experts" and farmers about agricultural and related problems.

Conclusion

The Tanzanian example clearly shows that the conventional system
evolved in the West is poorly suited to Tanzania's needs. Very
little has been written about agricultural extension in socialist countries whose model is perhaps more applicable to Tanzania.
At first hand it appears that no such system exists in these
countries. However, it is my view that as the continued learning of new skills and ideas by farmers is necessary for agricultural development, some system to facilitate this learning
must exist. We perhaps fail to recognize it because it does
not resemble our conventional model. In China, for example,
agricultural extension does not exist as a separate educational
system, but forms an integral part of a complex education-prod-
uction system providing continuous all-round mass education.

Tanzania is not unique in having a poorly adapted extension
system. As noted in the introduction, while the situation in
the LDCs and Western industrialized countries is drastically
different, and there are major differences among the LDCs, their
agricultural extension systems are remarkably similar. Agricultural extension is commonly regarded as ideologically neutral.
Because it concerns the introduction of new farming techniques,

it is believed not to support any particular ideology. As such
extension has been left in the hands of technocrats, to institute as they see fit.

The Tanzanian case study, however, clearly shows that far from
being neutral, extension is a definite force for the promotion
or maintenance of a particular concept of society. As Freire
has pointed out, neither education nor technology is ever void
of ideological content. The conventional concept of "extension"
itself rests on the assumption that knowledge is something which
can be given by those who have it (the experts) to those who
lack it (the peasants). It assumes a one-way flow of knowledge
from the extension agent to the farmer rather than the mutual
exchange of ideas in a dialogue out of which knowledge then
develops. As such, the conventional model can be seen as fostering dependency and being anti-development rather than educational and thus contributing towards genuine development.

The suitability of Western sociological, economic and political
models to the Third World has been questioned and many have
found them not only unadequate but a force for the continued
underdevelopment of the LDCs. Considering the widespread disappointment with agricultural extension, it seems high time to
question the conventional extension model and attempt to evolve
models specifically suited to the realities and aspirations of
the Less Developed Countries.

References

1. Barraclough, S. Training for Rural Development. Mimeo,
    Santiago, Chile. June 1973.

2. Cliffe, L. and Saul, J.S. (Eds.) Socialism in Tanzania.
    Vol. 1. Dar es Salaam, E.A. Publishing House. 1972.

3. De Vries, J. Has Extension Failed? A Case Study of Maize
    Growing Practices in Iringa, Tanzania, Eastern African
    Journal of Rural Development, 9 (forthcoming).

4. De Vries, J. and Fortman, L.P. A Study of Ujamaa Villages
    in Iringa Region. Prepared for FAO/UNDP Planning Team.
    Mimeo, Morogoro, 1974.

5. De Vries, J. and Hansel, H. Ujamaa Villages as a Strategy
    for Rural Development in Tanzania, in Hansel, H., De Vries,

154   J. De Vries

J. and Ndedya, P.C., Agricultural Extension in Ujamaa
Village Development. Morogoro University, 1975, pp. 19-27.

6. Cliffe, L., Lawrence, P., Luttrell, W., Migot-Adholla, S.
and Saul, J.S. (Eds.) Rural Cooperation in Tanzania. Dar
es Salaam, Tanzania Publishing House, 1975.

7. I.B.R.D., Tanzania Agricultural Sector Survey. Baltimore,
1974.

8. McKinsey et al., Reorganizing around the key tasks for
agricultural Development. Dar es Salaam, Ministry of Agriculture, 1973.

9. Nelson, R.D. and Kazungu, D. An Evaluation of the USAID
Extension Project in Uganda. Morgantown, University of
West Virginia, 1973.

10. Nyerere, J. Ujamaa - The Basis of African Socialism.
TANU, Dar es Salaam, 1962.

11. Raikes, P. and Meynen, W.L. Dependency, Differentiation
and the Diffusion of Innovation: a Critique of Extension
Theory and Practice, Annual Social Science Conference of
East African Universities, Nairobi, 1972.

12. Rodney, W. How Europe Underdeveloped Africa. Dar es
Salaam, Tanzanian Publishing House, 1973.

13. Schultz, T.W. Education and research in rural development,
in Turck, K.L. and Crowder, L.V. (eds.) Rural Development
in Latin America. New York State College of Agriculture,
Ithaca, 1967, pp. 391-402.

14. United Nations Economic Commission for Africa/Food and
Agriculture Organization Joint Agriculture Division. A
Comparative Analysis of Agricultural Extension Systems of
Eight East African Countries - With Suggested Guidelines
for Improvement. E/CN.14/AGRIP/10, Addis Ababa; ECA/FAO
Joint Agriculture Division, 1971.

Breaking the Monopoly of Knowledge: Research Methods, Participation and Development

Budd L. Hall

People cannot be developed; they can only
develop themselves. For while it is possible
for an outsider to build a man's house, an outsider cannot give the man pride and self-confidence in himself as a human being. Those
things a man has to create in himself by his
own actions. He develops himself by what he
does; he develops himself by making his own
decisions, by increasing his understanding of
what he is doing, and why; by increasing his
own knowledge and ability, and by his own full
participation — as an equal — in the life of
the community he lives in.

(Julius Nyerere, 1973:60)

Research is always and by logical necessity
based on moral and political valuations, and
the researcher should be obliged to account
for them explicitly.

(Gunnar Myrdal, 1970:74)

Background

Thinking about development, adult education and the role of
social investigation has undergone dramatic shifts in the recent
past. The "top down" concepts of education and development have
been widely questioned. Emphasis has shifted from concepts of
development based on urbanized expectations to the need to stimulate growth and change in rural areas. The importance and
necessity of increased popular involvement in decision making
in both rural and urban settings is accepted widely. Development is more and more seen as an awakening process, a process
of tapping the creative forces of a much larger proportion of
society, a liberating of more persons' efforts instead of a
"problem" to be solved by the planners and academicians from
afar.

Along with the shift in thinking about development has come a

general questioning in all fields of social science about the
relationship between the way in which research is conducted and
the overall values the researcher holds. This discussion within
the field of adult education has been particularly rich. There
are a growing number of adult education researchers who are ex-
ploring new methods. Kathleen Rockhill has suggested that adult
educators' search derives from three primary perspectives:

(1) The concern that quantitative research methods are
     not providing an adequate understanding of complex
     reality.

(2) The desire for 'practical' research that can be
     used as a base for setting policy and developing
     programs which will promote social justice and
     greater self-reliance.

(3) A humanistic view of human behaviour which sees
     individuals as active agents in their environ-
     ments rather than as passive objects to be re-
     searched.

                                              (1976:1)

What are the Weaknesses of the Most Commonly Used Research Methods?

If one examines the research in the field of adult education,
one would find that 90 per cent of the studies done represent
one form or another of the survey research approach. This
despite the fact that a vast range of other possible research
strategies exist. A number of shortcomings can be identified:

1) The survey research approach oversimplifies social reality and is therefore inaccurate.

In addition to the arbitrariness of instrument construction or
the class bias of such specific tools as semantic differential
tests and various other tests devised by those who work from a
primarily psychological base, these approaches have other weak-
nesses. A research process that extracts information from individuals in isolation from one another and aggregates this into
a single set of figures does so at the expense of reducing the
complexity and richness of human experience. Social responses
to problems by groups of people are not necessarily the same as
the total of individual responses of people acting alone. It is
of course correct to say that the use and interpretation of the
figures, "depends on the institutional and social context within

which the research is embedded" (Carr-Hill, 1974:30). But even
given an institutional framework that encourages popular participation or control of decision making, the representation of
population needs by a set of figures such as "22 per cent of
those interviewed said that their home environment has had the
most influence on their career choice", or "42.16 per cent of
teachers report problems", is inadequate, and unsatisfactory.
The illusion of accuracy through numbers has been long perpet-
uated by many of us at least partly as a way of hiding, obscur-
ing or mystifying research.

A second way in which survey research oversimplifies is the perspective of the forced choice. Information is sought through
interviews or questionnaires which provide a framework for the
responses. For example many questions ask people what is "most
influential", "least satisfactory", "first choice" or "most
responsible" regarding some specific attitude or decision when
attitudes, decisions and behaviour do not reflect a single cause.
The curious fact is that all of us have experience of this false
choice. We have often filled in forms or questionnaires and
have felt the desire to say, "that really isn't the right question". The forced choice approach reaches a fetish point in
some educational research as was seen in one case where a "diag-
nostic tool" was being employed to help in the analysis of new
adult students. Potential students of English were asked to
choose the one form of literature in which they were most interested from a list that included novels, short stories, poetry,
drama or non-fiction. Pity the person who either didn't know
the difference between the forms (this is likely enough in modern literature), wanted some of all, or was curious about a
specific period.

A third reason why one-time surveys oversimplify is their presentation of a static picture of reality, a photograph of a group
of people with neither a past nor a future. The very fact that
the survey is ahistorical is a severe limitation; social change
is a continuous process, a dialectic or movement from one pole
to another over time. The way people respond on one day under
one set of conditions by no means guarantees a similar reaction
at another time.

?) Survey research is often alienating, dominating or oppressive in character.

If one accepts Freire's point that teaching methods have ideological implications then the same holds true for research methods.

If one is concerned with increasing people's capacity to participate fully and gain some degree of control over their lives,
then research methods themselves can be part of this process.
Questionnaires or interviews designed in an office of a university or adult education institution are by nature onesided.
This process regards people as sources of information, as having
bits of isolated knowledge, but they are neither expected nor
apparently assumed able to analyze a given social reality. At
the extreme, researchers take up people's time with often badly
formulated questions and make interpretations based on little
experience in the area or social class the basis of programmes
which are then expected to be useful and relevant.

Research approaches of this style often create the illusion
among those who are the suppliers of information that research
is rigorous, highly technical, scientifically "pure" and that
the work can only be done by those who are university trained.
The abilities of people to investigate their objective realities
are not stimulated and the pool of human creativity is kept
within narrow confines. Those most familiar with the problems
and whose daily existence is affected by poor health, poor nutrition, low levels of production or past failures of educational
provision are effectively taken out of the active process of
making the changes which might lead to improvements. Control
is left to those who by definition and levels of training are
outside the experiences within which change is sought.

3) Survey research does not provide easy links to possible subsequent action.

Much research in adult education is action oriented. It may be
an attempt to determine a community's educational needs or an
attempt to modify existing programmes through an evaluation/
research process. In either case it is expected that when changes
are made the people in the community or the participants in the
adult education programme will participate more actively, more
efficiently or will gain increased benefits over what had existed before. Basic principles of planning stress that the likelihood of full and effective participation in any ventures — education, political or social — are improved by involving would-be
participants in the decision-making process. In addition to
resulting in a poor source of information, research which has
alienated, or at best treated respondents as sources of primitive
information, has little likelihood of creating the active and
supportive environment essential for change.

4) Survey research methods are not consistent with the principles of adult education.

The arguments put forward so far would apply to a critique or
research in social science generally. Within the field of adult
education there are additional criteria to be met in selecting
a research approach. To begin with, adult education is rooted
to a concept of social justice and equality in a way in which
other disciplines are not. Concern for the adult learner is
often concern for the proportion of the population that has not
had, for various reasons, an appropriate share of either national
wealth or social services. In Africa, Asia and Latin America,
adult education is directly linked to attempts to increase participation of citizens in national development and to provide a
minimum level of basic education to all people.

A reading of any or all of the basic adult education texts such
as Kidd, Knowles or Miller would produce a set of principles
that would most likely include statements such as:

a) Programmes should be based on adult needs.

b) Adults, unlike children, are more easily able to articulate
    their learning needs.

c) Although there are changes with age in the ways in which
    adults learn, the phrase "too old to learn" is a fallacy.

d) Adults work out often quite complex learning strategies to
    achieve desired goals on their own.

(Kidd, 1974; Knowles, 1971; Miller, 1964).

These principles, and many others, imply a faith in adults as
whole persons participating actively in the world. It is no
secret that the administration of actual programmes usually
falls short of these principles; but such principles do exist
and should serve as a basic guide for adult education research.
John Holmes has suggested that if educational research had been
working with adults instead of children, the concern with methods
would have arisen much earlier as some adults at least are not
passive and would not be as tolerant as school children and their
teachers (1976:150).

Instead, we find that the dominant research methods in use and
the ones being picked up as adult educators begin to do more
and more research are alienating, inaccurate as a means of identifying needs, and see some adults as marginal or incapable of

articulating their own needs. Research in adult education is at
an early stage of development. Within this specialization we
still have time to select research approaches that suit us
uniquely and thereby keep us one step ahead of other social
sciences now going through the throes of discarding an anti-
quarian pursuit.

Alternative Strategies

Some work has been done on finding an alternative approach. A
general dissatisfaction with orthodox approaches has been expressed in the work of Mead and Blumer (Blumer, 1969). Qualitative, as opposed to quantitative, strategies have made their
strongest entry with Glaser and Strauss, in The Discovery of
Grounded Theory (1967). Filstead's introduction in Qualitative
Methodology provides a useful discussion substantiating the need
for alternatives (1970). Pilsworth and Ruddock have described
an alternative approach based on a phenomenological position
(1975:33). Still other approaches have borrowed from anthropol-
ogy and stress the value of participant observation (McCall and
Simmons, 1969). Beltran has outlined convincingly the western
bias in social science research methods (1976). Helen Callaway
has similarly singled out the cultural trap which researchers
are prey to when attempting allegedly objective research in non-
western cultures (1976).

From Africa comes the work of Swantz and in some sense Malya
with his approach to providing follow-up literacy material and
investigation of a literacy environment (Swantz, 1974a, 1974b;
Malya, 1975). In Latin America, Freire provides useful ideas in
chapter three of Pedagogy of the Oppressed and a bit more in a
talk given to the Institute of Adult Education in Tanzania (1971,
1973). Vio describes some attempts at peasant participation in
Chile under the Allende government (1975:70). Beltran and Gerace
have developed important concepts of communication among peasants
rather than to them (Beltran, 1976; Gerace, 1973). These concepts of "horizontal communication" are important links. In
addition to Freire, Pinto has elaborated the forms of thematic
investigation (1969). Within the field of sociology, the Oli-
veiras have put forward a compelling set of similar ideas in
The Militant Observer: A Sociological Alternative (1975).

Participatory Research

The combination of community participation in decision making

with methods of social investigation results in the concept of
participatory research. The term refers to the efforts along
several lines to develop research approaches which involve those
persons who are the expected "beneficiaries" of the research.
The term deliberately focuses on involvement of those who are
traditionally the "researched" in formulation, collection of
data (widely interpreted) and interpretation of information.
There is on-going work by about 80 researchers in several countries with the support of the ICAE participatory research team
to work further in both formal and informal ways to outline and
test some of these concepts. Some of the guidelines which have
been put forward to date are:

1) A research process can be of immediate and direct benefit to
   a community (as opposed to serving mei'ly as the basis for
   an academic paper or obscure policy anaᵧᵣsis).

   Research cannot be justified solely as the basis for intellectual exercise or academic career building. It is important that the community or population gain not only from the
   results of the research, but from the process itself. This
   means, for example, that villagers or city dwellers should —
   as a result of participating in the research process — be
   more able to articulate problems themselves and to initiate
   processes to find solutions. In more concrete terms, the
   reports of the youth research in Tanzania by Swantz (1974b)
   and the agrarian reform work in Chile (Vio, 1975) stress the
   importance of the entire research team contributing to the
   productive work of the area. Such an approach has the added
   advantage of creating a better working atmosphere and providing a closer involvement with the community for the outside
   members of a research team.

2) A research process should involve the community or population
   in the entire research project from the formulation of the
   problem to the discussion of how to seek solutions and the
   interpretation of the findings.

   Here we come to what is perhaps the fundamental principle of
   participatory research and its point of most radical departure from both orthodox research approaches and such improvements as grounded theory. The research process should be
   based on a system of discussion, investigation and analysis
   in which the researched are as much a part of the process as
   the researcher. Theories are neither developed beforehand
   to be tested nor drawn by the researcher from his or her

involvement with reality. Reality is described by the process through which a community develops its own theories and solutions about itself.

3) <u>The research process should be seen as part of a total educational experience which serves to establish community needs, and increase awareness and commitment within the community.</u>

Research of this nature could be seen as a natural part of the educational planning or development planning process. It could be an accepted method of raising interest and increasing motivation rather than as a by-product of a research project which might or might not be picked up, depending on the circumstances surrounding the project.

4) <u>The research process should be viewed as a dialectic process, a dialogue over time and not as a static picture from one point in time.</u>

Roy Carr-Hill makes a compelling case for using questionnaires as consciousness raising instruments (1974). His point is that precisely because questionnaires are biased they can be used positively to create an awareness and to awaken in individuals powers of analysis which can then be brought to bear on the problem. I would agree with this point, but would want to make certain that in a participatory research process several additional aspects are made clear. The first is that the questionnaire represents only the first stage of the analysis, the basis for several discussions and interactions with the respondents. Secondly, that the interpretation of the questionnaire data is also shared and is not done solely by a single social scientist. Thirdly, one would want any action based on the research process to be arrived at by more than a social scientist and his or her bureaucratic counterparts. The one-time questionnaires, even in the hands of someone who is "pro-people", remains a static and limited tool. It does represent a way of arousing initial interest in a social problem, especially in industrialized societies where community and group interaction is extremely limited.

5) <u>The object of the research process, like the object of the educational process, should be the liberation of human creative potential and the mobilization of human resources for the solution of social problems.</u>

This statement is a value, an underlying assumption for
participatory research which will not suit everyone. But
then this type.of research will not perhaps be acceptable
to a number of people in any case. The focus of research,
learning and socio-economic development should be the same
— man. The more intellectual power and creativity that can
be brought to bear on society, the more likely a solution.
We need not more highly trained and sophisticated researchers
operating with ever more esoteric techniques, but whole
neighbourhoods, communities and nations of "researchers".

An analogy to medicine is appropriate here. Social science
research often appears to produce a situation in which a
medical doctor tries to diagnose a patient's symptoms from
around the corner and out of sight. The social scientist
uses his "instruments" to measure the response of the patient
as thought they were a king of long stethoscope. The focus
of the researcher has been on developing a better and better
stethoscope for going around corners and into houses when
the real need is for the researcher to walk around the corner, go into the house and begin talking with the people who
live there.

6) <u>A research process has ideological implications</u>.

There are two points involved here: First is the re-affir-
mation of the political nature of all we do especially in
adult education. Knowledge is power. A research process
which allows for popular involvement and increased capacities of analysis may also make new political actions possible.
At the same time it may be necessary at a certain time for
the researcher to choose one group or another within the
community to work with. The use of the term "participatory
research" will not prevent someone from using similar methods
to help a group of landlords work out a set of "tenant-tight"
rules and living arrangements. It may be necessary to make
the choice to work only for the tenants at an early stage.
What is reality for landlords and perhaps even some government officials is not reality for tenants.

<u>Conclusion</u>

We have created and are still creating a situation in social
science research which effectively denies recognition of knowledge creating abilities in most of the people of the world. In

our search for ways of adding to the "body of knowledge" we have
lost sight of the objectives of our work. For persons working
in participatory research the importance of keeping a firm eye
on one's values is crucial. Science is not a bag of tricks that
one learns by being trained at ever increasing degrees of detach-
ment from reality. We have created an illusion that we have come
to believe ourselves; that only those with sophisticated techniques can create knowledge.

Participatory research is not a set of ideas that can be applied
at random with predictable results. It is not neat, it cannot
be rounded off to two decimal points and it is even difficult to
make into charts. It does not eliminate the need to constantly
evaluate political implications of one's work. What it does for
those of us in adult education is to offer an alternative way of
thinking about research which may suit both the needs of our work
and our own values more closely.

REFERENCES

Adiseshiah, M.A. (1976) Valedictory Address, International Con-
    ference of Adult Education and Development, ICAE, Dar es
    Salaam, Tanzania, June.

Asian Action (1976) Newsletter of the Asian Cultural Forum on
    Development, 4 May-June.

Beltran, L.R. (1976) Alien premises, objects, and methods in
    Latin American communication research, Communication Re-
    search, Vol. 3, No. 2, April, 107-134.

Blackburn, R. (ed.) (1972) Ideology in Social Science. London,
    Fontana.

Blumer, H. (1969) Symbolic Interactionism. Englewood Cliffs,
    N.J., Prentice-Hall.

Bodenheimer, S.J. (no date) The ideology of developmentalism:
    American political science's paradigm-surrogate for Latin
    American studies, Berkeley Journal of Sociology, 95-137.

Buttedahl, P.G. and Buttedahl, K. (1976) Participation: The
    Transformation of Society and the Peruvian Experience,
    Convergence, Vol. 9, No. 3, pp. 16-26.

Callaway, H. (1976) Research for Development: Adult Learners within their cultural setting, presented at Conference on Adult Education for Development, Dar es Salaam, June.

Carr-Hill, R. (1974) Developing Educational Services for the Needs of Population Groups: testing some concepts (mimeo, Paris: UNESCO - E.P.P.), June.

Colletta, N.J. (1976) Participatory Research or participation put-down? Reflections on an Indonesian experiment in non-formal education, Convergence, Vol. 9, No. 3, pp. 32-46.

Draper, J. (1977) Research and Community, an Ojibway Case Study, in Hall, B.L. and Gillette, A., Participatory Research: An Approach for Change (forthcoming).

Economic Development Bureau, Inc. (1976) Appropriate technology for grain storage in Tanzanian villages (preliminary report).

Filstead, W.J. (1970) Qualitative Methodology. Chicago, Markham.

Fordham, P., Poulton, G. and Randle, L. (1975) A question of participation: Action and research in the New Communities Project, Convergence, Vol. 8, No. 2, pp. 54-69.

Freire, P. (1971) Pedagogy of the Oppressed. London, Penguin.

Freire, P. (1974) Research Methods, Literacy Discussion, Spring.

Gaynor, M.G. and Gaynor, E. (1976) Bibliographical compilation concerning "participation" in work organizations and in educational contexts in Peru, prepared for Conference on Adult Education for Development, ICAE, Dar es Salaam, June.

Gaynor, E. and Gaynor, M.G. (1975) A study of the effects of workers' participation in agricultural co-operatives involved in an adult education program in Peru, Department of International Studies in Education, Michigan State University.

Gerace, F. (1973) Communicacion Horizontal. Lima, Libreria.

Glaser, B.G. and Strauss, A.L. (1967) The Discovery of Grounded Theory. Chicago, Aldine.

Guttierrez, F. (1976) Creativity through cultural activity, paper presented at NORSECA seminar on adult education, Costa

Rica, August 10.

Hall, B.L. (1975) Participatory Research: An approach for cahnge, _Convergence_, Vol. 8, No. 2, pp. 24-32.

Holmes, J. (1976) Thoughts on Research Methodology in _Studies in Adult Education_, Vol. 8, No. 2, October.

Kennedy, T. (1973) The Sky River Project: The Story of a process, _Access_, Challenge for Change (National Film Board of Canada), Summer.

Kidd, J.R. (1974) _How Adults Learn_, 2nd edition. New York, Association Press.

Knowles, M. (1971) _The Modern Practice of Adult Education_. New York, Seabury Press.

Lindsey, J.K. (1976) Participatory Research: Some comments, _Convergence_, Vol. 9, No. 3, pp. 47-50.

Lotz, J. (1976) Whatever happed to community development, _Canadian Welfare_, 52, pp. 5-8.

Malya, S. (1975) Tanzania's Literacy Experience, _Literacy Discussion_, Spring, pp. 45-68.

Marsick, V.J. (1976) Grounded Theory: A research strategy for analyzing programs of non-formal development education, University of California at Los Angeles, Berkeley.

McCall, G. and Simmons, J.L. (1969) _Issues in Participant Observation_. Reading, Mass., Addison-Wesley.

Miller, H. (1964) _Teaching and Learning in Adult Education_. New York, McMillan.

Myrdal, G. (1970) _Objectivity in Social Research_. London, Duckworth.

Nyerere, J.K. (1973) _Freedom and Development_. Dar es Salaam, Oxford University Press.

Ohliger, J. and Niemi, J. (1975) Annotated and quotational bibliography on participatory research, _Convergence_, Vol. 8, No. 2, pp. 82-87.

Oliveira, R.E.M. (1975) The Militant Observer: A Sociological
    Alternative. Geneva, IDAC.

Pilsworth, M. and Ruddock, R. (1975) Some criticisms of survey
    research methods in adult education, Convergence, Vol. 8,
    No. 2, pp. 25-33.

Pinto, J.B. (1969) Methodologia de la investigacion tematica.
    Bogota, IICA-CIDA, No. 101.

Puerta, I. and Bruce, R.L. (1972) Data collection with low-
    income respondents, Department of Education, Cornell Univer-
    sity.

Reed, D. (1975) The militant observer: Redefining the role of
    the social scientist, Institute for Documentation of Cultural
    Action, Geneva.

Ribeiro, L. (1975) A village scenario: Action research in Goa,
    World Education Reports, No. 10, December.

Rockhill, K. (1976) The uses of qualitative research in adult
    education to "enlighten, enoble and enable", Department of
    Education, University of California, Los Angeles.

Rockhill, K. (1975) Alternatives for adults: Education for indi-
    vidual and social change. Graduate School of Education,
    University of California, Los Angeles.

Rogers, E.M. (1976) Communication and Development: The passing
    of the dominant paradigm, Communication Research, Vol. 3,
    No. 2, April, pp. 213-225.

Swantz, M. (1974a) Participant Role of Research in Development
    (mimeo), Dar es Salaam, BRALUP.

Swantz, M. (1974b) Youth and Development in the Coast Region of
    Tanzania, Dar es Salaam, BRALUP Research Report No. 6.

Swantz, M.L. (1975) Research as an educational tool for develop-
    ment, Convergence, Vol. 8, No. 2, pp. 44-53.

Tate, S. (1973) Anthropological perspectives on evaluation in
    development education, Interchange, Vol. 4, No. 4.

Vanek, J. (1975) and Bayard, T., Education toward self-management:

An alternative development strategy, _International Development Review_, 4, pp. 17-23.

Vio, F. (1976) Participation, Education and Agricultural Reform in Chile, paper presented at Conference on Adult Education for Development, Sar es Salaam, June.

Young, M.F.D. (1975) The ideology of educational research, _Times Higher Education Supplement_, Jan. 17.

Zuniga, R.B. (1974) _The experimenting society and radical social reform: The role of the social scientist in Chile's Unidad Popular experience_, paper presented at American Psychological Association convention, September 1, New Orleans.

Adult Learners within their Cultural Setting: Research for Development

Helen Callaway

The past decade has been one of marked innovation in educational
ideas and practice. However disappointing the results may seem
in meeting the present urgencies for development, this period has
brought forth both energetic criticism of existing structures and
concentrated efforts to create new and more appropriate forms of
adult education. New pedagogical techniques have been worked out
to encourage adult learners to take initiatives in solving their
own problems. Programmes of mass media have been set up to reach
the most remote and isolated villagers, who have formed study
groups to share and discuss the new information. Functional literacy (with its wider definitions) has been launched in many
nations. Attention has been given to the preservation and renewal of cultural heritages. Everywhere the emphasis has changed
from what now seems the artificiality of the schoolroom to the
wider framework of skill training on the job and literacy study
closely related to the improvement of everyday work and living.

But, in contrast, until recently there has been little experimentation in the concepts and methods of research used in adult
education. Although exceptions can be noted, research for the
most part has been undertaken along conventional patterns, following such prescribed methods as social surveys with fixed-
choice questionnaires and their resulting statistical grids which
set out the answers to the outsider's questions in the outsider's
categories. Some research procedures have been carried out almost automatically, as if a "right way" has become established.
Only a few educators, for example, have ventured to ask whether
the usual preliminary survey called "KAP" (knowledge, attitudes,
practices) designed by outside "experts" is the best approach
for a beginning inquiry at village level. Few have thought to
question whether the standard requirements for "control groups"
are always necessary in determining the advantages and disadvan-
tages of an innovative project. Evaluation studies have too
often been carried out as exercises in laboratory objectivity,
as if the creatures observed were rats going down mazeways rather
than mature human beings who are thinking, speaking, feeling,
acting and interacting according to meaningful patterns that
invest their world with significance.

An economist's analysis of development research

There are signs now, however, that research itself is being subjected to critical scrutiny. In his study, The Limits of Development Research (1975), the economic Paul Streeten sets forth
a comprehensive and searching analysis of the problems of co-operation in research across national boundaries. Contrasting two
views of development, he shows how research and the role of the
donor nation can be regarded as radically different according to
which view is accepted. The first is a linear, stages-of-growth
view of development which gives attention to obstacles holding
back the expected economic growth. With this perspective, research is seen as providing one of the missing components in
reaching the "take-off" stage. In contrast, the second and more
recent view sees underdevelopment as partly the historical result of the system of international relations, of malign exploitation or benign neglect on the part of the developed countries.
Those who take this view place primary emphasis not on economic
growth by itself but on strategies for the eradication of poverty
and the reduction of inequality. And here, research (by outsi-
ders) can be regarded as part of the oppressive or neglectful
system.

Streeten points out that it is quite legitimate to criticize
orthodox Western models in the social sciences for their exces-
sive claims, for their "intellectual imperialism". It is in the
interest of honest work to assert that in Africa, Asia, and
Latin America, at low levels of development, in another demo-
graphic setting, in a different place in the international system, etc., the order of things may be conceived in different
ways. While he concedes that the concepts, models, premises,
assumptions, paradigms, theories and questions in the social
sciences are in some respects based on their origins in time
and place, he concludes that the laws of logic and the criteria
for truth must be universal. It follows that the standards of
scholarship are universal, the commitment to the search for
knowledge knows no national frontiers.

The call for new directions in educational research

While no scholar (to my knowledge) has so far subjected the problems of international research in adult education and development
to such systematic analysis, yet here and there writers have
registered dissatisfaction with conventional modes of research
and have set forth new ideas. Jack Mezirow, guest editor of the

issue of <u>Literacy Discussion</u> (Vol. V, No. 3, Fall 1974) on
Program analysis and evaluation, noted in his introduction how
our academically revered methods of research have proven inadequate; in particular, he points out, they do not enable us to
understand the complexities of social interaction involved in
educational processes. Other contributors to this issue reiter-
ate this theme. During the past few years, the "anthropological
approach" of Malcolm Parlett and David Hamilton in <u>Evaluation as</u>
<u>Illumination</u> has gained wide recognition. More recently, a sus-
tained attack on conventional research with a fresh presentation
of alternative ideas has come from the authors whose papers make
up the special feature on participatory research (the approach
defined in an earlier paper by Budd Hall). These writers, with
research experience in varied settings, set out new directions
in research more consistent with current principles of adult
education as the liberation of human creativity and the mobilization of human effort for the solution of social and economic
problems.

These examples, and they are by no means exhaustive, illustrate
the growing awareness that research practices have not been
keeping up with our changing ideas on adult education and development. President Nyerere of Tanzania has spoken of development
as the interrelated process of economic growth, self-reliance
and social justics. We recognize that the conditions for economic growth and for social justice may require structural changes
or modifications from centralized government powers. But the
concept of self-reliance presents another perspective. This
suggests the view that the roots of change are in men's and
women's minds, that they are conscious agents learning from each
other as they confront the problems of their environment. And
it suggests, too, that village people in their social and economic activities are capable of finding new ways of doing things
to meet their objectives for community improvement. Educational
programmes may play a vital part in this process.

President Nyerere has written:

> Development brings freedom, provided it is
> development <u>of people</u>. But people cannot be
> developed; they can only develop themselves.
> For while it is possible for an outsider to
> build a man's house, an outsider cannot give
> the man pride and self-confidence in himself
> as a human being. Those things a man has to
> create in himself by his own actions. He dev-

> elops himself by what he does; he develops
> himself by making his own decisions, by inc-
> reasing his understanding of what he is doing,
> and why; by increasing his own knowledge and
> ability, and by his own full participation —
> as an   equal — in the life of the community he
> lives in (1973:60).

If we take this view of the self-reliant individual interacting
with others for a common purpose, then we need to rethink some
of the basic concepts in our research. It is abundantly clear
that the stimulus-response models of human action which dominated
research in education psychology for over 30 years are no longer
acceptable. Conventional research models for the most part are
based on ideas of human beings as passive objects rather than
creative subjects and of knowledge as something static to be
transferred rather than as a process of negotiations, adaptations
and innovations.

We might also ask whether there has been an over-emphasis on
quantitative research in order to meet the standards of scientific exactitude. Such research carries the underlying assumptions
that complex qualities of human experience can be adequately
registered in statistical stretches and meaningfully compared
in numerical tables. Certainly there are many areas in educational research where quantitative methods are necessary; for
example, to give the statistical dimensions of a problem for
administrative purposes, or to reveal correlations between varying factors. But at the same time we must also acknowledge other
areas where qualitative methods — for the gathering of empirical
facts and the continuing critical reflection upon these data —
yield practical insights. Can such methods be considered scientific? If we recognize that different forms of understanding
require different criteria for validity, then both quantitative
and qualitative methods are seen as necessary in our scientific
search for the knowledge of social reality (Cicourel, 1964;
Glaser and Strauss, 1968; Keat and Urry, 1975). Herbert Blumer
has written that given the nature of problems and data in social
psychology, its generalizations and propositions are not capable
of the validation that is familiar in the natural sciences.
"Instead they will have to be assessed in terms of their reason-
ableness, their plausibility, and their illumination" (1969:182).
When this point is accepted, perhaps there will be less effort
in research placed on verification and more on illumination.

The limits of objectivity

In the sociology of education (e.g., Young, 1971), recent discussion has centred on the rejection of an absolutist model of
validity which has its origins in pre-relativity physics. The
heart of this problem is found in a talk given as long ago as
1938 to an international gathering of anthropologists by the
distinguished nuclear physicist, Niels Bohr. The lesson which
was new at the time was the "principle of complementarity".
This had emerged from the consideration of the properties of
light; with the use of one set of measuring instruments light
is described as waves, while with another it is seen as parti-
cles; yet it is not possible to perceive light simultaneously
as both. The experimental methods are mutually exclusive; the
information each provides is "complementary" to the other. What
this revealed, Bohr pointed out, was the fact that the unavoidable interaction between the objects and the measuring instruments places an absolute limit to the possibility of speaking of
a behaviour of atomic objects which is independent of the means
of observation.

Bohr set out the conclusions for scientists. Physical experience
can be described in different equivalent modes. These depend on
the interaction between objects and measuring tools, or (phrased
another way) on the inseparability of objective content and observing subject.

While the social sciences differ from the physical sciences in
significant ways, this lesson would apply to both. Even today,
however, some educational researchers do not demonstrate their
awareness that their results are related to their measuring
tools, that the interpretation of the objective content depends
on value judgments of the observing subject. In a sense, this
relativity is obvious and experienced researchers perceive the
ways in which their choice of methods determines the selection
of relevant data, the emphasis on certain lines; yet some still
present their research findings as if these were independent,
completely "objective", a representation of "reality as it is".

In his lectures published under the title, <u>Objectivity in Social
Research</u> (1970), Gunnar Myrdal brings together insights from his
years of dedication to social research. He states unequivocally:

> Indeed, no social science or particular branch
> of social research can pretend to be "amoral" or
> "apolitical". No social science can ever be

"neutral" or simply "factual", indeed not "objective" in the traditional meaning of these
terms. Research is always and by logical necessity based on moral and political valuations,
and the researcher should be obliged to account
for them explicitly (1970:74).

Learners as subjects: their world of experience

A relatively neglected area of research, in my view, has been
the perspectives of adult learners within their cultural contexts. The Declaration of Persepolis (1975) set forth this proposition:

Literacy is therefore inseparable from participation, which is at once its purpose and its
condition. The illiterate should not be the
object but the subject of the process whereby
he becomes literate.

If this ideal is to be translated into practice, then greater
attention needs to be given to learners as self-directing subjects, as persons who live within as essentially meaningful social
world and carry out activities according to accepted patterns.
How do they perceive the transitions from these traditional ways
to such educational objectives as, for example, improving agricultural practices? What are the interactions, the mediations
that take place with the agricultural teacher, with other farmers, with members of their families before these learners take
on the new ways of thinking and acting?

In entering a village setting for such research, we would first
try to understand the cognitive world of the people: their
categories of language, their systems for organizing information
to give cohesion and meaning to the flow of everyday events,
their shared conceptual patterns of explanation and prediction.
We would need to investigate their modes of learning and communication, their arts and technologies, their disciplined activities for gaining a living, their vision of the possibilities of
social and economic change. What are the recurring themes of
their concerns? What is their configuration of values as expressed in their words and action? What traditions do they respect and preserve?

In adult education, it was Paulo Freire (1972) who first outlined

such an anthropological approach for discovering the meaningful
world of the learners and involving these adults both in the
preparation of materials and in the problem-solving discussions
during literacy classes.

Here and there others have taken up related themes. Lalage Bown,
for example, in her paper on "The traditional setting" (1974)
argues cogently for the study of traditional practices of education and communication in order to gain lessons from them for
contemporary adult education more consistent with Nigerian ways
of life. She notes in passing that many African societies were
based on the idea of continuous learning long before this concept was discovered by UNESCO!

From Tanzania comes the report of Simoni Malya of research on
"Traditional oral literature for post-literacy materials" (1976).
Here tribal elders who are highly regarded as story-tellers were
asked to take part in workshops for the recording of these traditional tales. This oral heritage is now being translated into
the national language and edited for publication as reading materials for adults. Malya shows how such an endeavour serves
many purposes: it acknowledges that those with traditional knowledge have something valuable to offer to present-day education;
it strengthens the continuity of culture; and, most of all, it
is appreciated by adult readers because they recognize the style
of humour in these stories as their own.

My final example does not have to do with research in the detached
way we usually consider it, but as part of an imaginatively-
designed exercise devoted to intensive training in the field.
This is described as "The operational seminar: a pioneering method
of training for development" in a UNESCO study by Marcel de Clerck
(1976). Sponsored by UNESCO, this seminar has been held in many
areas during the past five years as a means of training personnel
for the intensified work in literacy arising out of the Experimental World Literacy Programme. For a period of about three
weeks, national and international specialists come together <u>at
the educational setting</u> to work out specific requirements for a
particular project. The seminar participants become research
workers. They study local conditions by interacting with local
people within their cultural milieu. Their research is problem-
oriented: how to design sequences of educational action which
will help the people themselves to solve problems of their environment.

In his conclusion, Clerck states that the operational seminar has its place within the context of the renewal of education. "It meets the requirements of those educators who are anxious to free education from certain preconceived ideas, or from rigid or outmoded conceptions, and to introduce into it a greater degree of realism corresponding to the diversity of existing cultural, social and economic situations" (1976:53-54).

Perhaps we could now ask for a similar renewal of research with a greater degree of flexibility and realism about cultural diversity.

References

Blumer, Herbert (1969) _Symbolic Interactionism_. Englewood Cliffs, N.J., Prentice Hall.

Bohr, Niels (1939) Natural philosophy and human cultures, _Nature_, _143_, 268-272.

Bown, Lalage (1974) _The traditional setting_. Paper for Third Annual Conference, Nigerian National Council for Adult Education, Jos.

Cicourel, Aaron V. (1964) _Method and Measurement in Sociology_. New York, The Free Press.

Clerck, Marcel de (1976) The operational seminar: a pioneering method of training for development. _Educational Studies and Documents No. 20_. Paris, UNESCO Press.

Freire, Paulo (1972) _Pedagogy of the Oppressed_. Harmondsworth, England: Penguin Books.

Glaser, Barney G. and Strauss, Anselm L. (1968) _The Discovery of Grounded Theory: Strategies for Qualitative Research_. London, Weidenfeld and Nicolson.

Hall, Budd (1975) Participatory research: an approach for change. _Convergence_ _8_, 2, 24-31.

Keat, Russell and Urry, John (1975) _Social Theory as Science_. London, Routledge & Kegan Paul.

Malya, Simoni (1976) Traditional oral literature for post-literacy reading materials. _Prospects_ _6_, 1, 98-102.

Mezirow, Jack (1974) Foreword, <u>Literacy Discussion</u> <u>5</u>, 3, i.

Myrdal, Gunnar (1970) <u>Objectivity in Social Research</u>. London, Duckworth.

Nyerere, Julius K. (1973) <u>Freedom and Development</u>. Dar es Salaam, Oxford University Press.

Parlett, Malcolm and Hamilton, David (1972) <u>Evaluation as illumination: a new approach to the study of innovatory programs</u>. Occasional Paper, Centre for Research in the Educational Sciences, University of Edinburgh.

Streeten, Paul (1975) <u>The Limits of Development Research</u>. Oxford, Pergamon Press.

Young, Michael F.D. (ed.) (1971) <u>Knowledge and Control: New Directions for the Sociology of Education</u>. London, Collier-MacMillan.

National Statistics for Adult Education
E. A. Fisher

The purpose of this paper is to describe in general terms the
actual situation and future prospects with respect to the collection of national statistics on adult education, and to suggest
to Conference participants what they, as non-statisticians but
potential users of national statistics, might do to improve the
availability of data. The more technical aspects of statistics
will not be analyzed in this paper; they can be found in documents mentioned in the references.

Every country has statistics on the provision of regular school
and university education. Data exists on enrolments, teachers,
finance and facilities; these data are cross-classified or
broken down by socio-economic characterstics and provide the
statistical rationale for planning and evaluation. Thus, with
respect to regular education, statistical answers can be given
to the following types of questions:

— how many people are following the various types of educational
     programmes?
— to what extent do disparities exist in the provision of edu-
     cation for various socio-economic groups?
— what financial and human resources are invested in the prov-
     ision of education?
— at what rate has participation in various types of educational
     programmes been growing?
— to what extent have targets been met?
— what targets for the future can be set?
— what are the priority areas for growth?
— is the provision of education in one country greater than
     that of another?

But, when it comes to adult education, very few countries have
sufficient statistical data for any of the above questions to be
answered in quantitative terms. One is left to wonder how any
meaningful national or international policy on adult education
can be formulated in the absence of a relevant statistical base.
The fact is, of course, that most national and international
policy decisions on adult education are prompted by crisis conditions perceived in a subjective rather than an objective man-

179

ner; "management by intuition of crisis", one might say.

The reasons why the state of the art of adult education statistics is relatively so underdeveloped are generally widely known:
John Lowe (1) draws particular attention to the looseness of the
definitions of adult education that are employed; J.A. Simpson
(2) cites the heterogeneity of types of programmes and the lack
of coordination of direction of organizing agencies; another
reason (and perhaps the most important one), is that only recently has adult education gained sufficient prominence to be
considered as something more than a marginal activity and deser-
ving a government budget for the collection of statistics. In
many countries, adult education has in recent years been the
fastest growing branch of education.

In order to evaluate progress in education during the Second
Development Decade, all educational activities should be taken
into account. Thus the provision of adult education and special
education should be included in the broad evaluation of education. However, since for most countries statistics on adult
education are either non-existent or partial, the evaluation and
subsequent policy decisions will consequently tend to be limited
to regular and special education. Fortunately, the situation
with regard to the availability of statistics on adult education
has been improving. Individual countries and international organizations have made considerable progress over the last few
years and if the present momentum is sustained, by 1980 it may
even be possible to present comparable data for a sufficient number of countries for answers to be given to most of the questions
listed initially on a regional as well as a national basis.

Although several countries have started publishing national statistics on adult education, differences in the coverage and clas-
sifications used preclude inter-country comparisons. However,
apart from these efforts, many countries are actively studying
the advantages of using the International Standard Classification
of Education (ISCED) as a framework for collecting and presenting
statistics on adult education, on the basis of the UNESCO Manual
(3) which has been designed for this purpose. A pilot test of
the Manual was made in the Libyan Arab Republic, and other pilot
tests are being undertaken in Chile, Norway and Peru.

A series of national handbooks on ISCED are being published by
UNESCO in collaboration with Member States. The first handbooks
that have been issued are for the United Kingdom (England and
Wales)(4) and France (5), and others are planned for Egypt,

Argentina, Peru and Venezuela. The handbooks classify the main
programmes of regular, special and adult education according to
ISCED. They are intended to guide statisticians, researchers
and planners in interpreting national statistics classified by
ISCED. They will also serve as models for other countries with
similar systems of education. In addition, ISCED handbooks related solely to adult education are being prepared for certain
countries (e.g. Czechoslovakia, Denmark and New Zealand).

The impetus for this upsurge of interest in using ISCED as the
basis for defining and classifying adult education can be attributed to several causes, but a key reason is that as Member States
become more and more aware of the immense potential of adult
education for national development and individual and social improvement, decision-makers and planners at the national and international levels are realizing that they lack adequate national
statistics. ISCED came on the scene at an appropriate time, and
was quickly recognized as a useful basis for compiling and presenting statistics on adult education.

Various international conferences and meetings have passed resolutions calling on the adoption and application of ISCED. In
May 1975, the Seminar on Structures of Adult Education in Developing Countries, With Special Reference to Africa made a recommendation "that Member States should develop regular statistical
surveys of adult education activities along the lines of the
UNESCO Manual for the Collection of Adult Education Statistics"
(6). In September 1975, the International Conference on Education passed a Recommendation addressed to Member States, UNESCO
and other international and regional organizations, calling for
"the adoption and application of ISCED as a basic standard in all
international reporting of statistics on education" (7).

But what needs to be done to proceeed from the recommendations
to positive action? The answer lies in the development of a
suitable national infrastructure, which would include:

— a national coordinating body for adult education to provide
        a communications network for national activities,
        and
— a statistical unit to collect and publish these statistics.

If a national coordinating body already exists, it could make an
important contribution by compiling a national directory of agencies which provide educational programmes for adults. The existence of a directory in one form or another is a prerequisite to

a statistical survey, in order to mail questionnaires, monitor
returns and follow up on non-respondents. A good example of a
national directory is the one prepared by the National Council
of Adult Education for New Zealand (8). This directory is particularly useful for statistical purposes because it employs
ISCED codes to describe the types of programmes offered by each
agency.

When a national coordinating body has prepared (or plans to prepare) a national directory, it should press for the establishment
of a statistical unit which will be assigned the task of collecting and publishing national statistics on adult education. The
unit could be located within the Ministry of Education or the
Central Statistical Office (if one exists), or might even be
attached to the national coordinating body itself. Naturally,
adequate funds will have to be allocated for the purpose, and
qualified personnel will have to be recruited. Suitable provision should be made for clerks, secretaries, supplies and equipment, data processing and publication services.

Where no national coordinating body exists, then concerned individuals should lobby for its creation. The Adult Education Division of UNESCO has recently produced a document (9) which contains the titles and addresses of national coordinating bodies.
Let us hope that the countries cited in this document will soon
outnumber those not mentioned, as more and more national coordinating bodies are formed.

It is in the interest of adult educators, planners and researchers to do what they can to promote the regular collection of
national statistics on adult education. When the type of questions posed initially can be answered for adult education, then
adult education will assume its rightful place alongside regular
education in the evaluation and planning of the total provision
of education.

References

1. Lowe, J. (1975) The Education of Adults: A World Perspective.
    Toronto, OISE, and Paris, UNESCO Press, pp. 19-26.

2. Simpson, J.A. (1973) Feasibility Study in the Collection of
    Adult Education Statistics. Committee for out-of-school
    Education, Council of Europe, Strasbourg, p. 2.

3. UNESCO Office of Statistics, Manual for the Collection of
    Adult Education Statistics, CSR/E./15, Paris (1975).

4. UNESCO Office of Statistics, ISCED Handbook: United Kingdom
    (England and Wales), CSR/E/12, Paris, 1975.

5. UNESCO Office of Statistics, Guide de la Classification
    Internationale de l'Education: France, CSR/E/13, Paris,
    1976.

6. Final Report of the Seminar, Nairobi, May 1975, Recommen-
    dation 10.

7. Final Report of the Conference, Geneva, August-September
    1975, Recommendation 70.

8. National Council for Adult Education (1975) Directory of
    Continuing Education, Wellington, New Zealand.

9. UNESCO, Adult Education Division, National Adult Education
    Boards and Council, Paris, March 1976.

The Role of Short Cycle and Community Colleges in Development

P. L. Malhotra

Few will deny that "Education is the most important single factor in achieving rapid economic development and technological progress and in creating a social order founded on the values of freedom, social justice and equal opportunity. Programmes of education lie at the base of the effort to forge the bonds of common citizenship, to harness the energies of the people, and to develop the natural and human resources of every country" (1). It therefore implies that any educational system must measure its vitality by its response to the educational needs for the individual and the community. It has also to take into account the national resources available so as to make the maximum use of them. Short cycle education and the experience of community colleges in various countries is of tremendous relevance.

Resources are scarce. Leisurely and rather expensive approaches towards higher education which invariably create social and educational elites can no longer be afforded by even more developed countries, must less the developing world. The growth of community colleges in one of the most affluent countries of the world, the USA, is an example. It is also true that younger students and adults are also questioning the utility of spending four or five years obtaining a university degree. It is estimated that the cost per university student in the United States is above $4000 per year, whereas the cost per student in a community college is around $300 to $400 per year. Besides, many universities continue to remain neutral and negative towards the social realities and fail to relate themselves and their endeavours to the actual needs of the communities that surround them. This dichotomy and the divorce of higher education from the main stream of society is now being questioned increasingly.

To some extent the answer can be found in the community based education, more popularly called two-year community colleges. This education is primarily short cycle higher education. It is intended to serve educational needs of its community or a region and to be responsive to the changes that take place in a given society. It implies that in a given situation the community based education provides opportunities for studies at the intermediate level in accordance with the regional and national needs.

It also provides guidance to students in their educational and
vocational pursuits with opportunities for both of formal and
non-formal education, utilizing resources at a minimum cost.

The community college system has attracted the attention of many
educators as a thoughtful approach to solve some of the educational problems. Manpower studies in many countries have shown
shortages of technicians and workers at the middle level. On
the other hand, there has been an over production of degree hol-
ders. In the developing world it has often been observed that
higher education is either too professional or too general. As
a consequence many graduates remain unemployed and scarce resources of a nation go to waste. Therefore, a shorter cycle of education that interweaves liberal and vocational elements could be
an alternative in many developing countries. The developing
nations cannot afford to invest unlimited money in unproductive
educational enterprises while neglecting employable workers.

The community college system serves many purposes. These may be
characterized as: occupation education, transfer education,
general education, guidance and counselling and community services. The main programme is designed to meet the needs at the
middle level of business, industry, government and services such
as health. The occupational curriculum contains a significant
amount of instruction aimed at enhancing the social, economic,
civil and personal competencies of those enrolled. Education is
linked to employment and both with life, making education socially useful and productive. The aim is to serve the requirements of development — national, regional and local. Such institutions may not create employment directly, but they do provide
marketable skills to their graduates.

The community college movement became very popular in the 1950s
and 1960s in the US and a few other countries. Development first
took place in college preparatory courses. Increasingly the colleges began offering courses designed to train people for various
kinds of vocations and technical jobs as certain technical skills
became obsolete and others advanced. Along with curriculum div-
ersification, the community college became a genuine community
educational resource centre where adults interested in any field
of knowledge could enroll. Consequently, the two-year colleges
began to function as significant recurring education centres.

Another significant change took place in the 1960s as educators
accepted the responsibility to situate facilities where people
worked or lived rather than on a remote campus. Community col-

leges and their programmes were installed in factories, business
and governmental houses, hospitals, agriculture stations, wherever the programme could be most responsive to a community's
educational needs. These factors explain why the community college education has proved very popular in the US, Canada, and
Japan, and is growing in some countries of Asia, Africa, and
Latin America.

There is, of course, no need to copy the US or Japanese model;
but one can certainly gain from the experience of others. Dr.
Seymour Eskow, a well known American college president, has said:
"It is essential that you study the grain, the texture, the context of your community — of the things that you have, of the
people you have, of the training possibilities you have — and
then design the institution around these considerations."

When you use the local community, its geography, its people and
draw the curriculum from the community it is a genuine community
college. This philosophy will inevitably link education with
development. And the educational needs of most countries require
institutions that are focussed directly on economic, social,
political and cultural development.

THE CASE OF INDIA

In order to get a clear idea about what has been happening in the
developing countries which have a long colonial history and experienced the perpetuation of the educational systems introduced
by colonizing power, we will examine briefly some of the educational progress in India since independence. India in some measure represents the aspirations and problems of the Third World,
and this analysis may help us towards a better understanding of
the present phase of social transformation in India and the limitations to which it has been subjected since 1947.

Uneven Growth in Education

Expansion in the field of education at all stages, primary education, middle-school education, secondary education, higher
education, engineering, technical and other professional education has been phenomenal. In the last 25 years primary education
has increased by three times, middle-school education four times,
higher secondary education five times and higher education by
almost six times. Besides, public expenditure on education has

risen from Rs. 1,444 million in 1950-51 to about Rs. 10,000 million in 1975-76. If it is expressed as a percentage of national income educational costs rose from 1.2 per cent of the national income in 1950-51 to 2.9 per cent in 1965-66 and was estimated to be over three per cent of the national income in 1968-69.

For higher education statistics are quite revealing. We have over four million students studying in various colleges. In 1947 the enrolment was less than a quarter million. The number of universities has risen from 19 to over 100. There are over 4,000 colleges throughout the country. Between 1969-72 roughly 200 colleges were added every year, in fact almost four colleges per week.

Enrolment in cities has been much faster than in underdeveloped areas. This is amply evident if one analyzes the data from various village surveys conducted during post-independent period. From these it is clear that the spread of literacy and education is much more amongst affluently advanced sections of society than backward sections.

> All past experience shows that at the point of planning policy, greatest stress is laid on universal mass education, education of women, rural areas, schedule castes and schedule tribes. At the point of fixing quantative targets, proportionate expansion of all sectors is provided for. At the point of actual execution highest achievements are all in the field of urban education, secondary and college education, upper caste education and so on. The policy-wise priority sectors, including adult literacy, fall much behind target. (2)

The rationale for a programme of investments in education is judged by the social rates of return. A number of estimates have been made in India. All these calculations show that there is a general decline in the rate of return as we move from the lower to the higher stages of education.

> The rate of return of primary education for an illiterate person is found to be about 15 per cent, that of middle school after completing primary education about 14 per cent, completing secondary school following middle school about 10.5 per cent. The average rate of return for

> a bachelor's degree in arts, science or com-
> merce is estimated to be a little less than
> nine per cent . . . (3)

The other side of the picture is that our universities are elitist institutions in the sense of being class biased. A survey
of Indian Education tells us that 80 per cent of our university
survivors and graduates come from the top 20 per cent of our
society. In terms of university attainments as distinguished
from university enrolments, Malcolm S. Adiseshiah says that:

> The poverty sector — which is the majority of
> our people — is barred from these institutions.
> The 50 per cent wastage in general university
> education and 20 per cent in professional edu-
> cation coincides with the 50 per cent in the
> poverty sector of the country. (4)

What is happening in the sphere of education has in fact an ama-
zing parallel in the developments in the national economy so far.
Seventy-one per cent of the population is illiterate and about
40 per cent of people live below the subsistence level. A.R.
Kamath, an educationist, states in his excellent monograph on
education that:

> The accent on higher education in a largely
> illiterate society is not very different from
> the economic priorities where terylene, cosmet-
> ics and private cars have a preference over
> cheap coarse cloth and means of mass transport.
> The high subsidization of secondary and higher
> education in the present socio-economic order
> helps the same relatively well-off sections of
> society as are helped by most public investments
> in the cities and the countryside, in industry
> and agriculture. (5)

The educational crisis, therefore, is a part of the more fundamental crisis in socio-economic development. Yet it cannot be
denied that substantial developments have taken place in the
field of education which have also brought about social transformation (6). But the benefits have largely gone to the urban
elite and the emerging rural elite.

Need to Bring about Change

The Kothari Commission report of 1966 observed: "In the rapidly
changing world of today, one thing is certain: yesterday's educational system will not meet today's, and even less so, the
needs of tomorrow". The alienation of the educational system
from the mainstream of Indian society is lucidly explained by
Sir Iric Ashby:

> Looking at Indian Universities a century after
> their foundation, one cannot help but feel that
> they have failed to adapt themselves to the
> vast opportunities which surround them. As uni-
> versities multiply in number their academic
> standards — relating to those elsewhere — do
> not improve. And something even more serious
> happens: the universities remain alien implan-
> tations, not integrated with the new India.
> There is one reason why, to the observer from
> outside, the Indian intellectual remains a
> culturally displaced person nostalgically trea-
> suring his threads of communications with
> England.

Modern Indian educational thought and process has been the product of two opposing forces. First, it used to be geared to the
practical, administrative, commercial and elitist requirements
of the British Raj and second, the renascent idealism of the
Indian National Movement. The influence of the Raj proved stronger and the present structure is largely its legacy. Bertrand
Russell once said: "there is an imperialism of culture which is
harder to overcome than the imperialism of power."

This is not to say that the diagnosis of the ills of Indian educational system and the courses of studies in universities have
not been scrutinized. In fact, for the last 30 years there has
been much talk about the restructuring of our universities, but
little attempt has been made to act. Rather, with every passing
day even the great educational experiments embodied in Tagore's
Santiniketan and Zakir Husain's Jamia Milia — two genuine Indian
innovations — have come to resemble more and more the dominant
inherited imperial pattern of pre-independence India, and suffer
from its worst effects. Why has it been so?

The vested and entrenched interests (the bureaucracy, the affluent and the new rich) who have been the beneficiaries of the soc-

ial system have inhibited any change from the Oxbridge model.
They believe in importing the latest foreign models even if they
lack much relevance to the social needs. In this process the
educational needs of the new generation of learners who come
primarily from lower middle class or poor peasantry stand contin-
uously to be adversely affected.

Restructuring Higher Education

The restructuring of higher education should enhance the development of a social consciousness which is the immediate need of
our country and also in many other Asian and African countries.
The colleges must actively promote it through various educational
programmes of short cycle duration — from six months to two years
directed towards immediate community needs. In a relevant and
meaningful educational system "community experience" has an important place. The colleges can take a big step in bringing the
community and higher education closer for the enrichment of education itself. Work experience and practical training in some
area of the subject in relation to the needs of the community,
could bring in a new dimension to higher education in the developing world. In this respect colleges can become centres where
the community can seek guidance and the teachers and students
can find a training environment to raise relevant questions and
to find answers.

Work experience should extend into the socio-economic development
of the community. A community oriented education will stimulate
the evolution of relevant teaching in social sciences, in science
or in business studies. Continuing education courses, in-service
training and the practice of drawing upon the experience of people
from different walks of life, etc., should form a part of the
regular curriculum. Care will have to be taken to relate the
actual courses of study with community needs so as to strengthen
the relationship between actual work and education and between
the market requirements and the output of various institutions.
The courses will therefore have to be tailored to the needs of
the students and the community.

Relevance of Short Cycle Education

It becomes evident that establishing educational targets corresponding to the requirements of a developing nation like India is
by no means an easy task. For such a need short cycle two-year

education like the junior college or the community college may
prove an invaluable institutional device for national development. There is, of course, no need to be rigid about the duration but a relatively short period will help to make the best
use of the meagre resources and prepare large numbers of people
for useful and productive occupations. There is a definite need
to educate the public to the value which results from middle
level service in the community.

It is also evident that the short cycle community college system
is effective in providing an educational opportunity for those
whose expectations are rising but whose resources do not permit
them to embark upon an extended study programme. Within this
group lies the manpower potential for many of the middle level
programmes in trade, industry and agriculture. Another need is
for the in-service training of many personnel already on the job
who require enlarged capacities. These needs can probably be
best served by an institution of the community college type.

What is required is the inter-weaving of general education with
employment motivation. It may be emphasized that whereas general education creates understanding, vocational education helps
to prepare an individual to work effectively. Similarly, general education gives general information, vocational education
helps to provide special skills. This inter-weaving should lead
to increased social stability in the present time of constantly
changing social and occupational needs.

Gandhiji's Concept and International Perspective

The whole philosophy of education should emphasize the training
of independent and self-directed individuals who can face the
problems of life and of society. There is a common trend towards
this objective in many of the more developed countries including
the socialist bloc. In France, Germany, Sweden, USSR, USA and
China, and even in the United Kingdom, there is an increasing
emphasis on work-oriented education at the post-secondary level.

In conclusion it may not be wrong to say that the community college education is the extension of Gandhiji's idea of basic education made applicable at the post-secondary level. In 1937 he
said: "I would revolutionize college life and relate it to the
national necessities". Perhaps this may come to be true in the
international context, particularly when there is an all-round
awareness of relating post-secondary education to the needs of

the society and its development. It is imperative that we should
have some international perspective about the concept of short
cycle and community college system. There are a number of common
issues like peace, food, population. The stark problems of social and economic development might be reduced by greater international cooperation. One possible institutional framework is
World Community College, a college without walls, a college
without boundaries.

REFERENCES

1. The Third Five Year Plan (India), Chapter on Education, The
    Planning Commission, New Delhi.

2. Shukla, S.C. (1971) Notes on Educational Situation, Main-
    stream, 6 February.

3. Sen, A.K. (1970) The Crisis of Indian Education, Lal Bahadur
    Shastri Memorial Lectures, New Delhi.

4. Adiseshiah, M.S. A Restructuration, Seminar (New Delhi),
    Vol. 166, p. 14.

5. The Educational Situation and Other Essays, p. 305. New
    Delhi, People's Publishing House (1973).

6. India, for example, has the third largest trained manpower
    of scientists and technologists and other professionals.

Educational Mass Campaigns for Development

Daniel Mbunda

Among the most attractive features of adult education programmes in Tanzania are the mass campaigns conducted at intervals by the Institute of Adult Education. This potential as an educational tool is widening with each new campaign. First used in the late 1960s, we have now had about five including the two most recent ones: "Man is Health" (Mtuni Afya) 1973 and "Food is Life" (Chakula ni Ulai) 1975.

Basics of Mass Campaigns Have Longer History

In his recent study, "Mass Campaigns and Development: The Tanzanian Health Education Campaign and Related Experiences", Dr. B.L. Hall suggests that the Tanzania mass campaign approach to mass education, "is linked either historically or through shared characteristics with media and campaign experience elsewhere".

While not denying linkage with external attempts at mass education, the basic principles in this approach are not as novel as they appear to be. Hasn't traditional African society grappled with such problems long before the colonial rule came to Africa? Even during colonial rule, society had to seek a solution to problems of a global nature and educationists will not easily accept the idea that the solution to mass education dawned on Tanzanian soil with the campaigns in the late 1960s.

Just as socialism was not born with the Arusha Declaration in 1967 so also socialist educational approaches are rooted in our past. "We in Africa, have no more need of being 'converted' to socialism than we have of being taught democracy. Both are rooted in our own past — in the traditional society which produced us". (Nyerere)

A mass campaign is usually a programme designed to solve a problem with the following elements:

1) There is an urgently felt need.
2) The need involves many; it is felt to be common to all.
3) To satisfy the need, the cooperation of all concerned is

paramount.
4) This co-operation ought to be a result of participatory
    planning and commitment to personal implementation.
5) There is a set time factor.

In traditional African society there were also moments of specially felt needs which required urgent solutions through the
cooperative action of the members of the clan or tribe.

In my village there was an epidemic. Many people died for no
apparent reason. It was a public concern involving a number of
scattered villages. The problem had to be communicated to various groups who would discuss the alternatives open to them.
They would opt for the best approach and devise a plan within
the set time and frame of reference. It was a matter of global
concern; basic knowledge had to be transmitted as raw material
for subsequent discussions leading to joint action to satisfy
the need of the community.

We had no radio transistors but we had drums and horns. A certain blow of the horn or beat of the drum meant someone had an
important message to tell the community. The beat of the drum
rent the air — all ears became alert. The announcer standing on
top of a "kisanja", an elevated platform used usually for drying
maize or cassave, would cry out the essential message to be
passed on to the neighbouring villagers. The message would run
like this:

> Our village is faced with deaths which the local
> doctors have not been able to account for. It
> is a general concern. We need to find out what
> is wrong and how we can save our lives. Our
> neighbours in village X have found a doctor who
> seems to have a solution. Please find out what
> we can do and let us meet at Mr. so-and-so's
> tomorrow morning ...

The message would be relayed over a wide area that same evening
and people would gather round their meeting places to look into
the matter more closely. So, "study groups" would be assembled
and a group leader, the man who caught the message, or the local
leader, would initiate the topic.

After discussion they may agree that they have failed to find a
solution to the deadly disease. Therefore the proposed solution
may be acceptable to this group; that is, they will be prepared

to support the idea of calling the doctor and pay his expenses
and follow his directions. Or, a group may decide that they
know this would-be doctor, he is no good, he is a cheater, therefore they will not support the invitation. They may propose an
alternative solution.

Group leaders or some of the participants would then represent
their groups at the following day's meetings where the whole
problem and various group decisions would be discussed and a
joint decision taken either for or against inviting the doctor.
This information would be brought back by the group representatives and be passed on either at a meeting or by announcing it
on the "kisanja".

If the proposal to invite the medicine doctor was adopted, the
arrival day and place of the visitor would be announced and the
schedule of visiting the various gathering centres would be relayed to the public.

This was a rudimentary method of focusing the attention of a
community on a major problem and of procuring popular participation in finding solutions. The message was vital to the whole
community; it had to be communicated to them for their active
participation.

This is but one example where roots of our mass campaign can be
identified in traditional society.

Our modern campaigns have the advantages of the world of technology. One does not need to climb up the "kisanja" and shout
himself hoarse but now just steps into the radio studio and
softly speaks into the microphone to millions of listeners scattered over thousands of miles.

Objectives of Mass Campaigns

A campaign usually deals with a subject of a general nature that
touches many people and one which needs mass mobilization for
action. It is designed to give basic functional information on
health, agriculture, public security, politico-social duties or
many other burning issues that touch the life of a nation. This
is especially true in a developing country like Tanzania.

However, providing information is not the only objective of
launching an education campaign; it serves a number of other

equally important purposes. Some are general and long-term objectives and others are specific and short-term. In our Tanzanian context the former are basic and underlie all national campaigns.

General Long-term Objectives

Mass campaigns are fundamentally adult education programmes and
as such they serve the general objectives of adult education.
They are meant to liberate the participants and make them more
confident in their development, more responsible in their own
programme. This is an important objective for people who for
centuries took orders and decisions from masters and had lost
their right to make decisions affecting their lives. Since campaigns require participants to share ideas on equal terms, they
inculcate the sense of equality and socialism and they liberate
the participants from a sense of inferiority and subservience.
In short, the campaigns liberate man and bring about the emergence of a new man. In his opening address, President Nyerere
pointed out: "the primary purpose of education is the liberation
of man".

This liberating effect is very marked with women participants
who for ages had been colonized by men and relegated into the
background of the home and kitchen. In study groups they freely
participate in discussing and planning projects on an equal foot-
ing with men.

The purpose of the decentralization policy of the government of
Tanzania effected in 1972 was to give power to the people.
Realistically, participation at the grass roots level is the
only sure approach to implementation of this policy. One objective of our mass campaigns is to encourage the involvement of
group members in decision making which affects their lives:
politics in "The Choice is Yours" in 1970; health in "Man is
Health" in 1972; and nutrition in "Food is Life" in 1975. These
campaigns reinforce the active role of participants in matters
that affect their lives, their villages and their development.

President Nyerere has emphasized the peoples' participation as
being crucial "to true socialist development". The purpose of
both the Arusha Declaration and of "Mwongozo" (TANU Guidelines)
was to give the people power over their own lives and their own
development. He has stated: "The government's proposals are
worked out with these objectives in mind ... if these proposals

are worked through properly, the masses of the people will find
that it is easier for them to practise self-reliance in their
own development, and to take part in decision-making which directly affects them ... "

The Tanzanian campaigns are meant to instil the spirit of local
interest in national affairs. They are meant to make the participant central rather than structures, administrators, and equipment.

It is the learner whose sensitivity must be understood by the
group leader and the Government officials. If the approach used
in study groups succeeds, dictatorship will be virtually impossible in the lives of millions of Tanzanians. The people begin
to question orders given to them from above; they are helped to
accept plans that they have collectively decided upon or have
been consulted about. They learn to look at issues with a critical mind.

The study group methodology is a lesson to Party and Government
leaders as well. It teaches them participatory planning — the
bottom-up process; it teaches them the correct role of the government's appointees and that of the experts, that is, to respect the sovereign rights of the people.

One of the offsprings of bureaucracy is the compartmentalization
of services in the interest of empire-builders rather than the
benefit of the clients. How does this affect the poor farmer?
The rural people are exposed to the plans of the Rural Medical
Aid, Health Officer, Agricultural Extension Officer, the Community Development Officer, Party Functionary, the Nutrition Officer, and a host of other officers who seem to bring the peasant
more confusion than help. The question arises: Is development
divided in itself? Does man develop in pieces or does he do so
organically and harmoniously?

One objective of mass campaigns is to try to answer this question by establishing structures which organize, plan, supervise,
and evaluate the campaigns in an integrated way. A Coordinating
Committee was set up with members drawn from our political party,
the government, parastatal organizations, regions, and voluntary
organizations. The whole range of resources and experiences of
these groups was brought to bear on the question and a collective
strategy was decided upon to which all the members representing
their respective organizations felt committed. This system has
a multiplying effect on publicity, supervision, and mobilization.

On the National Coordinating Committee for the "Food is Life"
Campaign six ministries were represented: the Prime Minister's
office, Education, Agriculture, Social Welfare, Health, and
Information and Broadcasting. The following organizations and
institutions sent representatives: The Institute of Adult Education, the University, Kivukoni College, the Co-operative College Moshi, the Nutrition Centre, and Tanganyika Women's Union.
All these representatives worked as a team to help make development occur.

This is an example of integration at the planning phase of the
campaign. The training teams also reflect an integrated approach.
For a mass campaign of the "Food is Life" magnitude it is necessary to train some 70,000-80,000 group advisors. They were
trained through a series of staged seminars which start by training regional teams and division teams who then trained the 70,000
group advisors at the ward level. The integrated feature of the
trainers' team at the regional level presents development as an
harmonious and integrated process. In the "Food is Life" Campaign the 20 regional teams were required to come to the Institute of Adult Education for two-day orientation seminars. Each
team was made up of the following members of the regional administration: Health, Education, Community Development, Institute
of Adult Education, Agriculture, Nutrition, and Tanganyika Women's
Union. This bringing together of officers from different departments sometimes becomes the beginning of continuing cooperation
between people in different ministries and organizations.

Integration does not stop there. The evaluation and supervision
teams in the regions or districts are also made up of people from
various ministries and organizations. Such a structure needs a
high coordinating consciousness to make it work. Tanzania has
been blessed with the unifying force of the Party and the commitment of the people to adult education as a national concern.
And as the mechanism proves effective, development projects initiated by other agencies adopt the inter-agency integrated approach
as their strategy. Recently the Ministry of Culture and Youth
initiated a project "Jembe ni Mali" (Hoe is Wealth)   the symbol
of work, farming, culture and economy. The planning and evaluation structures are designed on the same pattern as the mass
campaigns conducted by the Institute of Adult Education.

Specific Objectives and Delivery System

In developing countries subjects that show people how to liberate themselves from their daily ills and which directly promote their well-being are indicators for a successful mass campaign. They carry a simple message that satisfies basic human longings. Man has a sincere desire to know and to understand the meaning of what is happening in him and round about him.

In Tanzania basic education issues — health, security, agriculture, and political consciousness are matters of national priority to combat ignorance, poverty and disease. Hence, themes taken from those areas have resulted in successful campaigns.

The "Man is Health" Campaign was planned to reach one million participants but the evaluation indicated that over two million participants were reached. The "Food is Life" Campaign was aimed to reach an equal number of Tanzanians and initial figures from the regions are already over one million in spite of the special problems this campaign had to face.

"Food is Life" was a reaction of the Tanzanian worker and peasant to the previous campaign — "Man is Health". Healthy environments call for healthy and strong bodies. But what is our food situation? How can we increase our food production by using simple and inexpensive techniques? How can we preserve food against bad days, by using traditional methods, or by new methods? What is the importance of balanced diets to expectant mothers, to children, youth, and adults? How can we improve our diet habits vis-a-vis taboos?

The peasants wanted to improve their own health and increase their life span. The workers wanted to bring a healthier atmosphere in the offices, factories and industries.

"Food is Life" was a down-to-earth campaign. Its message was simple and relevant but the delivery system had to be worked out properly to maximize its impact.

A specially prepared booklet on food production, preservation and nutrition was prepared jointly by experts from Agriculture, Health, Nutrition and the Institute of Adult Education. The target was the average Tanzanian, often a recent graduate of the literacy campaign. This reading material in his hand would reinforce his literacy skills. The simple message was printed in bold letters and in easy readable sentences. The booklet contains 96 pages with many pictures and illustrations. The short chapters are written in a discussion-leading style and end with a few questions designed to evoke a lively reaction from the

members of the study group. The cover with its familiar symbol
of the campaign has a photo of a healthy baby, a picture of a
group of adults engaged in discussing "Kilimo cha Kufa na Kupona"
(Farming, a matter of life and death). These painstaking planning details may seem unimportant but they have an immense meaning to the simple learner. The participants develop a sentimen-
tal attachment to their books, they want to have them, handle
them, read them, almost talk or discuss with them.

The "Food is Life" Campaign did not really measure up to satisfy
participants. First, due to a shortage of paper, not as many
booklets were printed as had been intended. Even those printed
came late, so the launching of the campaign had to be postponed
from May to June.

Although books are important in a campaign, the influence of the
book may stifle the objective of the study group members, that
is to get their active participation in solving their problem.
This applies equally to the potential stunting effect of the
radio programmes. The poor peasant may yield to the temptation
of relying on what the expert has said, what is written in the
book, or what the radio says.

To make sure that learners really share experiences, the planners
took a number of precautions in the "Food is Life" Campaign.
The group advisors were reminded of the danger of killing the
participants' initiative and were required to seek how they could
encourage the shy members into active participation. In the
evaluation form advisors were required to report how often members of the group had actively participated in the discussion.
At one study session of the "Food is Life" Campaign at the Institute of Adult Education, none of the members knew that one was
recording our participations. The evaluation report came as a
surprise the following day. It was found out that the Director
had intervened more than anyone in the group of ten. Academic
colleagues came second and the non-academic "participants" came
last. The advisors then encouraged us all to take part equally.
Matters changed greatly in the following sessions, especially
the women participants who became more articulate and contribu-
tive. In programmes like this we should be aware of the "covert
power" of the written word, the too strong group leader and the
overly-assertive participant.

The radio programme is a powerful mechanism in the delivery system. It overcomes distances, physical barriers, and enters homes
of millions. The transistor radio is a common asset in most

Tanzanian villages. However, the reception may not be of the
best quality. But the radio still seems to act as a rallying
point for the discussion group as well as a uniting, living
voice for groups all over the country. Tanzania's efforts to
settle the peasants in planned villages will make it easier to
organize listening groups with Community Centre radio sets.
Incidentally, the government has abolished radio licences to
encourage people to buy personal radio sets as they are an educational asset rather than a luxury.

A radio programme is meant to cater for large groups of listeners and the time set for airing the programme must suit the majority of the listening groups. This has been a big bottleneck
in the "Food is Life" Campaign as the third formative evaluation
report points out. Radio time was fixed at 3:30 p.m. every Mon-
day and Wednesday. The assumption was that all 70,000 groups,
or most of them, would meet at that time. The formative reports
say it has proved difficult to do so because of the local differences. Farmers across the country have different seasonal periods, children in primary schools could not listen to the radio
periods as nearly all had either closed or were about to close
the day, and people working in offices and industries would have
already closed by 3:00 p.m.

So radio as a delivery tool needs to be investigated further to
optimize its coverage. Regional rather than national campaigns
have been suggested as a partial solution to this and other problems. One mistake was made in that the fixing of the radio time
was done by the Institute's Radio Unit on the assumption that
this would be the most suitable time for the groups. Perhaps
groups should have been offered alternative times. Another solution may be campaigns beamed to a target group with the same
working routine, e.g. a campaign for the school population, for
industrial workers, and for office workers.

The "Food is Life" Campaign has not solved the problem of how
best the radio can be utilized as a communication instrument but
rather has highlighted the need for new discussions of the problems involved in radio support for mass campaigns.

One unique and effective means of publicizing mass campaigns in
Tanzania has been the use of textiles called "khanga" and "vitenge". Worn as dresses, skirts, head coverings or shirts, these
colourful and attractive materials are popular throughout Tanzania. Designers were co-opted for the Coordinating Committee
to design textile patterns that would convey the message of the

campaign through symbols, pictures and slogans. Textile firms
cooperated in the production and distribution of the materials
and found demand larger than could be met. In the farthest
areas of the country, women were met wearing the "Food is Life"
khanga, silently delivering the message as they walked to the
communal farm or to the well, selling vegetables at the market,
or going to church or to a wedding feast. The Third Formative
Evaluation Report recorded the effectiveness of these khangas
and vitenge in spreading the message of the campaign.

The delivery of the "Food is Life" message included the involvement of leaders at all stages. The chairman of the UWT opened
the training seminars of the team of trainers and the National
Executive TANU Secretary closed the seminar. As the stages seminars moved to the zones and regions the local TANU chairman,
the TANU secretary, or the regional district director either
opened or closed the seminars. The involvement of crucial per-
sonalities goes a long way to committing them to the objectives
of the campaign. In this way the projects born out of the campaign and the assignments that derive from the campaign are counted to be a part of the regional/district plans. An outstanding
example is the Chiwanda orchard project (fruit, vegetables and
poultry) where, because of the local authorities' commitment to
the "Food is Life" Campaign, five villages in Chiwanda Ward have
been especially selected for a local campaign integrated into
the district plans.

The opening of the "Food is Life" Campaign was given the greatest
publicity possible. President Nyerere launched the campaign at
the State House. In attendance were Mama Maria Nyerere and three
cabinet ministers for national education, health and agriculture.
The chairman of the National Coordinating Committee read an address to the President briefly outlining the theme, objectives,
and the strategies of the campaign. The keen interest of the
President in the campaign was a great inspiration and motivating
factor for workers and participants.

The Minister for Agriculture addressed the nation on the campaign
over the radio at 8:15 p.m. — the campaign was on!

I have dwelt rather long on the involvement of our country's
leadership in our mass campaign. Political and government leadership in many developing countries has a certain appeal which
can be well exploited to mobilize people into useful self-help
programmes. The influence which TANU leadership wields in Tanzania can work wonders in motivating and stimulating the masses.

Another crucial factor in the "Food is Life" delivery system was
the study groups themselves. Staged training seminars were conducted at national, zonal, regional, district and divisional
levels to train a sufficiently large number of study group advisors to handle the programme. These advisors were local people
and were trained close to their place of operation in order to
cut down expenses and to make the training more practical. Unfortunately, the advisors had only a day's orientation and this
fault had its repercussion in the group formation and handling.
Group advisors were expected to enroll potential "Food is Life"
participants on a voluntary basis. The group should have consisted of 10-20 members to allow participants ample opportunity to
participate actively during a session of one or two hours.

As it turned out, many of the group advisors were literacy teachers and they turned the literacy classes into study groups.
That is fine except that some of those classes were too large
for an effective dialogue. Also, literates did not like to join
literacy classes. In quite a number of cases the literacy teachers unfortunately turned out to be a lecturer, since there
had not been enough time to master group leadership techniques.

As a corrective measure visiting groups from the trainers' teams
were organized to visit study groups and try to help overcome
shortcomings. More time and more money should be allocated to
the training of the advisors and the visiting team plan needs to
be reinforced. Where, however, there was a competent group ad-
visor as in the 12 groups operating in the Institute of Adult
Education, the atmosphere was conducive to innovative learning
processes. Wider participation was offered, lively discussion
followed and well worked out plans of operation were written as
group resolutions. If most of the groups decided on a proposal,
the director and his administration were requested to take up
the matter. So it happened, for instance, that all the groups
resolved that the Institute start its own canteen. The administration took up the matter with the district Ujamaa and Cooperative Division. The Institute Cooperative Canteen was officially
registered and opened as a result of the "Food is Life" Campaign.
The initial evaluation reports suggest that a number of projects
have been started as a direct result of the "Food is Life" discussion groups.

Cost/Benefit and Self-Reliance

Education is normally an expensive social service. Non-formal adult education programmes attempt to reduce the costs by inspiring the spirit of self-reliance and self-help. The major financial burden of the campaign was borne out of a SIDA grant of 2.4 million shillings while the Tanzanian government contribution was partially borne in the various services offered by concerned ministries and organizations. The financial burden which the Ministry of Education would formerly have borne alone has become an interministerial and interagency responsibility. This is a socialist approach to shared work. A number of Tanzanian institutions have taken to initiating projects using this approach, including the Tanzania Food and Nutrition Centre, the Traditions and Customs Research Section of the Ministry of Youth and Culture, and the Tanzanian Community Development Trust Fund.

Until such time as we have all the necessary statistics it is impossible to say what is the average cost of this campaign. It was reported that the "Man is Health" Campaign cost per learner was about ten cents (US).

An over-riding element in the national campaign is the stress on self-reliance of the adult learner himself. "Food is Life", like any functional adult education programme, must have as its objective the transformation of the learner. "Food is Life" was meant to improve food production, diet habits, and food preservation methods. It was therefore expected that many practical resolutions would come up with concrete projects such as the adoption of better farming tools, better seeds, better and larger farms, opening up of vegetable gardens, fruit gardens, poultry units, better culinary utensils, the opening of canteens in offices and places of work, and the establishment of day care centres for children. These projects are not meant to overload the government, they should mainly be run on a self-help basis. The members personally subscribe some capital and render some of the services themselves.

In the Chiwanda project which aims at establishing communal fruit and vegetable gardens and poultry units, public funds are used to buy items, but services such as preparing the plots, bringing local manure, digging the holes, building the poultry pens are all done collectively by the villagers themselves.

One cannot over-emphasize the importance of implementing two of the necessary conditions mentioned in the Arusha Declaration — intelligence and hard work. The people themselves must generate and sustain their development by hard work rather than sit down and wait for the government to do the job for them. "Everybody

wants development; but not everybody understands and accepts
the basic requirements for development. The biggest requirement
is hard work."

"We should not lessen our efforts to get the money we really need,
but it should be more appropriate for us to spend time in the villages showing the people how to bring about development through
their own efforts rather than going on so many long and expensive
journeys abroad in search of development money." (Nyerere)

In-built and Decentralized Evaluation

The "Food is Life" evaluation system helped assess the approp-
riateness of structures, organization delivery systems, objectives, and the campaign facilitators, as well as campaign obstacles and problems; the instruments of evaluation were also evaluated.

It is difficult to devise and apply an evaluation system based
on a socialist approach, where the people involved in development
become themselves an integral and essential part of the evaluation unit. This was the basic consideration of the evaluation
section of the campaign. How best can the various groups of
people in the whole range of the "Food is Life" programme become
self-evaluators supporting the evaluation unit at the Institute?
The evaluation must be decentralized.

The people mainly involved in the campaign were the trainers of
the group leaders, the group leaders, and the group members.
All members of these three categories were introduced to basic
facts on evaluation, the importance of evaluation, and what role
each participant could play to make the exercise really useful.
The participants were encouraged to set their own objectives and
select strategies for achieving the desired ends. They were
introduced to recording their transactions such as time and place
of meetings, number of participants, level of participation, and
reasons why certain projects could not be accomplished.

The team of trainers were introduced to assessing the training
seminars, the tools of the study groups, and the organization of
the study circles.

Evaluation of the programme was presented as a procedure in which
each member must involve himself so as to ensure the success of
the learning process. Evaluation is not a job the expert does

for academicians. One of the encouraging results has been a
request from the teams of trainers and group leaders to do more
evaluation programmes with them. They have come to see their
usefulness and importance.

Another essential element in the evaluation was that each stage
was evaluated formatively to establish the existential stage of
the programme and serve to show indicators for the next developmental trends into the following stage.

As a result "Food is Life" Campaign has, apart from its evaluation guidebook, four official evaluation reports, namely the
first, the second and the third formative evaluation reports
written at the start, after three months, and at the end of the
campaign respectively. A fourth report will sum up the whole
campaign. All reports are a joint effort to assess the progress
of the campaign by the evaluation specialists and the participants. The former divided themselves into six groups and visited
six selected sample areas each time before they jointly wrote the
report. They stayed with the groups for approximately two weeks,
participated in the sessions, and lived with the group members.
It was through living with the participants that the evaluators
could really come to see the difficulties and progress of the
campaign. They were also in a better position to sift properly
the raw data they collected from the local reports.

Another source of the evaluation reports was the regular dispat-
ches from the regional and district adult education coordinators
as well as from the regional centres of the Institute of Adult
Education. Occasionally the members of the groups would write
to the staff at the headquarters for solutions or help which was
normally answered by letters or broadcast as a national feedback.

Even before the final summative report is completed, we have an
idea how well the campaign started and how it progressed. The
third report tells us what the campaign has achieved judging
mainly from the six sample areas: the increased consciousness
of the general public of the need for more food and cash crop
production; the establishment of vegetable gardens and poultry
units; improved diet habits; increased attendance at clinics
by mothers; the set-up of canteens and day care centres for
children; the abandoning of some traditional taboos and bad
practices about food. In all these areas the campaign seems to
have scored encouraging results.

The Role of Languages in Development
Mubanga E. Kashoki

After consideration of the multiple sub-themes inherent in the
subject of cultural pluralism, national integration and development, I have decided to restrict myself to only one aspect,
namely, how to reconcile the need to preserve the indigenous
cultures with the need for a unifying national culture. In Zambia this constitutes the single most critical issue, impinging
as it does on those most talked-about social and political topics
—"nation-building", "national unity" and "national language",
not to mention "tribalism".

A preliminary point needs to be settle concerning the meaning
we attach to "cultural pluralism". In Zambia and Central Africa
as a whole the term has been employed variously in the past. In
this paper I have divorced racial considerations from the concept of cultural pluralism. The term is restricted to its current commonly accepted meaning of the co-existence and interaction within the national boundaries of an indigenous population
consisting of an heterogeneous admixture of ethnic (itself an
imprecise term) or sub-national groups.

Cultural Development Without a Cultural Policy

In recent years, particularly in nations categorized as developing, economic development has characteristically taken place
under the aegis of "development plans". Two notable features
influence economic development: first, the theoretical "ideologies"; secondly, on the more practical level, there are the
"development plans". At the level of ideology, it may be noted
that Tanzania and Zambia respectively are pursuing economic policies circumscribed by their socialist and humanist ideologies.
Thus the national ideology provides both the basis and the context within which actual economic plans can be conceived and
executed. It is possible in these circumstances to talk of national education policies that are broadly in conformity with the
prevailing national ideology.

But developing countries, particularly in Africa, which are preoccupied with economic development are simultaneously preoccupied

with another type of development, that is, cultural development.
Typically, cultural development encompasses questions of preser-
ving and promoting one's cultural heritage, evolving a national
culture, forging a national identity, ensuring national unity,
and promoting and/or selecting one language as a national language. These national goals are often in conflict. It would
therefore seem important that an overall cultural policy, to direct and regulate the future of cultural development, should be
enunciated at the earliest possible moment if a nation is to
avoid serious political conflicts. It would certainly be in the
national interest if economic development took place in step and
harmony with cultural development.

It is precisely the conspicuous absence of such a policy in almost all the developing countries known to me that should be of
primary concern. In Zambia an overall cultural policy has not
been formulated and explicitly spelled out so as to be of assistance to workers and institutions concerned with such varied
matters as education, political unity, cultural identity, dance,
music and language. Of course one occasionally comes across
vague references to a notion of "unity in diversity" as being a
basic political principle for Zambia, but nowhere is this explicitly stated as Party or government policy.

The implications of policy vacuum may be summarized as follows:
(a) in general, there is no discernible sense of direction in
which meaningful and relevant cultural development can take
place, and (b) cultural programmes and activities that should
have a common basis within a wider philosophical framework are
conceived and undertaken with little or no reference to each
other and, in a great many cases, amid serious contradictions.

Perhaps it is in recognition of the vacuum discussed here that
the Organization for African Unity, in a welcome development,
has sought to provide a general cultural policy for its Member
States ("Draft Cultural Charter for Africa: Report of the Committee of Experts Meeting in Accra under the Auspices of the
OAU, October 1975). Article 2(c) states: "In order to fulfil
the objectives set out in Article 1, the African States solemnly
subscribe to the following principles:

> (c) "respect for national specificities and
> local peculiarities in the field of culture"
> (underlining mine). Similarly, Article 3
> states: "The African States recognize the need
> to take account of national specificities and

local peculiarities, cultural pluralism being
a factor making a balance within the nation and
a source of mutual enrichment for the various
communities." In further amplification of this
point, Article 4 stipulates: "Cultural pluralism and the assertion of national identity must
not be at the cost of impoverishing or subjec-
ting other cultures."

Within the context of these three articles of the draft Cultural
Charter (which is not ratified at the time of writing) the African Member States are presented with two clear choices: either
to pursue a policy of cultural diversity or one of cultural homogeneity. A mixed policy is of course also possible. However,
from the spirit of the draft Charter and its obvious bias, the
African States are being persuaded to consider diversity and its
promotion as being in their national interest.

Diversity or Homogeneity

The draft Cultural Charter before the African States is both an
invitation and a challenge to make a clear choice whether they
wish to pursue a policy of cultural diversity or one of homogeneity. There are many reasons wht this task may not be that simple. The choice whether to adopt one or the other of the alternatives is dependent upon one's understanding and appreciation
of all the relevant and contingent variables, historical, social,
economic, political and psychological. Almost invariably those
with the responsibility for making the choice do not fully appreciate all the factors to be considered. In the majority of
cases the political factor, e.g. possible national disunity,
will be singled out and dramatized out of all proportion in a
calculated effort to persuade the population that diversity is
necessarily anti-national.

And yet there is ample evidence to suggest that all loyalties
and institutions, including modern ones such as Party branches,
districts, provinces or regions and even educational systems,
are potentially divisive and from this standpoint anti-social
and anti-national.

A further point is that whether we perceive the nation-state
from a "traditional" or a "modern" perspective, all newly independent African states (including those considered culturally
uni-ligual such as Botswana, Lesotho and Somalia) are character-

ized by one kind of diversity or another. The presence of an
array of modern institutions is in itself a sign of diversity
within the nation-state. Despite the overwhelming evidence that,
whether looked at from a "traditional" (cultural) or modern perspective, African states are essentially nations of diversity,
why then is there a general reluctance to stress diversity as
perhaps the only realistic approach to socio-cultural development? Why do most African states consider these differences as
an index to the instability of the nation, and that their absence or removal is a necessary pre-condition to the soundness
and stability of the nation-state?

Problems of Definition

I hinted earlier that the difficulties arising in making the
proper choice towards more meaningful cultural development may
be explained by the fact that those responsible for making the
choice are not sufficiently alert to the many interacting
factors which need to be taken into account. One dimension of
this situation is definitional. It has to do with how we understand certain concepts or terms, especially those having a direct bearing on questions of cultural development. The choice
between diversity or homogeneity requires a full understanding
and appreciation of such notions as "nation", "national unity",
"national integration", "national identity", "nation-building",
"loyalty" and "tribalism". Each of these notions is likely to
play an important part in the formulation of cultural policies.

As anthropologists and linguists have in recent years come to
appreciate, the very concepts of "tribe", "dialect" and "language"
present their own definitional problems. For instance, it is
proving increasingly difficult to reach general agreement on
the definition of "tribe". And what precisely is a "nation"?
In the Zambian context, what is meant by ONE ZAMBIA, ONE NATION?
Is it diversity or homogeneity that is implicit in the two
phrases?

From all available evidence, "the general orientation" in Zambia,
as exemplified by the Cabinet memorandum referred to earlier,
"is to regard 'nation' as that condition or stage of nationhood
when there is only one language, a common pool of customs, a
common set of traditions, or in general a shared national experience".

Hence the never-ending search for a national dress and one uni-

fied customary law for the country, to give two obvious examples.
Implicit in this notion of nation is the assumption that until
a national consensus in all areas, cultural, political and social,
is attained, the nation-state is not a "nation". The task of
"nation-building" must go on. The question is: when is a nation
a "nation", only when there is absolute uniformity and national
consensus in all spheres of life?

Similar questions may be posed with regard to the other terms
enumerated above. In the following sections I attempt to deal
with only two of these, "loyalty" and "tribalism".

Beware of Tribal Loyalties

The assertion that national integration in newly independent
multi-ethnic, multilingual, and multicultural African nations
will be difficult to achieve if "tribal" loyalties continue to
be an enduring phenomenon pervades much of the social anthropological, sociolinguistic and political science literature concerned
with the future of these nations. We have been told that "tribal"
loyalties are primordial and immutable and that our only salva-
tion lies in eliminating them altogether. The frenzy with which
we are setting about trying to eliminate "tribalism" does not
give us the respite to sit down and critically examine the whole
concept of "loyalty", its nature, and how it is manifested in
our own countries.

I pose here a series of questions and suggest a new look at
"loyalty" and new approaches in bringing about meaningful national integration in the face of a multiplicity of loyalties in
our nations. But our primary concerns here are particularistic
loyalty and national loyalty. What are the measures required
to reconcile the two? What constitutes "loyalty"? Is loyalty
so a sub-national group indeed static and immutable as we have
been told? Or do we agree with Molteno (1974:100) who argues
that "it is possible for a person to behave successively in terms
of national goals and sectional goals"? Is loyalty therefore
variable?

An important point little appreciated in our circumstances is
that stressed by the Canadian Government's Report of the Royal
Commission on Bilingualism and Biculturalism:

>   Integration, in the broad sense, does not simply
>   mean the loss of an individual's identity and

> original characteristics or of his original
> language and culture. Man is a thinking and
> sensitive being; severing him from his roots
> could destroy an aspect of his personality and
> deprive society of some of the values he can
> bring to it. Integration is not synonymous
> with assimilation. Assimilation implies almost
> total absorption into another linguistic and
> cultural group. An assimilated individual
> gives up his cultural identity, and may go as
> far as to change his name. (Book IV, 1969:5)

In many African countries national integration has too often
aimed at total absorption or assimilation into some theoretical
socio-political entity called "nation" — something that is in
any case claimed not to exist.

At all times, the two phenomena, identification with the national
group and affiliation to one's ethnic or cultural group (or
class), exist to some degree in both individuals and groups of
individuals. The existence of diverse groups is not necessarily
disintegrative. How many of our nationals strongly identify
with their respective ethnic groups at the expense of the national will? How many of us as the result of "tribal" loyalties are
plotting to secede from the nation-state? Is it not possible
to be loyal to the "traditional" chief and the national President simultaneously? Do we deserve to be arrested for bowing to
the chief? So we need to abandon our language in order to be
truly national?

While pondering these questions, one must bear in mind that such
factors as intermarriage, education, economic interaction at
regional and national scales, urbanization, social mingling, and
social and geographical mobility are playing an ever greater role
in the integration of our people into the national fabric. In
these circumstances, sense of belonging and the will to exist as
a group are bound to be affected in fundamental ways.

But are cultural or ethnic loyalties static and immutable? Is
the only way we can become Zambian or Tanzanian nationals fully
and truly by rescuing us from our tribal loyalties? Molteno
dismisses the notion of static or immutable loyalties:

> ... leaders and followers act situationally.
> Depending on how their social situation appears
> to them, they will act in terms of nationalist

norms and identifications or sectional norms
and identifications. Moreover, on different
occasions they may act in terms of different
kinds of sectional ties ...

Consider the following hypothetical case. A
Zambian Minister flies to London to negotiate
a loan. He acts nationally as a 'Zambian',
since domestic sectional cleavages are irrelevant to his behaviour in the negotiations. On
his return to Lusaka he may involve himself in
a Cabinet dispute on the location of some development project in which sectional splits
follow linguistic or provincial lines. He may
then tour his home province and discover that
his leadership is being challenged. He then
aligns himself with sections in the province
which base themselves on dialectical differences or divisions among traditional leaders, or
geographical-historical cleavages, or commoner-
traditional ruler distinctions.

The same man can act successively in the various roles of 'Zambian', 'Eastern Province man',
'Tumbuka' or 'Tumbuka commoner'. He has a
series of social ties, group loyalties, institutional environments. How he acts depends
on his perception of what appears from his social situation to be most relevant at the moment.
In other words, a loyal nationalist might also
act as an ardent sectionalist politician.
(op. cit., pp. 88-89)

Tribalism, Ethnicity, Sectionalism, or Interest Groups?

Considering the remarks of the preceding section, what therefore
is "tribalism"? Gulliver (1969:7) suggests that "partly because
of the lack of an agreed definition, partly because of certain
derogatory implications attached to it in some contexts by some
people (i.e. primitive, uncivilized, conservative, inferior),
and partly because in contemporary conditions certain new elements, ascriptions and alignments have become attached to it",
those who object to the term "tribe" and its derivatives and
wish to see it replaced by a more apt term may have a point.

Molteno (1974:62-63) criticizes and dismisses the term "tribalism"

and prefers what to him is a more fitting term, "sectionalism".
He argues against a definition of tribalism which "plays down
the rational economic motivation that underlies the role of sectional groupings as interest groups in Zambia" (ibid: 63). His
other objection to the term is its apparent restriction to the
Third World. He points out that "Unlike the term 'sectionalism',
'tribalism' fosters the divorce between concepts and hypotheses
developed to analyze political behaviour in the West and those
evolved to study often essentially similar phenomena in Africa.
It is arbitrary to speak, for example, of the Flemings in Belgium
as a nation (and their political behaviour as 'nationalism') but
of the Lozi in Zambia as a tribe" (and what they do as 'tribalism').
(ibid: 63)

For the latter reason, many writers prefer the term "ethnicity"
to "tribalism". Cohen (1974:ix-x) defines "ethnic group" and
"ethnicity" more broadly than conventional definitions of "tribe"
and "tribalism" suggest: "... an ethnic group can be operation-
ally defined as a collectivity of people who (a) share some patterns of normative behaviour and (b) form a part of a larger
population interacting with people from other collectivities
within the framework of a social system. The term ethnicity
refers to the degree of conformity be members of the collectivity
to these shared norms in the course of social interaction" (un-
derlining mine).

From the foregoing, it is evident that an increasing number of
writers are now approaching questions of "tribe" and "tribalism"
from contextual, situational, and operational perspectives.
"Tribalism", "ethnicity" or "sectionalism" may be defined on the
one hand as the existence of interest groups competing for scarce
resources and on the other as the exploitation of existing differences (cultural, ethnic, political, economic, etc.) to further
their interests.

Our concern now should be with the absence of a full appreciation
in many African countries of the forces at work in our societies.
In Africa generally, the situations and processes involved are
often ill-understood and therefore insufficiently appreciated.
For this reason, the remedies we prescribe for ridding ourselves
of the dreaded "tribalism" are more often than not based on a
very imperfect diagnosis of the ailment. Some prescriptions
have, for example, suggested that all that is required is to
eliminate our cultural, ethnic and linguistic differences and
after that all would be well. The trouble with this suggested
remedy is whether it gets at the root problem at all and whether

it serves any useful purpose. Does one get rid of provincialism
by abolishing provinces, or does the solution lie in removing
those factors and tendencies that lead to exploiting regional
differences for personal gain?

In approaching contemporary problems of political and social
conflict, we are too prone to believe that it is our "tribes"
and our languages in themselves that are responsible for our
social ills. On the contrary, is it not the scarcity of our resources and the manipulation and exploitation of our differences
as a weapon for getting what we want that are at the centre of
our current conflicts? If it were the "tribes" which were the
only source of the problem, logically we should all be rallying
around our chiefs and headmen. But in fact it is our national
political leaders who are at the centre of the storm; it is
these leaders who are fanning the fires of sectionalism. Sectional conflicts are not generated by "traditional" rulers, to
perpetuate primordial loyalties; very often it is the modern
polit al leader — the Party official in search of a promotion
—who panders to cultural, ethnic, or linguistic differences on
the road to a Cabinet post. The solution then is not to do away
with the culture or language of the people being manipulated by
the leader, but either to remove such a leader, or to remove the
factors which result in such practices. In Zambia, for example,
one remedy may be to legislate against Parliamentary candidates
standing in their own ethnic or "home" areas.

The essential point being made here is that for most leaders,
whether political or non-political, the ethnic group — in the
absence of other interest groups to manipulate — is about the
only social organization available for exploitation in the stiff
competition for employment, housing, high positions, a place in
school, or favours. It is not the villager and his chief who
feel so aggrieved that they want to secede from the nation-state;
it is typically the national leader who has not got what he wants
who agitates against a certain individual, group, or even the
state itself in sectional terms.

It is the modern leader who tells his ethnic group that they
have no Cabinet minister, no tarred road to their area, and that
their language deserves to be included among those used in the
education system. In so doing, he politicizes and socializes
them into perceiving social, economic, and political ills mainly
in "sectional" or "tribal" terms. The people so manipulated
(only the leader is entitled to mislead the people) begin to see
the other "ethnic group" as their social, economic, or political

enemy. The consequence is that "once sectionalism gets a popular hold, it is difficult for a leader to act contrary to its
pressures" (Molteno, op. cit, p. 102).

Seen in this light, sectionalism as essentially a form of competition, whether labelled "tribalism" or "ethnicity", will not
go away merely by dint of eloquent sloganeering, by ineffectual
attempts at eliminating cultures and languages, or by prescrib-
ing one language as a national language. As long as people have
aspirations to be met, competition and the manipulation of social distinctions and differences will remain in one form or
another.

Language and National Integration: Is a National Language the Answer?

In much of the current socio-linguistic and related literature
it is commonplace to attribute to language inherent qualities,
whether positive or negative, which it does not possess. The
usual claim is that a commonly shared language unifies. For
instance, Abdulaziz (1971:164) asserts that "Swahili has played
a very significant role in the development of political values
and attitudes in Tanzania. Its integrative qualities (under-
lining mine) have influenced the style of Tanzania politics,
especially its non-tribal and egalitarian characteristics."
Despite the evidence adduced to demonstrate the integrative
qualities ascribed to the language, it is not clear whether it
is Swahili alone, in isolation from many other social, ideological, political and economic factors, which has brought about
the degree of national integration claimed by the writer. Until
Swahili can be isolated from other factors impinging on the process of national integration and shown to be the factor responsible for the emergence, for example, of "egalitarian characteristics" among Tanzanians, the evidence will remain inconclusive
and therefore of doubtful value.

There are two statements that could be made about language with
a measure of absolute certitude. The first is that, whether at
local, regional or international level, a common language facil-
itates communication. The second is that, to the extent that a
group of people sentimentally identify with it, language can be
a source of social solidarity. Beyond that it becomes extremely
tenuous to ascribe to language absolute or categorical attri-
butes. The claim that language unites or disunites a people is
a moot point. A language as a unifying or disintegrative factor

is conditional and contingent upon many social factors.

For example, a nation-state, e.g. the United States, while enjoy-
ing the advantage of one common language, English, may be subject
to considerable social unpheaval. Indeed, Black Americans, speaking English just like other fellow Americans, have found it necessary to agitate against the American nation-state — to assert
their rights — because of discriminatory practices and social
injustice based on colour. Moreover, it is possible for two nations, e.g. East and West Germany, to speak the same language
and yet not enjoy the close ties of solidarity and, in the event
of serious conflict, even go to war. It must also not be forgotten that in pre-colonial times our communities were not without
grave social and political upheavals even though their peoples
communicated in a common medium. I certainly know that the Bemba
occasionally went to war among themselves and not for want of a
common language.

From the point of view of national unity or disunity, a national
language alone is not the answer. Specifically, Kiswahili in
Tanzania is not the solution to all problems (cultural, political,
social, economic, psychological, educational) that Tanzania has
to face. Kiswahili along cannot be expected to bring about economic, political or social miracles. Other measures are necessary
to make Tanzanians believe that they have an enduring stake in
their country. A national language (where conditions favour the
selection of one language as a national language) must be comple-
mented by other equally important measures (such as Tanzania's
Ujamaa and Zambia's Humanism) if the nation is to survive as a
cohesive entity and if its people are to continue feeling a
sense of belonging and the will to exist as a national group.
Eliminating cultures and languages may prove to be a futile
exercise and may even be counter-productive.

In conclusion, I am inclined to agree with Kelman (1971:48) who
suggests that:

> "... the deliberate use of language policies
> for the purpose of creating a national identity
> and fostering sentimental attachments is usually
> not desirable. Rather, language policies ought
> to be designed to meet the needs and interests
> of all segments of the population effectively
> and equitably, thus fostering instrumental attach-
> ments out of which sentimental ones can then
> gradually emerge."

His final proposition is that:

> Even if one accepts the proposition that lan-
> guage policies should be designed to meet the
> needs and interests of all segments of the pop-
> ulation in the most effective and equitable
> way, he has to determine what specific policy
> is most likely to be conducive to this end of
> a given society at a given point in time. In
> some situations, a common national language
> may be most appropriate; in others, the recog-
> nition of two or more official languages; and
> in yet others, the combination of a national
> administrative language, with officially recog-
> nized local languages.

References

Abdulaziz, M.H. (1971) Tanzania's national language policy and
the rise of Swahili political culture, in Language Use and
Social Change, W.H. Whiteley (ed.). London: Oxford University Press (for the International African Institute), pp.
160-178.

Alexandre, P. (1968) Linguistic problems of nation-building in
Negro Africa, in Language Problems of Developing Nations,
J.A. Fishman, C.A. Ferguson & J. Das Gupta (eds.). New York,
John Wiley & Sons, pp. 119-127.

Cohen, A. (1974) Introduction: The lesson of Ethnicity, in
Urban Ethnicity, A. Cohen (ed.). London, Tavistock Publications, pp. ix-xxiv.

Dole, G.E. (1968) Tribe as the autonomous unit, in Essays on
the Problem of Tribe, J. Helm (ed.), American Ethnological
Society, pp. 83-100.

Fishman, J.A. (1968) Nationality-nationalism and nation-nationism,
in Language Problems of Developing Nations, J.A. Fishman, C.A.
Ferguson & J. Das Gupta (eds.). New York, John Wiley & Sons,
pp. 39-51.

Fishman, J.A. (1971) National language and languages of wider
communication in the developing countries, in Language Use
and Social Change, W.H. Whiteley (ed.). London: Oxford

University Press (for the International African Institute),
pp. 27-56.

Fishman, J.A. (1971) The impact of nationalism on language planning: Some comparisons between early twentieth-century Europe
and Southeast Asia, in Can Language Be Planned?, J. Rubin &
B.H. Jernuss (eds.), Honolulu: The University Press, Hawaii,
pp. 3-20.

Gann, L.H. (1958) The Birth of a Plural Society. Manchester:
Manchester University Press (for the Institute for Social
Research, University of Zambia).

Gulliver, P.H. (1969) Introduction, in Tradition and Transition
in East Africa, P.H. Gulliver (ed.), London: Routledge &
Kegan Paul, pp. 5-35.

Hymes, D. (1968) Linguistic problems in defining the concept of
"Tribe" in Essays on the Problem of Tribe, J. Helm (ed.),
American Ethnological Society, pp. 23-48.

Kelman, H.C. (1971) Language as an aid and barrier to involvement
in the national system, in Can Language be Planned?, J. Rubin
& B.H. Jernudd (eds.), Honolulu: The University Press, Hawaii,
pp. 21-51.

Kashoki, M.E. (1971) Language and nation in Zambia: The problem
of integration, Journal of the Language Association of Eastern Africa, 2, 2, 91-104.

Kashoki, M.E. (1973) Language: A blueprint for national integration, Bulletin of the Zambia Language Group, 1, 2, 19-49.

Mfoulou, J. (1973) Ethnic Pluralism and national unity in
Africa, in Symposium Leo Frobenius, Pullach/Munchen:
Deutsche-UNESCO Kommission, Koln Verlag Documentation, pp.
110-132.

Molteno, R. (1974) Cleavage and conflict in Zambian politics:
a study in sectionalism, in Politics in Zambia, W. Tordoff
(ed.), Manchester: Manchester University Press, pp. 62-106.

Workers' Participation for Development

J. R. W. Whitehouse

Purpose of the Paper

In response to the basic aim of the Conference, i.e. the need
to examine the meaning of development at the half-way point of
the Second Development Decade, and identify the role of adult
education in the development process at national and international levels, the purpose of this paper is two-fold:

(1) to disseminate information on the basic concepts, objec-
     tives and technical operational activities of the Workers'
     Education Programme and Branch, with a view to identifying
     areas in which the ILO may further assist workers' parti-
     cipation in the development process, and

(2) to convey some thoughts on popular participation and its
     practical implementation for development, with specific
     reference to the role of workers' organizations and wor-
     kers' education institutions.

The Workers' Education Programme of the ILO

The central role of workers' organizations in workers' education
developments was emphasized in the Report of the Meeting of ILO
Consultants on Workers' Education, Geneva, May 1971, which con-
cluded:

> "(16) it is up to the trade union organizations to
> assume the primary responsibilies for workers' edu-
> cation and to have control over activites which are
> carried out in this area."

Within this context the Consultants urged intensification of
the ILO Workers' Education Programme to:

> "(18) — help, on their request, the unions and workers'
> education bodies to help themselves in carrying out
> their functions better and in developing to this
> effect their educational activities ...

" — further in developing countries the creation and
development of institutions devoted to workers' education at different levels operated by trade unions
or bodies having the full support of the workers'
organizations ...

"(19) In furthering these objectives, the ILO Workers'
Education Programme should strengthen education services of workers' organizations and research services
of trade unions, promote workers' participation in
development through information and education ... "

It follows, quite naturally, that the development of workers'
education activities through the ILO has resulted in close collaboration between the Workers' Education Branch and workers'
organizations at the national, regional and international levels,
as well as workers' education institutions, including post-secondary institutions, "having the full support of the workers'
organizations".

The Concept of Labour and Trade Union Education

Workers' organizations in a rapidly changing world face more
complex and exacting challenges than ever before arising from
changing requirements and conditions of work, industrial and
social relationships, and most important of all the acceptance
of new concepts relating to the increasing rights and responsibilities of organized labour in the social and economic life
and development of the nation, local community and enterprise
in which they are employed.

Each of these challenges conjures up a response conditioned by
many factors but with its effectiveness determined by the intellectual equipment, operational skills, integrity and devotion of
working men and women, and the organizations which defend their
collective interests. Needs in the field of labour education
today emerge as complex and dynamic as the challenges themselves.

The expansing responsibilities of workers' organizations include:

(i) their traditional functions of seeking better working and
living conditions, security of employment, and a fair share
of the benefits of economic growth;

(ii) confronting broader questions of social and economic policy,

including the protection of real incomces, social security
and other benefits, through economic stability and orderly
processes of social change;

(iii) participation in developing, planning and implementation,
so as to bring greater realism and social content to development policies which workers and their organizations
can support;

(iv) direct contributions to development through union-sponsored
or union-supported co-operatives, credit unions and housing
projects, health and welfare programmes, family life and
planning endeavours, community services, literacy training
programmes, labour studies, curriculum development in cooperation with educational authorities, and advanced college and university-centred labour education developments,
etc.

Trade unions will continue to exert pressure to ensure the availability of comprehensive and universal public education for all
up to the level of each individual's needs and capacity; support
and encourage the development of adequate technical and vocational training centres; work towards the development of a learning
society through continuing adult education; and look to a reform
of formal school curriculum that will incorporate comprehensive
labour studies. But, I suggest, we do a disservice to an important participatory educative development if we confuse these
trade union educational concerns with Labour Education, as it is
now broadly emerging in major regions.

Clearly Labour Education encompasses, but extends beyond, the
traditional identification of Trade Union Training having to do
with knowledge extension and skill development to meet the on-
going organizational and administrative needs of the trade union.

It is useful, I suggest, to consider points of difference in objectives that differentiate trade union education from the more
traditional objectives of general adult education, and I suggest
further they may be found in aims and developments of a collective nature, using collective approaches and mechanisms, rather
than the individual development and upward personal job mobility
goals of broad fields of adult education, though both may result
from a labour education experience.

The basic goals of labour education are the development of skills,
knowledge and understanding for service within, and through, the

labour movement for the achievement of the broadest institutional, social and economic purposes.

Some of these concepts and thoughts are undoubtedly controversial, and require further clarification and development. They are shared with you for this precise purpose, and with a view to identifying an institutional vehicle through which workers' participation in the development process seems likely to be achieved.

Popular Participation and the Implications for Workers' Education

The concept of popular participation as a motivating force for, and integral part of, the development process is not new to the ILO for it has been firmly rooted in its fundamental principles.

In this connection, particular mention should be made of an extensive ILO study on Employers' and Workers' Participation in Planning, 1971, carried out as a follow-up to a resolution on the concept of democratic decision-making in programming for economic and social development adopted by the International Labour Conference in 1964.

As pointed out by this study "... the type of participation on which the ILO has concentrated its research in recent years is that concerned with the contribution made by individuals or organized groups of the economically active population to the acceleration of economic and social development".

Whatever the varying uses of terminology may be with regard to the term participation, for example, consultation, co-operation, sharing, etc., in the decision-making process for development, it is generally recognized that the concept of popular participation implies the spontaneous and democratic involvement of people's organizations in contributing to the development effort, with people sharing equitably in the benefits derived therefrom and in decision-making at all levels, with respect to goal-setting, formulating and implementing policies and planning for development.

With respect to popular participation in such fields as industrial relations and labour administration, for example, perhaps three basic conditions need to be fulfilled. First, it is necessary for the parties concerned to be able to adopt a positive attitude towards participation; second, it is indispensable that this attitude be accompanied by appropriate institutions and

systems through which participation in the decision-making process may operate effectively, and finally educational facilities
must be available through which the parties may acquire representative training and development for effective participation.

It would be appropriate also to note that participation in decision-making, as it relates to ILO's terminology in the context
of industrial relations, involves on the one hand participation
by the occupational and social groups, i.e. workers' and employers' organizations, at all levels in various public or semi-pub-
lic bodies set up for the purpose, and on the other hand participation in development in the form of action undertaken volun-
tarily by workers' and employers' organizations at the level of
the undertaking.

Trade union representatives at the level of the undertaking have
different educational needs depending on their particular functions. In some countries workers' representatives sit on the
board of directors or national enterprises, share in the management of economic enterprises and contribute to the functioning
of social as well as economic institutions.

Where workers' organizations engage directly in productive undertakings and invest union resources in economic development, trade
unionists with specialized functions need to be equipped with
practical knowledge for establishing credit unions and co-operatives of various kinds, promoting vocational training and literacy schemes, operating union health and welfare services, instituting workers' housing schemes and so on.

In many countries workers' members of national, regional or sec-
toral development commissions and specialized committees have to
acquaint themselves with the basic principles of development
planning and macro-economic tools such as national accounting,
employment and manpower planning and assessment, as well as economic and social policies relating to prices, income, money, credit and fiscal systems.

In several regions of the world trade unionists and labour educators need to understand the impact of economic integration on
living standards, employment, labour mobility and trade union
policies.

Trade unions now must grapple with the myriad facets of multi-
national companies and their impact on the earnings, job security
and union rights of workers. In order to understand and cope

with the complex structure and operations of worldwide enterprises, trade unionists must become concerned with international investment and capital movements, import and export controls, as well as comparative wages and other conditions of employment in different countries.

As union affairs become more complex, union treasurers and other officials dealing with financial questions need increasing knowledge of accountancy, banking and investment practice, as well as relevant elements of commercial and trade union law.

Trade unionists responsible for preparing briefs and other research functions need to develop their skills in analyzing complex facts and figures, obtaining and interpreting statistical data, and preparing union positions which advance workers' interests.

Many workers' organizations need educational programmes at the membership level to enable them to know their rights and responsibilities in the society in which they live and work, as producers, consumers and citizens, and to understand the meaning of trade unionism and the importance of self-reliance and collective action.

There is an evident need for developing the educational use of union journals and the labour press, as well as the media, including radio and television.

Special programmes have also to be conceived and carried out for particular groups of persons such as young workers, women, non-wage earning rural workers and migrant workers.

To carry out these various educational programmes there is a universal need for the training of union instructors and labour educators, involving methods and techniques of workers' education, as well as curriculum development.

Labour education requires teachers who are technically competent, sympathetic to labour's aspirations, and acceptable to the trade union learner. While certain specialists from universities and other educational institutions do meet these conditions and are increasingly called upon to help in teaching, the great bulk of workers' education is organized, administered and carried out by persons found within the labour movement.

Mandate of the ILO Workers' Education Programme

The development of workers' education activities through the ILO
has therefore resulted in close collaboration between the Workers'
Education Branch, and the national, regional and international
trade union organizations. The labour education programmes of
urban and rural workers' organizations have been supported, developed and strengthened particularly in developing countries
where the full development of the trade union movement is a condition for the achievement of worker, social and national objectives based on equality of opportunity and social justice.

From the point of view of framework it is again worth recalling
that the initial resolution concerning the concept of democratic
decision-making in programming and planning for economic and
social development, adopted by the International Labour Conference in 1964, calls upon governments to ensure that appropriate
methods of consultation and participation of free and independent
employers' and workers' organizations should take place in working towards and implementing social advancement schemes, and in
promoting national development at all levels, and to intensify
studies and research in the field of democratic decision-making
as well as techniques of consultation and participation in all
aspects of economic forecasting, programming and planning for
economic and social development.

Of regional significance are two resolutions, one on social participation in the development process, and another on action by
the ILO in the field, adopted by the Ninth Conference of American
States Members of the ILO, Caracas, April 1970.

These two resolutions call upon all governments of the region to
adopt effective measures designed to enable employers' and workers' organizations and youth organizations, to participate in
economic and social development, and to seek the collaboration
of universities, teaching, research and training institutes in
achieving these goals.

Reference should be made to two relevant resolutions and conclusions concerning popular participation adopted by the Asian Regional Conference of the ILO. The first is the resolution on
Freedom of Association for Workers and Employers and their Role
in Social and Economic Development, adopted by the Seventh Asian
Regional Conference, Teheran, 1971, and the second, the resolution
concerning Workers' Education Programme for Rural Workers' Organizations, adopted by the Eighth Asian Regional Conference, Colom-
bo, 1975.

The former resolution (paragraph 5) recommends that arrangements
for the participation of employers' and workers' organizations
should include tripartite machinery, such as national labour
conferences, labour advisory boards, councils or committees.

While emphasizing the need for strengthening workers' and employers' organizations, and the key-role which ministries of labour
should play in the elaboration and implementation of national
labour relations developments, the resolution draws attention to
the need for workers' education and training programmes.

The latter resolution concerning workers' education programmes
for rural workers' organizations calls for the implementation of
the terms of both the Convention and Recommendation concerning
Organizations of Rural Workers and their Role in Economic and
Social Development. The Recommendation provides that it should
be an objective of national policy concerning rural development
to facilitate the establishment of strong and independent organizations of rural workers as an effective means of ensuring the
participation of rural workers in economic and social development.

Objectives and Basic Principles

In refining objectives of an operational nature during successive phases of long-term planning, the following specific priority targets have been identified for the Workers' Education
Programme:

(1) strengthening the educational services of workers' organ-
     izations, particularly through the training of labour edu-
     cators;

(2) promoting and strengthening trade union research and docu-
     mentation services;

(3) strengthening other union services through the training of
     workers, e.g. co-operative undertakings and economic and
     social services sponsored or supported by workers' organ-
     izations;

(4) promoting workers' participation in development through
     information and education;

(5) dissemination of information, and extension of education on

labour matters through workers' education associations, universities, schools, etc.;

(6) developing and promoting the development, at country level, of study materials, audio-visual aids and methods and techniques of workers' education.

In recent years, increasing emphasis has been placed on the promotion and strengthening of labour educational activities of rural workers and peasant organizations, associated with trade union organizations.

Structure of the Workers' Education Branch

The work of the Branch is divided between several sections dealing with field development and technical co-operation; research and development; teaching materials and publications and technical administration.

As a result of decentralization five regular budget workers' education experts have been assigned to ILO regional and area offices in Asia, Africa, Middle East, Latin America and the Caribbean. In addition seventeen additional workers' education experts have been assigned to field projects funded by external funding agencies.

An important role is played by the workers' education consultants, appointed by the Governing Body, to assist the Office to develop appropriate policies and technical methods in workers' education. Apart from their advisory function in the development of policies and practices of the programme, the consultants keep the Office informed of trends and developments in workers' education, on their own initiative or at the request of the Office.

In the main the workers' education programme of the ILO is financed by allocations from the regular budget, though increasingly technical field co-operation projects, developed and administered by the Workers' Education Branch are funded through such multi-bilateral funding agencies as the United Nations Development Programme; the United Nations Fund for Population Activities; the United Nations Environment Programme; the Danish Agency for Technical Co-operation; the Norwegian Agency for Development, and the Swedish Technical Co-operation Agency.

Areas of Activity

Research: The research work carried out under the Workers' Education programme comprises two closely related categories:

(1)   educational methods and techniques (audio-visual aids and public media, etc.) and organizational aspects of workers' education (e.g. the role of universities and public authorities);

(2)   the substantive content of workers' education programmes. ILO research supports training by analyzing educational problems of such groups as rural, women or young trade unionists; training, in turn, creates the learning experience, and disseminates the results of applied research.

International Symposia and Seminars are arranged to draw upon the experience and knowledge of experts in selected areas of concern. For example, between November 1973 and February 1975, four such Symposia were held in Geneva, dealing with:

(1)   the role of universities in workers' education;
(2)   workers' education needs of migrant workers;
(3)   economic education for trade unionists; and
(4)   workers' education methods and techniques for rural workers and their organizations.

The proceedings and conclusions of these symposia, with additional research findings, will be published. A further conference on labour's involvement in educational reform is scheduled.

Regional Seminars are arranged with subject content related to expressed needs, e.g. labour participation in development; labour participation at the level of the enterprise; trade unions and co-operatives; trade union research services; family life and population problems; use of radio and television; residential workers' education; advanced techniques and methods (study circles, group dynamics), and so on.

Participation in external workers' education activities: Staff of the Workers' Education Branch participate in numerous international and regional seminars and courses organized by international trade unions and workers' education bodies. After the system of regional advisors was established, the participation in such activities by workers' education regional advisors was greatly accelerated.

Expert Missions: More than eighty workers' education experts helped trade unions or workers' education bodies in over fifty countries to improve the structure and administration of their workers' education services, to train instructors, and to develop content and courses for trade union leadership. Some missions had other specific objectives directed toward documentation and research services (e.g. Singapore, 1965; Kenya, 1969) or on the use of visual and audio-visual aids for workers' education (e.g. Malaysia, 1967) or on building up permanent workers' education institutes (e.g. India, Middle East, Caribbean).

Regional Advisers: The main roles of regional advisers are to provide advice on workers' education programming and institution building, to conduct direct educational activities, and to develop field projects with workers' organizations. A post of regional adviser was established in Asia and Latin America in 1966 and in the Middle East in 1969; three regional advisers or multinational experts are in Africa. They organized training for over 2,140 workers' instructors and union officers, with at least an equal number of others in courses conducted by the trainees and supervised by the regional adviser, up to 1972.

Fellowships: During the first seven years of activity, fifty-four fellowships have been awarded under ILO's regular budget. Many former fellows have become key persons responsible for workers' education in their own countries.

Manuals: Mainly designed for instructors to give an introduction to the subjects treated and provide concise material calculated to stimulate interest, discussion and further study.

Guides and Booklets: Are designed to be used as study materials for seminars or courses given by trade union or workers' education bodies. They are presented in the form of simplified texts with detailed outline of courses, indications about the methods and techniques to be used and the audio-visual aids proposed.

Labour Education Bulletin: This is a forum for labour educators to be informed of current problems, methods and techniques of workers' education, as well as new developments in the field.

Provision of Teaching Aids

Filmstrips and other visual aids: The relative low cost of filmstrips has enabled the ILO to produce its own filmstrips or

slide series of which multiple prints are easily made, distributed and/or donated to workers' education bodies. Flannelboard
symbol sets printed under the Workers' Education Programme since
1969, include 100 copies each of the Industrial Enterprise,
ILO Conventions and Recommendations; 300 copies of Your Role as
a Shop Steward; 100 copies of Teaching Methods and Group Dynamics. Three hundred flipchart sets on The Stake of Workers in
Population Questions were released in an English version in 1971.
Several other aids on workers' population education were produced
in 1974/75.

Films: Since labour studies films are effective teaching aids,
provision was made as early as 1956 for the purchase of films
and projectors to set up a lending library to serve labour education needs. As of 1972 the film loan service comprises 123
active titles, with 345 prints stored at ILO headquarters and
its various field offices. Incomplete statistics submitted by
the field offices indicated to the end of 1972, 97 loans, with
382 showings to 29,484 participants. Loans made directly from
Geneva total 214, with about 600 showings to approximately
15,000 viewers during 1971/72.

Equipment purchased for supply to workers' education institutions
and trade union educational bodies since 1960 include: 8 movie
screens, 24 film projectors, 6 duplicating machines, 40 tape
recorders, 31 slide projectors, and assorted equipment such as
loudspeakers, microphones, easels, flannelboards, etc.

Related Workers' Education Activities and Future Trends

In the field of workers' education specific reference should be
made to the paramount need to develop workers' education infrastructures at the country level, if meaningful and representative participation in the development process is to be achieved.

The ILO Workers' Education Branch in co-operation with the International Centre for Advanced Vocational and Technical Training
in Turin, recently responded to the need for workers' educator
training by the establishment of a union-oriented Trade Union
Training Section in Turin. Programmes are developed by the
Workers' Education Branch in co-ordination with a Trade Union
Course Design Committee, administered by Programme Managers and
Instructors drawn from the labour movement. Four 12-week residential courses in Trade Union Education Methods and Techniques
have been offered so far. With 20 to 25 labour educators in

each course, participants came from English-speaking Africa, French-speaking Africa, Asia, and a new rural workers' course drew campesino union educators from Latin America.

A subsidiary objective of this development, and in response to needs for adequate labour education training materials, is to develop, with participant co-operation, two training packages, Participant Guides, Study Notes, Teacher Manuals and Audio-Visual Aids related to urban and rural workers' educator needs in the field.

Emphasis on the infra-structure building objectives of the Workers' Education Programme can be further illustrated by reference to a 1976/77 major rural field and research project designed to assist in the development of organizations of non-wage-earning rural workers, in co-operation with existing rural workers' organizations: the development of documentation and manuals on the structure and functions of wage-earning rural workers' organizations: the ILO/SIDA workers' education project for Asian Maritime Workers, and the ILO/DANIDA project to assist the Malaysian Trade Union Congress develop a research and library unit.

This tendency towards self-help, action-oriented assistance, rather than international assistance through subject-matter, dissemination of information-oriented workers' education activities is pronounced in most of the emerging concerns of workers' organizations in the developing world.

It is certainly true in rural development fields. The size and complexity of the organizational problems of rural workers makes it a priority concern in social and economic development. Without viable peasant organizations and other social institutions of rural workers, there can never be the spirit of organized self-help and confident dynamism essential for successful and just rural development.

Labour education institutions and agencies need to develop field studies of peasant organizations, economic and social problems and other obstacles to organization as a prerequisite to the organization of rural workers' organizations. Action-oriented programmes need to be devised that help urban and industrial workers understand the problems of rural workers, leading to an alliance of peasants and industrial workers united in a search for social justice.

Educational programmes for rural workers should be planned on

the basis of revealed needs and aspirations of rural workers and
planned with their full participation. The interdependence of
education, organization and problem-solving action needs to be
fully recognized and accepted in programme planning.

Related to this major development, but not confined to it, is
growing recognition in the developing world that eradication of
illiteracy, and the development of functional literacy programmes
and materials appropriate to the needs of the worker-learner,
should be a labour education concern. This attitude, I suggest,
stems from realization that (a) illiteracy is a high barrier to
organization and meaningful participation in the affairs of the
union and society, (b) the knowledge that after a decade of
effort by the world project to eradicate illiteracy there were
800 million illiterates in 1975, compared to 735 million in 1965.

Obviously, only the concerted efforts of all segments of society,
public and private, including the trade union education institutes and systems, can provide the full response to illiteracy.
This was a significant theme of the recent ILO Seminar on Participation and Development of Workers' Education for trade unions
in English-speaking Africa, held at the Ghana Labour College,
Accra, November 1975, and the First Arab Regional Conference on
Illiteracy Among Workers in Arab Countries, Baghdad, February
1976, which recommended that the International Confederation of
Arab Trade Unions should, without delay, establish a special
literacy department within ICATU's Office of Workers' Education.

The emergence of new problems, a common characteristic in both
the industrialized and developing countries, will require flexibility and/or participatory community development approaches, in
a constant search for new dimensions and approaches in labour
education.

New responses and initiatives are already evident to meet needs
related to:

(1)   analysis of ways of improving the economic knowledge of
       trade unionists as related to trade union concerns; plan-
       ning and implementation of programmes of labour economics,
       development of teaching methods, preparation of study mat-
       erials and promotion of research work. Reference can be
       made to the Report of the ILO Symposium on Economic Educa-
       tion for Trade Unionists, Geneva, December 1974, and the
       Report on the Seminar/Workshop on Labour Economics for
       Caribbean Trade Unionists, held at the Trade Union Education

Institute, University of the West Indies, Jamaica, April
1975;

(2)   educational programmes for rural workers and peasant organizations, such as the trade union education techniques and
methodology course for rural organizations jointly developed
and offered by the Workers' Education Branch and Turin, and
particularly rural projects related to the identification
of needs and organizational structures for the non-wage-
earning peasant, tenant farmer, etc. Reference can be made
to the Report on the ILO Symposium on Workers' Education
Methods and Techniques for Rural Workers and their Organizations, Geneva, February 1975; the ILO Convention and
Recommendation on rural workers and their organizations,
and Labour Education, No. 28, a special rural workers' issue.
Such projects and the Landless Rural Poor in India and
Aurangabad Experiment, and Organization of the Rural Poor,
Kalan Area in Ghazepur, India, are well documented, and a
new book by Jeremias Montemayor, the founder and President
of the Federation of Free Farmers, The Philippine Agrarian
Reform Program, adds to our understanding of the problems
and concerns of tenants, farm workers and small owner-culti-
vators;

(3)   development of new forms of study materials and new techniques and methods of labour education. In this respect
the Workers' Education Branch has produced, or is producing,
six films during the past two years: It Can Be Done, Bar-
bados; They Call it Griha Pravesh, an attempt to illustrate
the Aurangabad Experiment. This film was submitted for
showing at the HABITAT Conference on Human Settlements in
Vancouver, June 1976, and a Swedish language shortened version is under production in Sweden; The Man-made Miracle,
Singapore, an attempt to illustrate trade union concerns
with human and social environment; The Future Began Yesterday, dealing with industrial relations and developments in
Papua-New Guinea; Discovering the Co-operative, filmed in
Kenya, and Investment in Safety, now under production in
co-operation with trade unions in the Federal Republic of
Germany. Environmental attitudes of the trade unions in
Zaire are the subject of another film produced in May 1976.
Other instructional aids that should be noted are Which Way
to Turn, two sets of educational cubes, designed for use in
Asia and the Caribbean, explaining in juxtaposition the
pros and cons of economic family life, and How to Make a
Slide Show, filmstrip with accompanying text. An instruc-

tors' manual on environment is under development;

(4) promotion of college and university collaboration in labour
     education and service to trade union movements, basically
     requiring a joint Union/university approach to labour ser-
     vice academic structures, curriculum development and instruc-
     tional resources; representative participation, and con-
     sensus on trade union values, interest and objectives.
     Reference can be made to the ILO publication The Role of
     Universities in Workers' Education, based upon the proceed-
     ings and conclusions of the November 1973 International
     Symposium, and the paper College-centred Labour Education:
     A Statement of Basic Principles;

(5) workers' concerns with participation in decisions at the
     enterprise level, and in this regard we can refer to the
     summary of discussions at the ILO Symposium on Workers'
     Participation in Decisions within Undertakings, Oslo, Aug-
     ust 1974;

(6) specific approaches to social and labour education for
     trade union youth, women trade unionists, migrant workers,
     (reference is to the Report on the Symposium on Workers'
     Education Needs of Migrant Workers, Geneva, October 1974)
     and, finally,

(7) the reform of educational systems, school curricula, etc.
     at various levels to ensure adequate trade union partici-
     pation and the inclusion of accurate and balanced labour
     studies subject content. An ILO/NORAD Seminar on Trade
     Union Concerns with Educational Reform, was held in Oslo,
     May 1976.

At the level of the undertaking, ILO experts have participated
in educational programmes for members of boards of directors of
nationalized industries in Egypt, Iraq, Peru and Tanzania, in
the training of shop stewards in Argentina, Kenya, Mexico,
Venezuela and Zambia.

Another interesting example is the extensive programme carried
out in 1968, in collaboration with ORIT with a view to training
union officers in both participatory techniques and teaching
methods. This programme included three sub-regional courses
held in Costa Rica, Nicaragua and Honduras for sixty participants, followed by a two-month course in Cuernavaca.

The educational approach to labour's participation in such developments is exemplified by the series of ILO/Danish inter-regional and regional seminars on trade unions and co-operatives
organized under the Workers' Education Programme. The first
seminar, which was inter-regional in scope, stimulated several
of its trade union participants to initiate or plan co-operative
activities, so that the regional seminars in Africa and Asia,
which followed, included increasing numbers of trade unionists
responsible for union/co-operative affairs within their own
organizations.

The range of co-operative activities sponsored by trade unions
has expanded from credit and savings societies, consumers' co-
operatives and other basic units, to such sophisticated forms
as housing and land co-operatives, insurance, medical and dental
co-operative undertakings. A one-year ILO mission to advise and
assist the Co-operative Insurance Commonwealth Enterprise Ltd.,
established by the Singapore National Trade Union Congress,
stimulated organizations of administrative and operational procedures, and training sales personnel to promote co-operative
industrial life insurance.

College and University Centred Labour Education and Labour Studies

An emerging objective of the Workers' Education Programme is the
development of union-centred labour education structures and
programmes at the post-secondary educational level, and the
stimulation of labour studies curricula throughout the formal
school systems.

A major effort was started in recent years in the form of a
research project on the role of universities in workers' education, carried out with the collaboration of Prof. Marcel David,
a pioneer of university workers' education in France. The first
results of the project were studies based on fact-collecting
missions in a number of countries, which were then analysed on
a comparative basis to identify the reasons for success or failure of university efforts in workers' education and to provide
guidance to labour educators in developing countries. Subsequently an international symposium on the role of universities
in workers' education was held in Geneva, November 1973. The
published report The Role of Universities in Workers' Education,
containing papers, proceedings and conclusions of this study and
symposium, will be known to most of you.

Internal Concerns of Labour Colleges

The on-going concern of staff of labour colleges and workers'
education centres for (a) exchange of experience, (b) joint
examination of course requirements, (c) method of participant
selection, (d) evaluation of teaching practices and methods,
and (e) evaluation of learning experiences is reflected in activities directed to these ends.

For several years the Asian Trade Union College, New Delhi; the
International Institute for Co-operative and Labour Studies, Tel
Aviv, and the Asian Labour Education Centre of the University of
the Philippines, organized biennial seminars, with these objectives in view. (To a large degree this inter-regional Seminar
is an extension of that process.)

In November 1974, an ILO/DANIDA Seminar on Caribbean Labour Colleges and Trade Union Education Institutes attracted staff from
nine labour colleges and institutes in the Caribbean to the Bar-
bados Workers' Union Labour College, for precisely these purposes, and a report was published.

In order to establish permanent machinery to deal with these
problems, labour colleges, universities and colleges, with labour education centres, in Canada and the United States created
the University College Labour Education Association to which
some 39 labour education centres are affiliated.

National labour centres are taking their own initiatives, a good
example being the descriptive and evaluative survey of trade
union education, including the Labour College of Canada, by the
Adult Education Research Centre of the University of British
Columbia at the request of the Canadian Labour Congress and published in 1974 as Union Education in Canada.

Perhaps an assumption that may be drawn is that there is a need
for the collection, analysis and dissemination of existing information on labour colleges and labour education generally, through
information retrieval systems, or data banks at the national,
regional and international levels, computerized if feasible.
In many areas such information, if systematically organized,
could be fed into existing documentation and library data bank
systems.

In conclusion it is suggested that there is a growing recognition
that a potential weakness in processes designed to achieve social

and economic development objectives arises when there is failure
to achieve the active involvement of the people in determining
the needs and objectives of development policies, as well as in
the implementation of these policies.

It is further suggested that development is not just a question
of integrating the various technical, structural and administrative aspects of both urban and rural development, but also of
integration of the population themselves in the development process, and at least one way of achieving this is through effective and knowledgeable organizations of peasants and workers.

Distance Teaching Alternatives in Education and for Development

Tony Dodds

Two themes dominate much contemporary thinking about the expansion of education in the Third World. First is the growing commitment of countries, especially in Africa, to provide universal primary education in the shortest possible time. Even in a country like Nigeria, which by African standards is comparatively wealthy, this commitment will strain the available resources. At the same time "Life-Long Learning" is gaining new prominence in discussions about the ideal education system. The former unavoidably increases the potential demand for the latter yet it diverts most of the resources into primary and away from continuing education.

Alternative use of some of those resources could lead to a post-primary educational network through which much larger numbers of students can be offered opportunities for continuing education than can be reached in the foreseeable future by traditional and institutional methods. This presentation is mainly speculative, since few comprehensive experiments exist to support the proposal. Its purpose is to draw on the scanty evidence that exists and to make a case for larger and more carefully controlled experimentation. First, a brief analysis of some of the problems of the existing formal system, and the recent scattered development of non-formal alternatives.

The Educated and the Uneducated: A Statistical Profile

The thirst for education in the Third World is now almost proverbial. Education is seen, both by the leaders and the people as a whole, as the means of moving out of poverty and subsistence existence into "the better life". To both, education means the primary and secondary schools and higher education colleges of the traditional formal system. The foundation of this — and perhaps of any — system is the primary school. Thus governments throughout Africa have committed themselves to achieving Universal Primary Education as soon as possible — or even sooner. Just as the achievement of this purpose comes within reach, however, the primary school leaver can no longer expect to obtain paid employment in the modern economy. The educational planners

react with attempts to make the primary school curriculum more
relevant to citizens who will receive no other formal education;
the consumers — both parents and children — react by a demand
for continuing post-primary educational facilities. A brief
look at the educational statistics of Nigeria helps to set the
scene.

The Federal Government of Nigeria has set 1980 as its target
date for the full achievement of Universal Primary Education.
The first universal age-group enrolment was scheduled for September 1976. UPE will represent an increase of 65% in primary
enrolment in less than 10 years. In 1973 only approximately 4%
of secondary-school age children were enrolled in secondary
schools of any sort; by 1980 the plan is the 15% will be enrolled.

To make possible an increase in primary school enrolment from
35% to 100%, the Third National Development Plan (1975-1980)
proposes to spend approximately 20% of its capital educational
expenditure; to provide for an increase from 4% to 15% in secondary level enrolment it devotes nearly 60% of its capital
educational expenditure.

It will not be until the year 2005 that all 25-year-olds and
below will have attended primary school and not until 2015 that
this will apply to all 35-year-olds and under. By the year 2000
at least 85% of 30-year-old Nigerians will never have attended
secondary school.

Formal Institutional Education is too Slow an Answer

The problem of educational deprivation for the majority of citizens in countries such as this — and Nigeria has more resources
for education than most others in Africa — will not simply go
away by increasing the number of school places. Moreover, the
economic burden of providing secondary school places, by traditional methods, for a majority of children in the near future
would seem to be far too heavy to bear.

This suggests the need to develop a system of post-primary provision radically different from the traditional system of secondary schools. It must be much cheaper, it must make facilities
available to much larger proportions of the population, and it
must cater both for the children who are unable to obtain places
in secondary schools today and tomorrow and for the adults who
were unable to do so yesterday.

The present secondary school system is largely derived from an imported model. It grew to cater for the needs of colonially-controlled societies, and those needs, the values on which they were based, and the curricula and testing methods which were adopted, took little account of the indigenous cultures, values and problems of the societies which inherited them. In particular they failed, and in most countries are still failing, to relate directly and realistically to the development needs of the nation whose future citizens and leaders are their present students.

One of the main purposes of primary education is to provide students with basic learning skills and attitudes such as literacy, numeracy, and enquiring minds. It is at post-primary level that specific and detailed knowledge is acquired whose application enables social, political and economic changes to be brought about in the communities. Such changes can only be brought about by the people themselves. They cannot be imposed.

Rote learning of remote and academic facts, however, which is still a dominant characteristic of formal schools, is no way to train students to participate in development through the immediate application of what they have learned to the problems they find around them. But participatory teaching and learning require higher-calibre teachers and teaching materials than are currently available. The "generation gap" between the introduction of new methods and curricula in teacher training establishments and their implementation in the schools prolongs this problem. Any alternative or parallel system must be linked more clearly and more immediately to the realities of life for the majority of people in a developing country.

Non-Formal Adult Education: A Superficial Critique

During the last 15 years there has been increasing attention given to non-formal adult education. This has been largely in recognition of the delay between secondary school teaching and its effect on actual development, and of the remoteness of most secondary school curricula from the real problems. Many attempts have been made to devise courses and learning opportunities for adults and out-of-school youth related directly to their own communities. In the last few years there have been various surveys of such projects and their impact. The evidence, sparse as it is, would suggest that within the limits, both financial and geographical, in which they have operated many such projects have achieved remarkable success.

The Brigades in Botswana; Farm Schools and Farmers Training
Centres in Tanzania, Kenya, Nigeria, Mauritius and many other
countries; Vocational Improvement Centres; the Intermediate
Technology Training Centre (now part of the Integrated Education
Project in Zaria and Jos) and the Opportunities Industrialization
Centre (in Lagos) in various parts of Nigeria; the Lushoto
Integrated Development Education Project in Tanzania; and Child-
care and Nutrition Centres in various countries, all give evidence that training and education can be related to real life
problems, can attract people to learn, and can have an immediate
impact on the life-quality of the students and their families.

The surveys give a panoramic impression of inventiveness, initiative, and low cost. At the same time the projects generally
seem to have very limited geographical and numerical coverage.
They are largely short-term learning experiences for small groups
of people. When compared either with the spread of formal education or the need for such services, their overall impact on
development would appear to have been peripheral.

Three general problems seem to emerge. First, wholly inadequate
resources are made available to enable them to reach out to the
enormously scattered population. This is an indication of low
political priority. It is aggravated by the inevitable limitations on numbers imposed by their institutional nature and their
dependence on person-to-person communication. Secondly, they
generally seem to have great difficulty in creating motivation
for sustained and long-term learning; this is caused, or at
least made worse, by the problem of obtaining recognition for
participation in such courses either for entry onto further education courses or for vocational promotion. Thirdly, they are
largely unconnected and unco-ordinated, even in the same country,
and do not usually offer any opportunity for a systematic accumulation of knowledge or the progression through learning experiences toward an ever-higher level of knowledge and competence.

A Distance-Teaching Alternative

Distance-Teaching combinations, especially the linking of correspondence courses, broadcasting and occasional face-to-face learning may be a means through which alternative or parallel systems
of post-primary education can be set up. Such a system must
draw on the advantages of both the formal school system and the
non-formal adult education experience and is worth examining
only if it can overcome some of the major problems of both.

Such a project would require that courses be provided by correspondence and supported by broadcast series. These would be partly studied by individual students but designed to include group
discussion and occasional face-to-face tutorials, which would
take place under the auspices of a network of local social organizations: co-operative societies, for example, might be the
base for economics and agriculture groups; women's clubs for
child-care and nutrition study courses; youth clubs for wood-
work courses; trade unions, religious organizations, social
clubs. Local schools and welfare centres would supplement the
organization's own premises by way of study accommodation and
facilities.

Students would enter the network at whatever point their interests and activities created a desire to learn, and brought them
into contact with the facilities available. From that point
they would be provided with information and guidance about other
relevant courses and how to follow them. By accumulating related modules students would prepare themselves to progress to
higher levels of knowledge. They could either specialize in a
single subject or accumulate course credits covering several
subjects, thus providing themselves with a broad understanding
of society.

A wide range of practical subjects would be included, drawing
on the experience of adult education bodies, including vocational, agricultural, health, and social topics. They would
cater for the living concerns of the various categories of citizens for whom they were prepared: farmers and technical and
industrial workers, men and women, employed and self-employed,
young and old, trade unionists, politicians, social workers,
housewives, teachers.

The choice of course combinations would be made by the students
themselves. In most cases they would probably be guided initially by the range of subjects provided to the organization
which had introduced them to the system; by providing course
modules specifically to meet the needs and interests of such
organizations the system would ensure the practical relevance
of its courses. This approach would give a loose coherence
through the network of social organizations by which the courses
were being serviced. Careful tutorial guidance, however, both
by correspondence and through itinerant face-to-face tutors,
would ensure flexibility and the opportunity to move from one
set of courses to another. The students would be guided in
their choices, but the choices would be theirs, as would the
choice of speed, order and timing of their progress.

The organization of study would also be flexible. In some cases,
particularly for young people who have recently left primary
school and have not yet settled into jobs or family responsibilities, arrangements might have to be made whereby the majority
of the student's time would be organized. The Half-Work, Half-
Study Schools of China offer an appropriate model here in which
students were participant in local production activities inter-
spersed with seasonal periods of study. Similarly, a Mauritian
experiment in part-time Further Education Centres using a distance-teaching delivery system linked with group study and tutorials offers a pertinent example.

Where workers wish to follow training which requires practical
application of the skills being studied, arrangements must be
made for occasional part-time use of workshops and laboratories.
Such arrangements would have to be outside their normal working
hours. The Vocational Improvement Centres of Nigeria offer
guidelines to situations where apprentices and untrained arti-
sans can obtain practical and theoretical training through the
part-time use of technical training workshops, or public engineering workshops.

To obtain recognition of student achievement by following these
courses, and therefore to maintain their motivation, the curricula would probably have to be so organized that at various
stages their progress and the standard of their knowledge and
skill acquisition could be easily equated with progress through
the formal school system. This would make it necessary to devise
testing and measurement mechanisms based on the practical and
real-life curricula of the parallel system. It may, under certain circumstances, be advisable to make these tests comparable
in standard, though not in content or method, to whatever exams
and qualifications framework is applied in the formal school
system.

It is important that this concession to the prestige of the formal system should not undermine the very different approach to
curriculum building which the alternative system would adopt.
It may be appropriate, however, to allow for some movement back
into the formal system, especially at more advanced levels beyond
which the alternative system might not go. Lessons can be learned
here from the Cuban "parallel system of education" in which a
network of alternative vocational, workshop, and prevocational
work/study schools have been set up to enable formal school failures and drop-outs to re-enter the system.

The most complex aspects of the system would be the development
of comprehensive but flexible curricula, and to devise effective
teaching materials to put them across. Much of such curriculum
development would have to be specific to individual countries
and could only be carried out after careful assessment of the
particular national situation. The example on the next page,
therefore, is crude, incomplete and quite possibly wrong for any
one place. It is put forward to illustrate the sort of pattern
which might emerge if such a project were set up and the necessary detailed assessment carried out.

Such a curriculum, linked to vocational and social realities and
to student activities, would make available the essential knowledge and skills which the secondary school sets out to teach,
though often in a way which divorces the content from the experience and environment of the students.

It must be stressed that this system is not put forward as an
alternative to replace either the existing formal or non-formal
systems. It would be intended to exist side-by-side with them
and to complement their services.

Conclusion: Life-Long Learning for Life

The proposed system is based on four themes. First is the need
for economy. The suggested system makes use of existing organizations and communication media, and the learning is organized
on a part-time basis, thus allowing students to remain productive
members of society while following their studies. By using distance-teaching methods is also allows learning to reach out to
large numbers of students far removed from the teachers.

Secondly, it sets out to base initial motivation for study on
the immediate and real concerns of the students and to provide
for longer-term incentives by allowing for educational progression. Thus students may enter the system at many different
points, follow various and individually appropriate course combinations, and at the same time see their way through to higher
levels of educational achievement, and the resultant benefits.

Thirdly, it is a system in which the student participates fully
in the design of his curriculum, and controls and content, progression, speed, place and time of his studies. Even the course
materials will be revised and expanded — and sometimes devised —
in response to the progress, the problems, the comments and demands fed back from the students.

SECONDARY SCHOOL CURRICULUM	ADAPTATION FOR A FARMER	ADAPTATION FOR A SMALL-SCALE MOTOR MECHANIC	ADAPTATION FOR A HOUSEWIFE
LANGUAGE	Letter-writing Comprehension of instructional manuals Writing reports and keeping records of production, etc.	Letter-writing Comprehension of instructional manuals Writing reports on repair projects	Letter-writing Comprehension of recipes/health manuals Writing reports on health or housing problems, etc.
SOCIAL STUDIES	Civics Village development Co-operative principles Agricultural economics Population education	Civics Trade union organization Economics Business management Population education	Child development Civics Co-operatives Population education
MATHS	Farm budgetting Pricing Produce recording Mechanical and construction design Stock-keeping	Mechanical drawing and calculation Budgetting Pricing Stock-keeping, etc.	Home budgetting Calculation of dietary combinations, etc.
SCIENCE	Animal husbandry Soil science Plant biology Basic mechanics, etc.	Mechanics Motor combustion principles Electricity Metalwork, etc.	Health and child-care Human biology Nutrition Hygiene Home repair hints, etc.
SCHOOL Institutions used	Co-operative Farmers union Village organizations	Trade union Town clubs	Co-operative Women's clubs/associations

Finally, each course module, while forming part of an elaborate educational structure, is of immediate and practical value in itself. Each part is problem-based and is related to everyday concerns. Any module can be followed in isolation, or fitted into a comprehensive pattern.

It is not difficult to produce evidence of the problems of the existing educational system and of needs which are not being met. There is very little proof that alternative systems have yet been devised to overcome these problems. The present expansion in primary education, however, calls for radical and comprehensive approaches to the creation of alternative systems of coping with the demand for post-primary opportunities which will inevitably follow. Distance-teaching may perhaps offer a vehicle through which such radical alternatives can be made available.

References

Government of Nigeria (1975) Nigerian Third National Development Plan 1975-1980, Lagos.

Sheffield, J. & Diejomaoh, V. (1972) Nonformal Education in African Development, African American Institute.

Wood, A.F. (1974) Information Education and Development in Africa, Institute of Social Studies, The Hague.

Berenson, R. (1964) Half-work Half-study Schools in Communist China, USA Dept. of Health, Education and Welfare.

Dodds, T.A. (1975) The Mauritius College of the Air - The First Two Years, IEC, Broadsheet on Distance Learning No. 7, Cambridge.

The Educational Core of Development

Per G. Stensland

The Relationship Between Development and Education

In all development there is an educational core. A central aspect of development actions, whether local, regional, national,
or global is purposeful learning. Whether overtly or not, development always is interwoven with education. Thus, education
cannot be planned or put into practice as something separate.
It must always be part of a wider totality.

For this analysis education will be regarded as purposeful and
organized learning from the standpoint of the learner and from
the standpoint of the educator as "the deliberate, systematic
and sustained effort to transmit and evoke knowledge, attitudes,
values, skills, and sensibilities". Development similarly will
be seen as purposeful and organized change from the standpoint
of the recipient of development efforts and, from the standpoint
of the developer, as "a deliberate and continuing attempt to
accelerate the rate of economic and social progress and to alter
institutional arrangements which are considered to block attainment of this goal".

The major value systems that have underlain economic and social
development in the last couple of centuries have been associated
with production. Thus, education to a large measure has been
valued as a contributor to production. Myrdal, in several contexts, has laid bare the influence of production valuations on
development policies. "The overriding importance of physical
investment" and the use of development models "centred on the
concept of a capital/output ratio" have tended to dominate economic planning in so-called underdeveloped countries. One of the
results has been the justification of education as "investment
in man". Fortified by traditional economic models, development
planners have defended outlays for education as the price to pay
for "human capital". Myrdal wryly observes that economists,
unable to explain the process of economic growth, discovered
investment in man "while all the time they were apparently un-
aware of the thinking and writings of students and practitioners
who specialized in this field". In an appendix to Asian Drama,
he underlines the failure of development planners to view educa-

tion as an integral, not isolated, part of development, while
"experts in health and education have long been aware that expenditures to improve the quality of the population may often
be more important for development than physical investment".

A capital investment justification of education obviously often
is at variance with the idea of education as serving "the highest development of the intellectual and moral aptitudes of the
individual, rather than the training of producers". Even so,
this view has held a key position. The establishment of public
school systems, the legislation to guarantee the right to education and enforce the obligation to attend, the growth and development of professional education, the efforts to further scientific inquiry into educational processes — all these fit into
the argument that society should invest not only in machines and
real estate, but in human capital. Thus it is not surprising
that even in a recent analysis Harbison regards "nationwide learning systems" as part of human capital formation. Simmons, re-
ferring to earlier expositions by Walsh, Schultz and Becker,
suggests that this human capital theory has underpinned most
justification of education both to increase labour skills and
productivity and to reduce social inequities.

There are obvious pitfalls in relating development and education
as if they were mainly production matters. Human capital formation cannot be regarded as a simple input-output transaction,
since obviously a vast variety of institutions contribute to the
education of human beings. Nor is this solely a matter of production. Both development and education involve consumption;
both take place in formal as well as informal settings, as well
as through a great variety of activities, making any reliable
estimate of either "input" or "output" in capital formation virtually impossible.

Related to the justification of education as investment in human
capital is the idea that education is part of the "infrastructure"
that societies must build on for their development. The major
drawback of the infrastructure argument is its over-simplifica-
tion. Formal education agencies cannot be isolated from other
institutions that educate — thus "infrastructure" would equal
"total life structure". Coombs and Prosser have convincingly
shown that possibly the most powerful structures are non-formal
and non-traditional mechanisms of learning. Thus, infrastructures are already there. What would make most sense is to fit
formal and publicly organized learning efforts into existing
non-formal and private structures.

Ultimately, the valuation of "investment in man" falters because
it skirts the issue of ends. If education, as Whitehead once
put it, is "the acquisition of the art of utilization of knowledge", one has to raise the old question "To what end?" Like
other human undertakings, education functions within an intricate
framework of valuations that does not permit the luxury of posing
"investment" as the single or most important purpose. The use
of knowledge and skill depends on values and choiced embedded in
moral commitments. Educators are not only in an economic transaction, but in a moral one. One now has to face the sobering
fact that the worth of ultimate ends does not lend itself to
objective measurement.

Ironically, rational analysis itself is questionable, even if
one were to accept "human capital formation" as justification of
education. Measurements and indicators of development are as
shaky as attempts to pin down the effects of education expenditures. The use of out-of-place economic concepts, irrelevant
development models, and inadequate measurements, has now been
effectively challenged by scientists like Myrdal, Higgins, and
Simmons, and educators like Coombs and Sheffield, exposing the
inadequacy of measures, and, behind measures, the looseness of
definitions and concepts. Price tags on development, summarized
into production figures, like the Gross National Product, end up
being imprecise if not meaningless. They fail to include a number of "products" that cannot be measured in money nor included
in any national balance sheet. True credit calculations should
(but do not) include, for example, increase in quality of life,
work by family members in the home, non-marketed services. Similarly, on the debit side, estimates of the national product
should (but do not) include, for example, depreciation of resources, business failures, loss of time and skill through unemployment, military expenses.

With capital investment valuation as the basis, and in the absence of reliable statistics and meaningful study procedures,
educational planning has too often had undesirable results,
visible especially in so-called developing nations. The end
product has been expansion of the existing system rather than an
effort to ameliorate problems not taken care of by these systems.
Too often educational programming has been misbalanced, and opportunities have been meted out to those already educated or to the
privileged classes. Thus, the gap between educated and uneducated has widened rather than lessened. Educational programmes
are often inimical to development. For example, school and university have offered a chance to escape from disliked manual

work. Indeed, there is now mounting evidence that "benefits of
schooling may not always have a significant impact on productivity" and "the contribution of education to growth and development has been less than we would have expected".

Causal relationships between educational investment and economic
growth are in doubt. Sometimes the latter has preceded rather
than followed the former! The effect of schooling on unemployment, on more equitable income distribution, or on job performance is not demonstrable. Socialization and modernization,
often the stated or unstated reasons for education investment,
especially in developing countries, are also under question.

New Development Concepts

New alternatives may initially come not from a reconsideration
or reshaping of education, but rather from a reconsideration of
the process of growth and development. Development planners,
rather than educators, may well be the first to change. Planners
have started to include in their models less traditional "inputs"
and "outputs". Among these are appraisals of the existing social
and institutional framework surrounding development and education,
institutional forms of enterprise, the processes of capital accumulation and of supplying entrepreneurs, the prevailing system of
social values, family patterns and obligations, leisure preferences, social prestige patterns, values about saving and time
use, options for numbers of children in the family, ethical
values.

Here Myrdal's concept of development comes into full force. Defining development as "the movement upward of the entire social
system", he includes "all non-economic factors, including all
sorts of consumption by various groups of people; consumption
provided collectively; education and health facilities". Breaking with orthodoxy, he adds to this list "the distribution of
power in society; and more generally, economic and political
stratification; broadly speaking, institutions and attitudes
... and, as an exogenous set of factors, induced policy measures
applied in order to change one or several of these endogenous
factors."

Such a development concept implies circular causation, making
all factors in development interdependent and often giving them
cumulative effect. In trying to determine causation and effect
from the standpoint of whether particular acts contribute to

development, one has little use for an ordinary GNP, or for
traditional calculations of cost and benefit. All the factors
involved are indispensable and thus dependent upon parallel ad-
justments.

The implications for education of such a model of development
are profound. Instead of merely putting children, youth and
adults in school or giving them educational opportunities within
the old system, one works toward structural change involving all
sectors of society.

The new development concept permits a realistic treatment of a
factor often excluded in planning, namely, distribution. Excluding distribution has led to neglect of one of the central human
issues: equality. A recent report by the Organization for Economic Cooperation and Development (OECD), building on studies by
Galtung and his collaborators, issues a harsh and direct indict-
ment of the present state of affairs. "Economic growth is accompanied not only by economic inequality, but also by concomitant
educational growth and education inequality — and the latter seems
at present to be increasing both within and between countries."
Reversing this disastrous trend calls for a shift in the whole
social system: "Societies must be prepared to consider the lessening of disparities as a major political, social and educational goal."

New Learning Concepts

A second kind of challenge to simple input/output reasoning has
come from scientists who have analyzed the dynamics of social
changes. Among them, Benne and Lippitt, building much of their
reasoning on Kurt Lewin's field theories of some forty years ago,
tend to look at intervention, group processes, and client-agent
systems as purposeful learning systems. Consequently their models for development and planned change, whether they refer to
management, therapy groups, or schools, become learning models.
Elsewhere, the author has suggested that "development is purposeful change with the participation of those involved". Clearly,
development and education include similar dynamic elements:
both imply a shift from a present state of functioning to a more
advanced state; both imply purposefulness; both imply an ag-
reed-on relationship between an agent (a developer, planner,
educator) and a client (a nation, community, student).

In his Asian studios, Myrdal observes that Western ideas of

development have built on such value premises as rationality,
rise of productivity, rise of level of living, social and economic equalization, improved institutions and attitudes, national
consolidation and national independence, political democracy in
a narrow sense, democracy at the grassroots, and social disci-
pline. It is easy to recognize these values as premises also
for education.

INTEGRATION OF DEVELOPMENT AND EDUCATION: THE FUTURE

Alternatives to Present Major Approaches.

If one accepts education and development as related processes of
purposeful and organized change, then presently favoured assumptions of straight-line, cause-effect associations between the
two or computer-like input-output connections need to be replaced.
In their place alternatives must be found that permit integration
of the two human activities. In an integrated system neither
education nor development could be isolated, even in deliberately
discrete analyses and assessments. Development is the action
strand interwoven with education, both moving the whole system
upward to higher levels of quality or forward to new bases. The
consequences of such an integrated approach to change affect both
developers and educators.

To illustrate: a school, a discussion about building a bridge, a
village meeting to hear an outside expert, literacy campaigns,
a family planning class, a pamphlet on land reform, a health
education broadcast — all these education activities would relate to development actions.

Integrated approaches are not new; they have been promoted and
tried for some time. In the United States, regional development
leaders several decades ago advocated integration in theory
(Ogburn) and in practice (TVA). Internationally and nationally,
community development, which got under way in the 1930's but
started in earnest only after the Second World War, also pre-
supposed integration in theory.

Nevertheless there are still formidable barriers to the treatment of human problems as parts of an integrated whole. Thus,
education and development still are mostly separated by administrative, political, and professional walls and barricades.
Skeptics say that the road is strewn with development projects
that have failed and theories that never were put into practice.

Cautious observers would add that integration, if at all present, is only rarely used as the basis for programmes. Building
of an irrigation dam in a country with high illiteracy is not
automatically combined with education campaigns against illiteracy. Conversely, literacy programmes do not always relate words
and sentences to matters that have meaning to dam builders or
irrigation farmers. Traditions, prejudices, power conflicts,
political policies and professional pride have too often hin-
dered integration, branding it impractical, uneconomical, un-
timely, or simply out of question. Thus it is encouraging to
note recent forces at work towards integration among scientists,
educators and country development agents.

Towards Integrated Theory

A first prerequisite for future advancement toward integration
is a confluence of thought and theory from many sciences. This
would assume effective collaboration of professionals and experts across their disciplinary boundaries. The collaboration
has to go beyond multidisciplinary efforts in research and training and involve interdisciplinary programmes, far more taxing
and threatening to scientists. The result of interdisciplinary
collaboration may be either a new science, like biochemistry, or
a new professional specialty, like biomedical engineering. The
end product may be an international scientific event like the
classic Manhattan Project or a local experiment like the ongoing
pilot projects in health care delivery in Thailand and Colombia.

In their now classic study of development in Peru, Whyte and
Williams insist on interrelatedness among economic, social and
psychological factors and variables. They visualize "how economic data may be fitted into the schemes of anthropologists,
sociologists and psychologists".

"As long as we communicate as scientists only in the abstract
terms peculiar to our own disciplines, we shall never forge
links in an interdisciplinary theoretical chain." Rejecting any
monoscientific approach to development, the two scientists put
the major emphasis in variability and on systematic differences.
With practical implications for change agents, they propose to
develop strategies based on "the theoretical integration of
economic, technical, social and psychological variables".

While laying their foundation for an integrated theory, Whyte
and Williams discard unproductive and misleading common ideas

held by many planners and developers, including educators. Among
the ideas they discard are the following: Any change is like
any other change. People naturally tend to resist change. The
major task is to discover the psychological and social techniques
that will allow the change agent to overcome resistance successfully. They call for joint research into the nature of specific
social change, into the ways people look at and react to change,
and into the actual psychological processes at work in resistance
since these processes may well be utilized rather than overcome.

Recurrent Education — Opportunity for Integration

An unexpected incentive to integration has now come from social
scientists and education planners who see the concept of a learning society as an integrating principle. Educators like Sweden's
Husen and France's Faure tend to look at the total human environment as the relevant framework for "learning to be". In the
currently fashionable recurrent education movement, integration
of education and action is a prerequisite. This movement, especially vigorous in OECD countries, exemplifies a concerted effort
to bridge the gaps between education and action.

With the bold new concept of total, lifelong education, integrated planning is within reach. A great variety of new ways in
which education and work interphase needs to be explored: ter-
minal education might not exist; there might be no graduations,
no final diplomas, no finished degrees. There might be an in-
finite number of mixtures of study and work geared to individual
preferences, aptitudes, and needs. Throughout life, a person
would enter at several points from education into the world of
action and go back at other points into education from work,
action and development.

Country Development as an Integrative Principle

Recent moves in developing countries tend to justify educational
efforts for children, youths, and adults in terms of development
of a society. The major thrust of arguments to strengthen adult
education in Tanzania have had their base in the reality of a
new nation. The President, Julius K. Nyerere, insists that the
core function of education is to establish conditions for a
nation's growth and development. Nyerere sees the prime role
of education to lay groundwork for sound country development and
to establish a favourable climate among the carriers of development, the citizens.

To be effective in a nation's service, education should strive
(1) to define social needs and problems, (2) to prepare effective
contributors to social development, (3) to apply knowledge to
the solution of development problems, (4) to strengthen education
at other levels than higher education, and (5) to help society
to define values and purposes.

Obviously, education processes are put to work not only in the
service of development, but as part of the development process
itself. Opportunities to learn necessary skills and gain knowledge needed for effective action must be available to high level
policymakers as well as to middle level managers and front line
workers. In one of his reports, the UN Secretary General urges
that education programmes accompany all development plans, argu-
ing that they are "essential for producing human talent and manpower". Swedish planners, in a later memorandum to the United
Nations, spell out the role they feel training should have in
development programmes and specify that training would be particularly important in such problem areas as population, employment, migration, environment, and trade.

What emerges is a double function of education, which itself
furthers integration: participation in development and preparation for development.

Social Action as Basis for Integration

A country development and local community development can act
as effective vehicles for integration of education and action
processes, so can action in social movements.

The Danes over a hundred years ago demonstrated this dramatically.
They taught "new ways" through adult education. In their folk
schools, the leaders Grundtvig and Kold advocated the rebirth of
a nation offering liberal, humanistic, untraditional education
to farmers in their own rural villages. The result was to be
not only a new Denmark, but resourceful innovative farm coopera-
tors. The popular movements in Sweden, which began in the 1880's,
included in their study circles and folk schools not only social
and cultural subjects, but also preparation for action in such
groups as unions, cooperatives, temperance lodges, dissenter
churches, and political parties.

A latterday advocate of this kind of integration of development
and education has been Paulo Freire. In his literacy and devel-

opment work in Brazil and Chile in the 1960's, Freire developed
a special approach to basic adult education that may well serve
as a model for future needed efforts to build bridges between
education and action. Critical of most education in the Western
world, Freire protests against education that builds on what he
calls "the banking principle". By this he means that which con-
fers on students the right only to receive, file and store knowledge and skill that teachers and instructors deign to dispense.
In its place Freire proposes "the development of the awakening
of critical awareness". What he called "conscionziaciao" will
not appear "as a natural by-product of even major economic changes, but must grow out of a critical education effort based on
favourable historic conditions".

A New Educator

Integrated approaches to development and education call for a
new kind of educator. Professional educators will no longer
have a monopoly of the teacher role. In a "learning society"
the educational function will be carried out by a great variety
of people. This is poignantly true in developing countries where
manpower resources are limited and where colonial traditions have
stymied innovation and imaginative planning. The barefoot doctor in the People's Republic of China, the *promotora del solud*
in Colombia, the community health aide in Jamaica, already play
a key role in educating for better health conditions in rural
communities. A recent shift in policy in the World Health Organization, from illness cure and disease eradication to rural
health care development, signified the importance that international health leaders place on an integrated approach to a
basic human need.

Development needs have created needs for new education agents,
dramatically changing the scope and character of the educational
enterprise. The new educator is the doctor, the nurse, the
skilled worker, the farm leader, the journalist, the lawyer, the
sanitation inspector, the bridge construction engineer, the
irrigation expert, the policeman. Education and development have
become the legitimate property of all who are responsible for
cooperative action in our communities, developing or developed.

This expansion of the educator concept has consequences for future planning of education and development. New strategies have
to be devised to attach to all development schemes provisions
for training the actors involved, regardless of their previous

preparation, professional or not. In a very personal way the
action agents will become the educational core of development,
their own actions the core of education.

To Summarize

1. As education and development are related change processes,
   the framework for planning and programming should be a social
   change model rather than current economic productivity models. The relationship between the two human activities
   should be seen as a process of continuous interaction rather
   than as a cause-effect connection.

2. Development must be based on valuations and choices applied
   to the whole society, not individual sectors or aspects.
   Thus, education must always be planned as part of a totality,
   closely related to other parts, such as health, housing,
   work, and leisure.

3. Theories in social and related sciences must move toward
   integration. Without losing their identities or special
   characteristics, the many sciences with bearing on human conditions must permit close interrelationship both in theory
   and practice, allowing the scientists joint explorations and
   collaborative utilization of findings.

4. The goals of a learning society demand innovative patterns
   of interweaving action with education, work with study. New
   combinations of formal and non-formal learning need to be
   explored, allowing for lifelong learning based on full use
   of the many educative opportunities and resources in the
   human community.

References

1. Coombs, P.H., Prosser, R.C. and Ahmed, M. (1973) New Paths
   to Learning for Rural Children and Youth. Prepared for the
   United Nations Children's Emergency Fund by the International
   Council for Educational Development. New York: IECD.

2. Debeauvais, M. (1971) Factors Contributing Towards Modernization and Socio-Economic Development. Approaches to the
   Science of Social and Economic Development. Paris: UNESCO,
   pp. 144-159.

3. Faure, E. et al. (1972) <u>Learning to Be: The World of Education Today and Tomorrow</u>. Paris: UNESCO.

4. Freire, P. (1973) <u>Education for Critical Consciousness</u>. New York: Seabury Press.

5. Freire, P. (1970) <u>Pedagogy of the Oppressed</u>. New York: Herder & Herder.

6. Harbison, F. (1975) Education: Nationwide Learning System, <u>Teachers College Record</u>, LXXVI, 539-562.

7. Husen, T. (1974) <u>The Learning Society</u>. London: Methuen.

8. Educational Development (1975) <u>Education in the Nation's Service, Experiments in Higher Education and Development</u>. New York: IECD.

9. Kellen, D. and Bengtsson, L. (1973) <u>Recurrent Education: A Strategy for Lifelong Learning</u>. Washington, D.C.: Organization for Economic Cooperation and Development.

10. Michanek, E. (1971) <u>The World Development Plan: A Swedish Perspective</u>. Uppsala, Sweden: The Dag Hammarskjold Foundation.

11. Myrdal, G. (1968) <u>Asian Drama, An Inquiry into the Poverty of Nations</u>. Vols. I & III. New York: Pantheon.

12. Myrdal, G. (undated mimeograph) <u>What is Development?</u> Paper in honour of the late Professor Ayres.

13. Organization for Economic Cooperation and Development (1974) <u>New Learning Opportunities for the Underprivileged Adult: Problems, Policies and Programs</u>. Report by the Secretariat, Paris.

14. Phillips, H.M. (1970) <u>Literacy and Development</u>. Paris: UNESCO.

15. Sheffield, J.R. (1974) Educational Policies for Developing Nations, <u>Teachers College Record</u>, LXXVI (September), 89-100.

16. Sheffield, J.R. (1975) New Perspectives on Education and International Development, <u>Teachers College Record</u>, LXXVI (May), 523-38.

17. Simmons, J. (1974) Education, Poverty and Development.
     Bank Staff Working Paper No. 188. Washington, D.C.: Inter-
     national Bank for Reconstruction and Development (mimeograph).

18. Stensland, P.G. (1962) Community and Development. Saskatoon,
     Canada: Centre for Community Studies.

19. Van Rensburg, P. (1967) Education and Development in an Emer-
     ging Country. Uppsala, Sweden: The Scandinavian Institute of
     African Studies.

Conclusions

INTRODUCTION

Be not afraid of going slowly; be only afraid
of standing still.

Japanese aphorism

The Conference in Dar es Salaam was never seen as a simple discrete event but rather an important stage in a lengthy development process. There were many conclusions but no closure other
than that people went away to continue the communication through
their respective organizations. It is anticipated that annual
assessment will follow concerning action and results.

The Conference representatives adopted unanimously a concensus
report. It encouraged all concerned to cooperate in implementing
the UNESCO recommendation on adult education and similar measures
by other intergovernmental organizations. It left with the Board
of the International Council for Adult Education the task of
shaping proposals for action drawn from many sources into a concrete Design.

Following the conference statements of conclusions and recommendations are appearing from national and regional organizations
and from such major interests as workers' education. These,
plus the papers selected for this book, and particularly the
Design for Action, provide an agenda for study and action for
the next decade, one that will be decisive for development.

Paulo Freire conducted a number of seminars during the meetings
in Dar es Salaam. An interview about his thought and its origins,
and about education for development was recorded on videotape
soon after and is available from the Canadian Association for
Adult Education. Extracts from this interview are provided with
these conclusions because in many ways his remarks convey the
spirit of the conference.

"As Educators we are Politicians and Also Artists"

An Interview with Paulo Freire

INTER-
VIEWERS: People are interested in your writings but they notice
in those writings someone who would just as soon teach
as write about teaching and likes to engage in direct
dialogue. I'd like to know something more about what
you now regard as your formative experiences in Brazil
in developing your sense of mission as well as the
ideology that emerges.

FREIRE: Your question leads me back to my youth in order to
re-see myself working in the beginnings and also to
think of what I am doing in order to understand better.
Since I was very young I worked with peasants and with
workers in the field of education, in adult education.
At the beginning, many years ago, I tried above all to
establish relationships between the parents and the
teachers mediated by the students, the children, trying
to discuss with the parents some problems which their
children had at school. It was maybe the first challenge I had when I was 22 years old, working in adult
education. But when I try to see me again at that
time, first of all I perceive how much I learned from
the parents, workers, peasants and secondly, how naive
I was also. For example, I remember discussing with
the parents about relationships between them and the
children. They were sometimes violent and aggressive
with the children, not because they did not love them
but because of the concrete situations in which they
lived. In discussing with them about that I remember
that I made reference to Piaget. Of course my naiveté
was not to talk with them about what Piaget said, it

271

was to quote Piaget: they could not know who was Piaget.

INTER-
VIEWERS: Were these poor parents?

FREIRE: Yes, workers and peasants. But I also worked at that
           time with groups of families in the middle class, in-
           tellectuals too. Nevertheless, I preferred much more
           to work with the peasants and the workers because in
           the last analysis, to the extent that they were exper-
           iencing themselves in a very difficult situation, they
           were much more open to understand the situation than
           the other class who were conditioned by university
           studies. Since the beginning of my experience I per-
           ceived many times that it is easier for us to discuss
           some concrete facts with the peasants, trying to under-
           stand the *raison d'être* for the facts, than to discuss
           the same subjects with the teachers.

INTER-
VIEWERS: Let me ask a question that's put to me about you. Did
           you think of yourself primarily as an educationist, a
           teacher who chose social activities to advance educa-
           tion and social development or did you think of your-
           self as a social revolutionist who chose education as
           your means? I realize the question is black and white.

FREIRE: I think that we cannot dichotomize these dimensions.
           Nevertheless, an acquaintance said to me recently:
           "When I met you for the first time many years ago I
           had the impression that you were an educator but now,
           more and more, I perceive that you are a politician."
           When I say politician I am not saying necessarily par-
           ticipating in this or that political party. At that
           time I was not so clear about the political implica-
           tions of education. Hence the impression I gave that
           I was exclusively an educator.

INTER-
VIEWERS: You said that at that time to be effectively an educa-
           tor you had to become or had to be also a politician.
           Is that related to particular circumstances in Brazil
           or is that an argument you would make about any educa-
           tor in any society?

FREIRE: Being together the educator and the politician is not
           a privilege of Brazil! I am convinced about this.
           As educators we are politicians and also artists.

INTER-   You've helped the rest of us get some understanding
VIEWERS: that there shouldn't be a dichotomy between education
and politics. At the international seminar at Persepolis there was unanimous agreement that education must
be at the centre of the social and political process.
A year later when we met in an international conference at Dar es Salaam, people took it for granted:
they didn't debate it any more, they accepted it.
Whether they are working at it in any way is something
else. What circumstances are there that prevent people
from seeing what seems obvious to us? You've said
earlier, on a number of occasions, that you are an
itinerant apostle of the obvious. But the irony is
that it isn't so obvious to other people. What prev-
ents it from being obvious that, as adult educators,
we are also artists and politicians?

FREIRE: I don't have a categorical answer but I will tell you
how I see it. First of all, I have the impression
that we have been conditioned to looking at education
as something above concrete reality even though we
talk about reality, even though we talk about education
and development, about education and social change.
But I have the impression that many times we talk about
these subjects but using the concepts in a bureaucratized way as if they were emptied, without having the
contents, the material conditions they express.

INTER-   They talk about education _for_ development, not educa-
VIEWERS: tion _inside_ development.

FREIRE: Yes, yes. Yes, as if education were here and development there.

INTER-   Does keeping them separate support some particular
VIEWERS: interests?

FREIRE: I think so. The more we teach students in education
courses that education is a neutral tool, a neutral
instrument, that we have to measure everything with
numbers, the more we say to the students that teachers
are neutral beings at the service of the humanity, and
the more we are training teachers not to analyze in a
critical way the conrete reality, the less chance to
find possibilities for changing education. If you act
to achieve change some people say that you are no

longer educators, no longer scientists, but ideologists.
For me I think that position is itself an ideology. By
saying that education is neutral <u>they</u> are ideologists.
When they deny the very process of ideology they are
making ideology.

INTER-   I would like to press a related question, going back
VIEWERS: to your past when you were 20 years of age. One thing
              that distinguishes you from many teachers is your res-
              pect for the learner. You say that the teacher must
              go to the learner and first learn from him. How did
              you get such a view? Many teachers don't, even in a
              long career. When and how did you become conscious of
              the capacity of the learner?

FREIRE: I think that one of the sources was in my relationships
              with my parents. My father, for example, was a fantas-
              tic open-mind. I was the youngest of four children and
              when he died I was 13 years. But his influence on me
              was so great that until now I feel him as if he were
              here. It's very interesting you know, my identification
              with him. He was always a man looking for, searching,
              and all of us had the right to say "no" to him. It's
              fantastic because at that time it was not usual in
              Northeast Brazil. He was not Christian although he
              had a certain respect for Christ. My mother was Cath-
              olic and is — she is very old now. I remember when I
              was seven years old I went to my father and said:
              "Look father, the coming Sunday I will make my first
              communion in the Catholic church." And he looked at
              me and said: "Congratulations son, this is your choice
              and I will go with you." And he went to the church
              without believing, but with total respect for the choice
              of his son.

INTER-
VIEWERS: At seven years?

FREIRE: Seven! And he kissed me after that and he came back
              home with me. Of course, the next Sunday he did not
              go to the church. I tell you this to tell you how he
              respected us. Nevertheless, it does not mean that he
              left us by ourselves. No. He never talked about his
              authority because he knew that he was authority. Also
              I learned with him and my mother since my early days
              to dialogue. This was my first source. For example,

I learned how to write and to read with him and my
mother under the shadow of the trees in the back yard
of the house in which I was born, writing on earth
with pieces of a stick, and the words they used to
introduce me into the literacy process were <u>my</u> own
words. It's very interesting to note that many years
after that, when I began the process in Brazil of adult literacy, I started precisely with the words of
the illiterates and not with the teacher's words. I
am now writing a book I could not finish yet because
of my travels. It is not an autobiography but it's an
attempt to analyze the experiences I've had. But of
course I am making some references to my childhood and
the more I do this the more I discover some elements
which are associated with my parents. When I went to
the primary school I already knew how to read and write;
I learned under the shadows of the trees.

INTER-   I would like to ask another question. What was it you
VIEWERS: were doing that brought you into conflict with the
              Government? Most educators don't think their work is
              likely to lead them into direct conflict and into exile.

FREIRE: In my career I was invited by the Minister of Education
              to go to Brazilia, the capital city, in order to start
              a national plan for adult education starting from the
              literacy process. I accepted; we began to work with
              teams in the country and also training teams in each
              city of the country; and we developed a national plan
              believing it should be possible for us at that time
              almost to eliminate the literacy problem in Brazil.
              Our approach began with the sometimes misunderstood
              word <u>conscientizacion</u>. It means that the adult liter-
              acy process which we tried to put into practice was
              not confined to a process in which the adults could
              read and write quickly but one in which they could be
              challenged, they were challenged, to understand the
              context of their lives, <u>and that is dangerous</u>. We once
              again see that there is no possibility of neutral ed-
              ucation. Our kind of education worked in the favour
              of the dominated class but not in favour of the domi-
              nant class; so I was dangerous and I was subversive.

INTER-   You have been working a good deal in Guinea Bissau
VIEWERS: where there has been a recent revolution. To what
              extent has adult education given strength to the people

who were carrying out — under very difficult conditions
— that revolution and to what extent is revolution a
good prelude for adult education?

FREIRE: I think that first of all, the conflict, the struggle,
is the midwife of consciousness: shapes consciousness,
re-shapes consciousness. This is one of the most important aspects you can perceive in Guinea Bissau.
When we talk with a peasant, for example, who had the
experience of fighting in order to be himself with the
others, he can be or she can be illiterate from the
linguistic point of view but not from the political
point of view. They are so <u>clear</u> concerning what they
want to do, what they need to do. For example, some
months ago I was there assisting a discussion in a
literacy course when one of the soldiers wrote a word
on the blackboard. The word *luta* which means struggle.
And the educator — a soldier also — asked him to talk
about *luta*, about struggle, and of course he spoke a
lot about his experience during the revolution. But
in a second moment he said: "Our struggle of today is
the same one as yesterday, with some difference. Yesterday, with the guns in our hands we fought to expel
from our country the invaders. Today, with our guns
gone from our hands, our struggle is for production in
order to recreate our society." It was fantastic, you
know. It was said by him, an illiterate man who nevertheless is politically literate. It is the result of
the experience of the struggle. The experiences in-
side the popular army were very good. The soldiers
learned how to read and to write quickly, to the extent
that they know, first of all, why they need to read
and write because they know that they are engaged in
an important process for them to help their country.
They don't come to the cultural classes to learn how
to read and to write or because they are seeking to
get a good job or to get a diploma. They learn because
they know that it is important for them to read and to
write so they can become much better prepared to help
the reconstruction of the country.

INTER-   In your writing, Paulo, one of the interesting things
VIEWERS: is that you treat the oppressor as a learner as well
as the oppressed and you point out the dynamics that
incline the oppressor to learn how to be an oppressor.
Now, it seems to me a commitment to learning is the

opposite of violence.

FREIRE: Every time people ask me questions about violence I
always ask: "Violence from whom, or of whom against
whom? Violence for what?" because I think that if we
take the concept as a metaphysical category we cannot
understand the real social process of struggle. One
should look at the relationships between the oppressed
classes and the oppressor classes in a concrete situation because they don't exist in the air and one exists because of the other. More oppressors equals
more oppressed and vice versa. In my point of view,
while for the oppressors violence is absolutely necessary in order for them to preserve their status quo,
the violence of the oppressed must be developed in
order to suppress violence. I don't know whether I am
clear? Theoretically, the oppressors cannot continue
to be oppressors without being violent — not necessarily every time killing people. The violence of the
oppressors sometimes is expressed by manipulating the
people, by giving even sweets to the people. At the
moment in which I prevent you from being, from expres-
sing yourself, from deciding, even though I give you
good fillet of roast beef and a good car, you are
oppressed and I am making violence against you. Then,
while the violence of the oppressors is necessary for
the oppressive situation to continue to exist, the
violence of the oppressed must be done in order, by
transforming materially the social conditions, to suppress the possibility of violence. This is how I see
it. Revolution is a right of the oppressed. It is
almost a kind of right for survival. That is, in a
certain moment of the confrontation the violence of
the oppressed is necessary. For example, let us take
the concrete situation of Guinea Bissau. For six long
years the people of Guinea Bissau had accepted not to
be violent instead of beginning to fight, and they
started fighting only when they exhausted all the other
attempts ... However, a day came when the Portuguese
killed hundreds of people in the port of Bissau because
of a strike. After that the people of Guinea Bissau
discovered that they would have to fight. If they had
not done so there would not have been a day of freedom
in Lisbon, in Portugal. The change in Portugal was
made by the Africans, was made by the struggle of the
Africans and not by the Portuguese army. Of course

the Portuguese army finally carried it out but after
being conscientized not through seminars but through
their experience in Guinea Bissau. The soldiers began
to see that they were dying and that they were killing
in a lost war; politically speaking and also from the
military point of view it was a lost war. Therefore,
they had to change Portugal in order to stop the war.
When I went to Lisbon I talked with the military and
also the educators and I said: "You should go in pro-
cession to Guinea, to Mozambique, to Angola, to tell
the people, thank you very much."

INTER-   It's sometimes said that violence begets violence. In
VIEWERS: history there are both cases where people get inured
                to bloodshed and others who seem to learn from it and
                grow and transcend the violence. Would you be reason-
                ably hopeful about the Portuguese-speaking peoples in
                Africa being able, because of their revolutionary ex-
                perience, to transcend the killing and find other
                means for their purposes?

FREIRE: Yes, yes. For example, one thing which impresses me
                by talking with the people in Guinea is the lack of
                hate. They talk about the struggle, about the atroci-
                ties of the Portuguese without any kind of hate, or
                the expression of hate. I remember I was talking last
                year with a young soldier about terrible atrocities
                committed by the Portuguese soldiers and I asked:
                "Look, when you could take these soldiers, these Port-
                uguese soldiers, after such an act, did you castrate
                them?" Of course I asked the question characteristic
                of the petite bourgeoise intellectual. My gun is my
                pencil. My gun is my word. But his gun was GUN
                really and not the words of the pencil, of the paper.
                He looked at me and he could not understand my ques-
                tion. He understood my tongue but not my language.
                It was as if I were speaking Greek. Finally, he looked
                at me and he said: "Comrade, our great leader, Cabral,
                always said to us — every day, every day — we have to
                respect the enemies even though the enemies don't res-
                pect us." And he looked at me again and said: "And
                do you think that you could respect the enemies by
                castrating them? We could not touch them. We would
                have to punish them yes, but respect them as human
                beings." I became so excited by his words, and also
                ashamed, so ashamed for us.

INTER-   Staying with the violence issue for a minute. Violence
VIEWERS: does involve killing from time to time. At the point
of the need for violence where is the teacher? What
happens to you or anyone else as teacher? At the moment of killing someone you are in effect saying: "You
are no longer permitted either to learn or to teach.
I will not allow that and the only way to deal with
that is to kill you."

FREIRE: No, I would tell you that even at this moment you are
teaching because you are teaching the others and also
yourself.

INTER-
VIEWERS: What about the one you kill?

FREIRE: He has had the last opportunity to learn. I recognize
it is very difficult but it is a fact. I would like
very much that humanity had to to a level in which the
contradictions could be solved like this meeting around
a table. But that is not yet the level of humanity.
If the French people, the Polish people, the Dutch
people, the English people, the Canadian people, the
American people, the Brazilian people, the African
people, had not fought, had not killed the Nazis, do
you not think that Hitler would be there yet?

INTER-   Much of your work has been around consciousness arou-
VIEWERS: sing, in alerting people, involving, engaging. At the
early stage in a revolution the goals are pretty clear.
I wonder if you have reflected much about the later
stages when a sustained effort is needed, when there
must be a re-engagement of people who may have become
tired. This is a problem in all societies. What will
now happen in Guinea Bissau and these other countries?

FREIRE: This is also one of my preoccupations. I am convinced
that the process of the awareness which comes also
through the struggle must continue and be increased
after the fighting is over ... the first difficult
moment was to expel the invaders, the colonizers, but
they must not stop now the process of increasing critical consciousness, critical understanding, the process
for you prefer to say "learning". If they stop now,
the result will be that the people will become bureaucratized from the mind point of view and then instead

of continuing the re-creation of society which must be
a permanent process they will become adapted to the new
reality. This is one of the points which makes me
sympathetic to the cultural revolution in China. You
have touched on one of the most important aspects of
a revolution because if the leadership is not able to
continue to establish its communion with the great
mass of the people, inviting them every day to participate in the creation, in the re-creation of their
society, the tendencies are very strong for leadership
to become static, bureaucratized, rigid, as if they
are the owners of the people and also of the knowledge
about reality.

INTER-   Because some revolutions have simply been coups the
VIEWERS: result is a change in rulers but the conditions go on.
             It's in relation to sustaining consciousness that rel-
             igion might be important. Religion, I suppose, can be
             an "opiate", it can be irrelevant. But you must have
             faced this question often ... can religion be functional,
             can it be relevant in maintaining concern, alertness,
             involvement, engagement of people?

FREIRE: Sometimes in my journeying around the world some people
             ask me if I am not contradictory by thinking and writ-
             ing and trying to do what I am trying to do while wor-
             king for the World Council of Churches, and at the same
             time saying that I am a man trying to become a Chris-
             tian. I say: "trying to become a Christian"; I never
             say that I am a Christian because I think that we are
             not; we are becoming or not becoming Christian. It
             is a permanent process of dying and birth and being
             born again. Sometimes, when I am very tired, I say,
             yes, I have the right to be contradictory. But some-
             times I elaborate something more, like now I think,
             as you, that religion has been lots of times an opiate
             of the people. Because of that I prefer to talk about
             my experience of faith instead of my religious exper-
             ience. I am much more a man trying to clarify, to
             express my faith than being a religious man. And I
             also say something that sometimes appears contradic-
             tory. I went to the people, to the peasants in my
             youth, as an educator to the workers because of my
             Christian faith. But when I arrived there the people
             sent me to Marx. Of course the people never said to
             me: "Paulo, have you read Marx?" But their reality

sent me. Then I went to Marx and when I met Marx I
did not find any reason to stop meeting Christ on the
corners of the streets. On the contrary, the more I
studied Marx the more I could re-read the gospels in a
different way. I am convinced that the traditional
church has nothing to do with increasing critical consciousness, no more than what I used to call the "modernized church", which is nothing but the traditional
chuch which becomes modern in order to become much more
efficiently traditional. Both these churches, in my
point of view, will die in history without resurrec-
tion. Only the prophetic church which is as old as
Christianity without being traditional; which is as
modern as it has to be without being modernized; only
the prophetic church, in my point of view, will survive
in history to the extent that the prophetic church knows
that in order for it to be, it has to become. The
prophetic church does not have fear of dying because
it knows that by dying this is the only way to be
resurrected.

INTER-   In the same way that the prophetic teacher isn't afraid
VIEWERS: of learning.

FREIRE: Yes, yes. The prophetic educator is not afraid to die
            as educator because he knows that in order for him or
            her to be really an educator he or she has to be born
            as a learner.

Design for Action

A programme of action resulting from the plenary
sessions, working groups and regional seminars
held at the time of the International Conference
on Adult Education and Development. It is the
action counterpart of the Address by President
Nyerere, "Development is For Man, By Man, and
Of Man".

INTRODUCTION

The Design for Action presents the practical and immediate steps
for the next five years that were formulated in 20 working groups
and approved by the more than 500 delegates representing some
80 countries at the International Conference on Adult Education
and Development held in Dar es Salaam, Tanzania, in July 1976.
It stands as the action counterpart of the statement by President
Nyerere of Tanzania on the goals of adult education and development, which was unanimously accepted by the Conference as the
Declaration of Dar es Salaam.

The Design outlines actions and programmes; it is an inventory
of the essential steps that must be taken to give substance to
the decisions of planners, politicians, and educators. It is
put forward by the adult education community as a compact of
commitment to the urgent needs for adult education all over the
world. The time schedule is five years.

The document is not unique in its proposals. The intent is to
bring together and sharpen the focus of concepts, needs, and
actions on which there has been emerging global consensus. Thus,
while the Design sets out the conditions and actions necessary
to strengthen and mobilize the capabilities of adult education
for development that were recommended at the Dar es Salaam Conference, it also draws on a number of recent international documents such as the Declaration of Persepolis from the International
Symposium for literacy, the UNESCO Recommendation on the Development of Adult Education, the Framework for a Comprehensive Policy
of Adult Education by the Organization for Economic Cooperation

and Development, and various conventions and recommendations by
the International Labour Organization concerning workers' education. Some of the proposals arise from projects or meetings
associated with intergovernmental organizations and have also
been the theme of regional meetings in the Arab States, in Africa,
in Asia, and in Latin America.

International conferences in the past few years have alerted the
conscience of the world community to such critical human problems
as food, population, environment and equitable economic policies.
The Design supplies the adult education component and learning
dimension that must accompany every economic, social or political
change if the human condition is to be secured.

To establish the framework, to clarify planning and to identify
the responsibilities of and environments for action, the Design
is presented in four sections. The first introduces the general
directions. The second centres on organization: action through
intergovernmental and international non-governmental organizations, through nations, regions and institutions. The third is
directed to proposals concerning the process of learning: research, training, content, particular needs, media and communication. The fourth is a brief statement of a commitment to ensure that recommendations are implemented.

Main emphases of the Design
Certain emphases recur throughout the Design for Action and form
the central focus of its recommendations. These include:

   i   the educative dimension of all strategies for economic,
         social, cultural and political development;
  ii   participation of the people in decisions;
 iii   policies responsive to basic human needs;
  iv   implementation of the UNESCO Recommendation on the Develop-
         ment of Adult Education;
   v   regional and national organizations to develop adult edu-
         cation capacity;
  vi   action to assist countries least developed in adult educa-
         tion;
 vii   training for adult education through regional centres;
viii   accent on particularly deprived groups in society: women,
         illiterates, peasants, migrants;
  ix   research that emphasizes participatory methods of investi-
         gation and evaluation;
   x   integrated rural development;
  xi   workers' education for those in the rural sector;

xii   promotion of and respect for <u>indigenous cultures</u>;
xiii adult education <u>content</u> concerned with development issues
      of food, health, environment.

GENERAL DIRECTIONS

The Design for Action recognizes that general directions for co-
operative action and programmes of education for development
should be as varied as the needs and cultural backgrounds of
human beings. Nothing proposed interferes with the responsibilities of governments or institutions in providing educational
programmes for their citizens. The initial step is to achieve
agreement about the process and the sharing of experiences and
resources so that responsible action is possible particularly in
countries or regions where development has been impeded.

This does not mean the advocacy of some generalized and homogen-
ized "curriculum" contrived through compromise or that ignores
cultural or political differences. Action should build upon a
wealth of cultural contributions: strategies for development
should contribute to the creation and understanding of, and respect for, the diversity of customs and cultures.

Development means justice, freedom
The objective of integrated, balanced development is to achieve
social, economic and political justice that leads to the liberation of mankind and in so doing eradicates such scourges as mass
poverty and mass illiteracy. The existing strategies, in a
large number of countries, have failed in this objective and
have served to strengthen the structure of privilege and power.
Adult educators, in cooperation with others concerned with social
justice, should engage in a continuous critique of development
strategies so that failures are eliminated and equitable conditions obtained.

The political process
An emergent consensus, and one that was stated clearly and accepted at the Dar es Salaam Conference, is that balanced development
calls for major national and international structural changes
that are not only technical or economic or educational concerns
but are rooted in political decisions. For if the quality of
human life determines the goals, it is the political process and
the exercise of political options that will define the means and
set the pace for development.

Adult education — which encompasses the human, educative and political dimensions of society — can prepare the ground within countries and between countries for the hard political decisions that have to be made, as well as acting as an instrument of popular participation so that such decisions are not manipulative and elitist but humanizing, egalitarian and liberating. Transformations of political and socio-economic structures may not be acceptable to all countries or establishments, but for many adult educators the fight for education for development centred on humanity, on liberation, on participation, and on justice must still be carried out even while acknowledging the limitations and impediments encountered.

Participation crucial to development
It is increasingly clear that participation of the total society is crucial to development. It is equally clear that participation can be distorted, such as when the learner becomes an object, not a partner, and when education is used to pacify or neutralize rather than as a process of consciousness-raising, participation and change. Since participation is a political process, in that it includes involvement and the exercise of options, adult education has a major function to identify and implement those processes of participation and those forms of consensus that make political, social and economic structures responsive to, and based on, human needs and aspirations.

Adult education can be a powerful factor in sensitizing individuals, groups, and communities — particularly the last privileged — to their role as self-reliant participants. The Declaration of Persepolis identified literacy not as a mere skill process but as "a contribution to the liberation of man and to his full development". The most favourable structures include those that "tend to bring about the effective participation of every citizen in decision-making at all levels of social life: in economics, politics and culture".

Leaders, administrators and policy-makers are urged to acknowledge and act upon the understanding that participation is not only necessary but welcome — and to trust it. They are to seek ways to participate more deeply themselves in the lives of the people and to see this process as essential to their own education and to their effectiveness as leaders. Thus, both policy-makers and the people they serve should be assisted to establish a participatory dialogue for planning, implementation, and assessment of results.

Integrated development strategies

The continuing education dimension of all development strategies should be included in development programmes of governments, ministries, and international agencies and be incorporated into national policies The condition of women must be an integral part of policies and strategies. Some of the most critical indicators of under-development relating to health, education and economic opportunities apply predominantly to the women of the developing world. The essential elements of new development strategies should include:

— orientation toward basic human needs so that goals, institutions and processes are revised to ensure that adult education is a more central component of development;
— social and political processes of participation that lead to an increasingly egalitarian and cooperative society;
— structures that provide and maintain productive work;
— infrastructures that enable individuals to effect control over and change their lives and their environment;
— decentralized production systems geared to goods and services needed by the majority of the population;
— an educational dimension that animates, guides, and appraises the process and the results.

Adult educators should take a lead in interacting with decision-makers and technical planners to identify, evaluate and implement such strategies.

ENVIRONMENTS FOR ACTION: ORGANIZATION

1.   ACTION THROUGH INTERNATIONAL COOPERATION AND ASSISTANCE

International collaborative action, essential to the global dimensions of development, can take place through a variety of channels: intergovernmental organizations, international non-governmental organizations (NGOs), and many national and regional organizations.

Conditions for assistance

It is recognized that much international assistance in the past has had consequences deeply detrimental to the interests of developing countries. International cooperation should be encouraged only if and when it is truly cooperative and results in balanced development based on self-reliance and shared resources. A priority for international assistance should be adult education programmes that contribute to development by the following means:

— assisting in the building up or strengthening of national
    systems and structures of education that benefit all people;
— primarily using indigenous personnel and resulting in the
    training of such personnel;
— supporting indigenous cultures and leading to the growth of
    self-reliance.

Programmes of adult education for development have rarely been
supported with international assistance funds. There are exceptions, such as the Experimental World Literacy Programme, but in
the main the record is one of neglect. There are several reasons;
negative reasons which must now be turned into positive action:

— governments in few countries have assessed adult education as
    of high priority in their development goals or in their
    requests for funds;
— few persons who make decisions about social programmes within
    countries or in international assistance agencies under-
    stand the significance and impact of adult education in
    fostering development;
— adult education organizations and personnel have not been
    successful in developing strategies that result in assis-
    tance funds.

To the extent that international assistance funds are required,
and can be used effectively, better strategies for obtaining
them must be employed.

Specific fields
Education for development often can be fostered through international cooperation related to specific fields or special targets.

For example, while the Experimental World Literacy Programme had
mixed achievements and never equalled some of its aspirations,
this product of international cooperation between two intergovernmental organizations (UNESCO and UNDP) and touching many countries, did have an impact on development and has produced valuable "lessons learned" that can now be applied generally.

The achievements in some countries during International Women's
Year respecting the education of women and the charting of policies and actions to achieve equality is another example and one
that must be carried further.

There are encouraging examples where concerted international
action, such as for workers' education, rural self-help projects,
and managerial and technical training for rural men and women,
have resulted in human development achievements as well as the
attainment of specific project goals.

The present and future "paper famine" which does and will seriously jeopardize educational and development goals (such as for
post-literacy materials) is an area demanding cooperative effort.
International action is needed to obtain access for all countries
to stocks from major paper-producing countries and also, most
importantly, to initiate research into the use of indigenous
fibres.

International cooperation can serve as an educative forum for
worldwide understanding of the contribution of different cultures
to world development and to national development. Adult education should contribute to respect for the diversity of customs,
cultures and languages, both internationally and nationally.
The cultural heritage of regions and peoples should find expression in education for development.

UNESCO Recommendation
An immediate focus for international action by countries and by
adult educators is the UNESCO Recommendation on the Development
of Adult Education which is an example of the normative and
standard-setting function of international cooperation. The
Recommendation is realistic about objectives and the resources
needed to attain them; it does not chain governments to false
expectations or costly innovations. It is a human-centred document because its implementation depends upon the initiative and
participation of many people, notably adult educators. The regular reports by governments on their actions to implement the
Recommendation opens up opportunities for study and public debate on performance respecting adult education for development.

2. ACTION THROUGH AND IN SUPPORT OF INTERGOVERNMENTAL ORGANI-
    ZATIONS

Several kinds of international collaborative efforts are needed
during the balance of the Second Development Decade through intergovernmental organizations that have direct interest in adult
education for development, including UNESCO, ILO, FAO, WHO,
UNICEF, UNEP, UNDP, World Bank, the United Nations University
and the programme of the United Nations Conference on Trade and
Development (UNCTAD).

Adult educators, their organizations and agencies need to keep
themselves informed about, and involved with, the plans and programmes of intergovernmental organizations whose strategies contribute to, and strengthen, education for development.

Initiatives for action
In order to take effective action through and in support of intergovernmental organizations, as well as NGOs, adult education organizations in every country should:

— take the initiative in fostering national plans for the imple-
    mentation and monitoring of their governments' action re-
    garding the UNESCO Recommendation on the Development of
    Adult Education;
— develop systematic means and programmes for interpreting the
    significance of adult education to decision-makers in nat-
    ional, regional and intergovernmental roles, as well as to
    the public, and specific audiences within the general pop-
    ulation;
— become proficient in developing realistic proposals for inter-
    national assistance through all effective channels, but
    particularly through "country programmes" of intergovern-
    mental agencies;
— initiate and/or support education measures that lead to the
    understanding of, and cooperation with, the development
    goals of programmes of such intergovernmental agencies as
    ILO, WHO, FAO;
— ensure that educational and development national policies con-
    tain provision for workers' education that includes direct
    participation of urban and rural workers' organizations.

For funding agencies
It is recommended that funding agencies concerned with international development assistance give priority to programmes that:

— develop a strong adult education infrastructure, particularly
    in countries where adult education is least developed;
— identify levels of training and self-help needs in terms of
    competence, management, delivery, and evaluation;
— assist workers' organizations now actively engaged in the
    organization and development of the rural poor;
— make direct provision for the equal integration of women into
    social and economic development;
— help the public to understand the momentous issues of the
    New International Economic Order and of environmental edu-
    cation for survival.

Issues relating to these and other priorities are contained in
further sections of the Design.

3. ACTION THROUGH AND IN SUPPORT OF INTERNATIONAL NGOs

Many of the major programmes in adult education in the future
will involve cooperative projects such as the UNESCO-UNDP Experimental World Literacy Project or the involvement of ILO in workers' education which features literacy for rural workers. The
participation of strong international NGOs should be a part of
programmes of intergovernmental agencies particularly to build
up a system and infrastructure for adult education and to foster
programmes of education for development within and through these
organizations.

Variety of support
There are many non-governmental organizations concerned with
adult education for development and whose experiences and services can be used more directly. They operate in such fields as
community colleges, universities, women's education, rural development, cooperatives, libraries and museums, educational technologies, publishing and broadcasting.

Recognizing the need for an integrated approach in solving the
problems facing practising adult educators and the fact of limited financial and manpower resources, it is recommended to all
organized teaching and other professional organizations that they
lend their support to adult and continuing education activities
within their country and region.

Enlarged role for NGOs
Because of their international membership network, NGOs should
be encouraged and supported for an enlarged role in the provision
of experienced personnel, the monitoring of projects, and the
production and dissemination of information.

For example, a precondition of new development strategies and
programmes, particularly for integrated rural development, is
knowledge of the experiences — successes and failures — of similar or related programmes elsewhere. International NGOs can
play a major role in identifying and disseminating such information to national policy makers.

The regional centres and offices of international NGOs can similarly serve policy needs through inventories of projects, inno-

vations and research as well as to provide indigenous personnel
for project teams to develop regional training facilities, evaluate new programmes and projects and assist with the monitoring
of such activities.

4. ACTION THROUGH REGIONAL ORGANIZATIONS

The strengthening of regional action through regional and/or
area organizations, the establishment of a training centre in
each region, and regional sharing of experiences, information
and personnel, are among the core recommendations from the Dar
es Salaam Conference. Regional organizations for adult education are now established, or under active consideration, in Europe, Africa, Asia, the South Pacific, the Arab States, South
America and the "Norceca" countries of North and Central America.

Immediate action needs
How to assist established, newly formed and about-to-be-formed,
regional associations to be more effective and to implement,
coordinate, and finance regional collaboration is a recommendation for immediate action.

As a practical aim for the balance of the Second Development
Decade, the improvement of capabilities for adult education should
be proceeded with, particularly in Africa, the Arab States, Asia,
the South Pacific, Latin America and the Caribbean. In many
cases, a regional organization may serve some national needs
until it is possible to create national associations. The region
can be the locus of such needed common services as training, research and information-sharing.

Regional priorities
Certain priorities for regional organizations have been identified at international and regional conferences:

— to establish one or more regional training centres to augment
    national training, using senior staff from the region;
— the training centres to incorporate research and evaluation
    components, particularly in methods and practices of par-
    ticipatory research and action research, and related to
    indigenous cultures;
— provision of direct assistance to least developed countries
    or sectors in the region;
— an effective two-way information and documentation exchange
    featuring the main languages of the region as well as the

international languages. These centres should also use
services and materials from UNESCO (particularly the International Bureau of Education), other intergovernmental
agencies, and international NGOs;
— exchange of personnel and informational visits;
— development of reading materials for new literates.

In any regional organization all the countries should be represented as well as major adult education interests and institutions
and groups and agencies involved with development work. A central purpose of the regional organization should be the advancement of education for integrated development, particularly with
respect to increase of food production, health, nutrition, poverty, unemployment, illiteracy, and the problems of rural movement to urban centres.

The participation of international assistance agencies should be
invited in the provision of experience, materials, funds and
personnel, but only through the initiative of the regional organization and under its direction.

Areas for action
Each country in a region should draw up an inventory of its innovative programmes, the areas where its adult education is strongest, and the areas in which it seeks to improve its performance
and to learn from others. For Asia and the South Pacific, an
inventory could be based on the survey of non-formal education
conducted by the South East Asian Ministers of Education Organization and expanded to include other countries.

The establishment of a pilot project in integrated rural development in each country of a region is also recommended. This
would lead to an overall plan of action for the integration of
adult education into solutions to various regional problems.

One or more specific projects or studies should be designed
within each regional grouping to explore how the efforts of adult education may be adopted and refashioned to serve the growing and urgent need to see the total community as a true learning base and to integrate learning into every phase of life.
The International Council for Adult Education should foster and
animate such projects, monitor them, and publish the results.

The evidence of closer cooperation among countries of the regions, and between regions and international organizations, is
commended. Governments are urged to endorse such actions and

make adequate financial contributions towards their realization.
A specific recommendation urges the strengthening of existing
pan-Arab and regional institutions such as ARLO and ASFEC, national adult education institutions and UNESCO national commissions; the establishment of a regional adult education research
and training centre; and support for the formation of an Arab
Adult Education Association.

5. ACTION THROUGH NATIONS AND NATIONAL ORGANIZATIONS

It has been recognized at the UNESCO World Conference on Adult
Education at Tokyo that adult education cannot and will not
flourish unless in each country there is a commitment to it, a
national infrastructure for stimulus and coordination, and the
cultivation of cadres of trained and experienced personnel to
sustain and enlarge it. Without these essential factors neither
adult education as a field nor adult education for development
will have much chance to be effective.

Agreement on needed structures
National meetings and international seminars, and the UNESCO
Recommendation on the Development of Adult Education, make it
clear that coordinating structures, actions and programmes are
needed in every country and that these be considered a basic
investment if adult education is to become an active agent in
development. The section on Structures in the UNESCO Recommendation begins with this statement:

> Members States should endeavour to ensure the
> establishment and development of a network of
> bodies meeting the needs of adult education;
> this network should be sufficiently flexible
> to meet the various personal and social situ-
> ations and their evolution.

The agreement in the UNESCO Recommendation is that each country
should have an appropriate mechanism for bringing together on a
regular basis those most responsible for education to determine
national commitment, decide on allocation of resources, and design sound policies and coordinated programmes for adult education for development.

Such a coordinating body would involve government departments
(such as health, agriculture, economic production, cultural services, education); universities and colleges; organizations

concerned with workers, rural development, trade unions, women, the aging, ethnic minorities, managers and employers, professional personnel, broadcasters and publishers.

Realistic target for action
A realistic target for the balance of the Second Development Decade is to assist every country that is willing to cooperate in developing the means to:

— stimulate and coordinate adult education nationally;
— hold regular national meetings for establishing targets and programmes of education for development;
— establish and maintain a system of information exchange;
— plan an appropriate infrastructure;
— initiate training and research;
— develop indigenous studies, languages and cultural expression.

Persons who have had successful experience in developing such policies are still few in number and their experience should be shared with other countries. An important objective for the next five years is the recruitment and training of such persons.

Action for national associations
Adult educators are urged to work in association with governments, wherever appropriate, for the establishment or strengthening of national associations/boards and other adult education coordinating organizations so that they become cooperative agencies for promoting and implementing development issues and programmes.

It is through an adult education association that educators can develop systematic efforts to make government planners aware that the goals of adult education and of workers' education are in keeping with the goals of integrated, balanced development. By such means adult education can strengthen its formal and informal linkages with agencies and ministries responsible for development.

National associations should recognize the significance of workers' education and equip themselves to respond to, and cooperate with, programme needs identified by workers' organizations and cooperatives.

It is also recommended that respective national associations in each region investigate and cooperate on activities now underway to refashion the formal school system so that work and service may become a part of the general curriculum and thereby

enable youth to participate in the concepts and practices of
development, self-reliance, social participation, and lifelong
learning.

Improvement of training

A priority for national associations is to work together for
improvement in the quality, type and accessibility of both long-
term and short-term adult education training for women and men.

Short workshops could focus on effective adult learning and
teaching to groups of full-time adult education organizers who
are in a position to disseminate their learning to teachers of
adults. In some cases, a resource team may travel to one country in the sub-region to take a course; in other cases, a course
may be held in a central location so that educators from neighbouring countries can attend.

Other recommendations related to training are contained in following sections of this document such as Action Through Institutions, Recruitment and Training of Personnel, and Research and
Development.

Regional action for national associations

While every country will need to plan for appropriate training
and research as well as for an adult education infrastructure,
as indicated earlier, some of these essential services may be
provided in part, at least temporarily, through regional, national and international cooperation.

It is recommended that regional organizations work for the establishment of national adult education associations in countries
where they do not exist, wherever possible making an approach
through the country's UNESCO national commission.

A practical step is for the regional association to offer to run
a workshop in a particular country with the aim of encouraging
the formation of a national association. Inter-country visits
to innovative projects can strengthen national and regional
associations and result in the publishing of case study inventories on such projects. International agencies and NGOs should
see funding assistance as a priority for improving the capability of adult education associations and their cooperation.

Action through governments

Fundamental to all discussion on adult education for development
is the need for governments to express in concrete terms their

political and moral commitment to adult education as an integral
part of overall national goals and objectives. This can be
accomplished by the following measures:

— defining the concept of education for development with full
   knowledge of how adult education can play an appropriate
   role by integrating its services and resources into national development plans;
— ensuring that the central focus of development is on human
   development and on real-life problems identified and faced
   by individuals and communities;
— creating an atmosphere favourable to the participation of individuals and groups — including leaders at national and
   local levels — in the planning and execution of development programmes;
— integrating adult education and non-formal education with the
   formal system in order to revitalize the total educational
   system and strengthen its orientation toward development;
— fostering the establishment of appropriate coordinating adult
   education infrastructures that will reflect the multi-
   disciplinary nature of adult education and thus provide a
   holistic view of national needs and priorities;
— reviewing the methods of financing adult education so that
   budget allocations are increased to such ministries and
   agencies;
— committing development and education policies toward the
   achievement of self-determination for women.

It is recommended that governments recognize, encourage and support the work of international NGOs engaged in adult education
and development such as the International Council for Adult Education.

A wide range of useful adult education expertise exists among
the membership of NGOs and within consultative bodies such as
UNESCO and its national commissions. Governments and associations should avail themselves of such liaison in the planning
and implementing of development policies.

Action for literacy
Governments should pledge themselves to literacy as an integral
part of national programmes and involve illiterates themselves
in the formation of such plans.

As far as possible, the functions and responsibilities of literacy and/or adult education programmes and the organization and

training of personnel should be located within one national coordinating body with the help of various ministries or organizations concerned in order to minimize competition for funds and
reduce inefficiency in implementation.

The recognition of literacy as a primary medium for social,
economic and political development means that increased budget-
ary allocations are essential. It also means the design of comprehensive and multi-disciplinary programmes that provide for
post-literacy projects and access to further education and training.

Culture and development

Governments should become more aware that a vigorous overall cultural policy is necessary to direct and regular the future of
education for development and that development must have a functional relationship to cultural traditions, customs and languages of groups and sub-groups within a country. Linguistic and
cultural diversity should be seen as a rich resource rather than
as a threat to unity.

Costs and funding

In view of the burden of educational costs on national budgets,
and while pointing out that adult education is a relatively low-
cost component of education, certain recommendations are made
for the reduction of educational costs through:

— use of locally available materials, resources, and skills;
— mobilization of available voluntary and part-time personnel;
— ensuring that para-state and private enterprise take due
    responsibility for the education and training of their
    workers;
— fuller use for adult, workers' and non-formal education of
    existing physical facilities, such as schools, community
    halls, churches, temples and mosques.

Participation of learners

Development programmes must be based on the principle of participation from pre-planning through to evaluation, thus creating
an opportunity for every participant to be both a teacher and a
learner. The involvement of learners in systematic needs assessment and in the evaluation of all publicly funded programmes
should be a part of funding priorities.

Workers' education

Since workers' education is an important and growing sector of

adult education, recommendations for workers' participation in
development planning are based not only on social justice but
also on the greater realism and social content it injects into
planning. Emphasis is placed upon the promotion of strong and
viable organizations of wage earners and non-wage earning rural
workers and their involvement in the planning and implementation
of rural development policies and programmes.

Educational and development policies should be so oriented that
the education of individual workers can be translated into par-
ticipatory contributions by their organizations, in line with
ILO Recommendation 94 on Consultation and Cooperation Between
Employers and Their Role in Economic and Social Development,
Convention 140 and Recommendation 148 on Paid Educational Leave.

6. ACTION THROUGH INSTITUTIONS

There is a conspicuous role in a design for action for every
organization and institution of adult education; indeed for
every learner. Because circumstances are so varied, plans for
institutions must be made by those engaged in the institutions.
However, there are steps that must be taken to support the quality and effectiveness of adult education.

Training role
The need for training programmes at regional, national and local
levels requires the active involvement of colleges and universities, government departments, professional associations, and
trade unions.

Documentation is lacking on the precise nature of existing under-
graduate and graduate instruction in adult education offered by
universities and similar institutions in various parts of the
world. A descriptive inventory of courses and a meeting of such
universities could create a "consortium" of expertise and information for the development and coordination of training programmes. Thus, institutions capable of providing training for
adult education could be helped to undertake such training and/
or to enlarge their efforts.

It is recommended that the training of adult educators for administrative, extension and field work have practical orientation.
For example, in addition to training rural extension personnel,
universities and colleges of agriculture need to work cooperatively to orient their courses to the practical needs and prob-

lems of field workers and to develop workshops and seminars for
in-service and refresher training.

Need for new forms of adult education

There is increased recognition that certain countries and regions
may lack particular forms of adult education that are specific
to their needs, such as literacy, workers' education, rural development, education for women, distance education, etc.

Specific kinds of institutions appropriate for development may
also be lacking, such as workers' universities or community colleges. Regional and/or international cooperation can support
the development of specific and needed kinds of service institutions and programmes in selected countries.

However, any development of new institutional forms, and their
programmes, should be rooted in the context of indigenous cultures and languages and be created with the full participation
of the communities and people they are to serve. In some countries the renewal of earlier cultural forms and institutions,
such as the mosque universities, can offer examples of admirable
community-based learning centres which still have contemporary
significance.

So that there may be an education dimension in all development
strategies, it is essential to adapt, extend, or establish a
variety of institutions and/or agencies which would be:

— based on identifiable local communities;
— sensitive to the specific development needs of those commun-
      ities;
— a resource for local leadership recruitment and training;
— an agent for the conservation and promotion of local cultural
      heritages;
— committed to the education of women;
— part of a network for coordinated research and evaluation,
      documentation, and dissemination of information and mat-
      erials on adult education.

The contribution of workers' organizations to social and economic
justice needs to be more widely recognized by education ministries to ensure that all institutions — schools, teachers' colleges, polytechnics, adult education centres, universities and
colleges — include labour studies in the curricula and that workers' organizations are adequately represented on governing
bodies and/or advisory councils.

The role of adult education for development needs continual interpretation to general and specific publics. The institutions of adult education can individually and collectively supply much of the infrastructure by ensuring that their collections of print and other media are accessible and well-distributed and that such information sources as cinema, radio and television, libraries, museums and art galleries are organized for the support of learning, particularly learning associated with development.

ENVIRONMENTS FOR ACTION: THE LEARNING PROCESS

1. RESEARCH AND DEVELOPMENT

Research for the development of adult education as well as for education for development is a crucial need in most countries. Emphasis should be given to those kinds of research that will assist decision-makers and result in improved performance over the next five years. This is not to question the value of long-range research but only to recognize that agencies and institutions already exist for long-range tasks and that research directed to informed decision-making is infrequent and usually ineffective.

Research to be participatory in nature
Research should be recognized as an integral part of adult education for development and be participatory in nature. All those taking part can be involved in the necessary research — learners, educators, planners, administrators, specialists. Participatory research thus becomes a system of continuing discussion and investigation conceived and organized to result in direct benefit.

Further principles of participatory research are that the research process should (a) involve the community or population from formulation of the problem to discussion of solutions and interpretations of the findings; (b) be seen as a total educational experience which serves to identify community needs and to increase awareness and communication within the community; (c) be a continuing dialogue over time, not an isolated exercise; (d) be of immediate benefit to a community and to decision-makers.

Training in research
All adult educators should receive training in the theory and practice of participatory research as well as in complementary quantitative research techniques. This training should be carried

out preferably in the field with appropriate support from nearby
institutions. For the new emphasis on participatory methods of
social investigation, training manuals and materials need to be
devised. International and regional seminars are necessary to
evaluate and consolidate the best uses of participatory research
and to further exchange of information and experiences.

Cooperative linkages

The development self-reliant capability is a fundamental approach
for research in adult education and one that needs broad international exchanges and mutual aid projects to contribute to the
variety and effectiveness of research. Encouragement should be
given to publications and research information at national and
local levels, as well as through international annual or bi-
annual publications on research.

For universities to contribute effectively to research in adult
education an essential condition is that they multiply their
contacts with other institutions and intensify their participation on ongoing adult education processes and the needs of national and local communities.

Stronger cooperative links are recommended between rural extension and research. Researchers should work on basic agricultural, social and economic problems; carry out field trials;
and be able to advise on appropriate technology. Such research
programmes should yield suitable results on the use of good
economic infrastructures for rural development including pricing,
marketing and distribution.

Because of legitimate demands on limited financial resources,
research projects, while considered as a priority investment,
should be designed with minimum costs and, where applicable,
with the cooperation and participation of other agencies and
personnel so that adult education can be strengthened and extended as economically as possible.

Among the special objectives of research is the recommendation
that these focus on better understanding of traditional and popular means of communication and informal learning (including
theatre, dance, music, art) and on how these media can be used
to stimulate and enhance learning and participatory development.

2. RECRUITMENT AND TRAINING OF PERSONNEL

Training programmes are needed at several levels — regional, national and in territories within nations. This will require the active involvement of colleges and universities as well as government departments and such general purpose organizations as trade unions. There are many kinds of personnel who require further training; most of them are in the important "middle management" area such as:

— those able to carry out education and training programmes for others;
— those instructing and providing non-formal education;
— organizers of adult education and training at all levels, including literacy, workers' education, agriculture and rural development, continuing education of managers and professional personnel;
— planners and decision-makers respecting education and training;
— managers of "delivery systems" of education in fields such as health, food, nutrition, social and political organization;
— producers and users of various media programmes, print, oral and visual;
— library, museum and gallery personnel.

Regional training centres
As indicated in the section on Regional Organizations, the immediate need is for training facilities and programmes to serve those countries that are not yet able to mount the kinds of training required to improve the capability of adult educators in the development process. A cooperative programme of regional training centres is recommended for mutual assistance in regions where there are bonds of culture or ideology or language, or geography and communication, or economic association.

— In each of the regions (Asia, Africa, Arab States, Latin America) at least one or more training-research centres should be established with indigenous leadership but assisted through international cooperation.
— These centres should be established, as soon as conditions of effective work are possible, over the next three years.
— Part of the strategy for these centres should be to have a systematic means of exchange of experience between centres and evaluation of procedures and results.
— These centres should serve the training needs of many kinds

of personnel listed above, and should utilize training experience and services available through governments, universities, unions, management, media.
— Intergovernmental agencies such as the World Bank and other
  agencies capable of rendering assistance should be invited
  to support the work of these centres particularly efforts
  concerned with development problems.
— Institutions capable of providing training for adult education should be involved in regional centres as well as in
  inter-regional cooperation.
— Participatory research should be part of the training component with regional seminars planned to build up regional
  capacities for research that assists education for development.
— The centres should use existing information services as well
  as foster development and exchange of materials relating
  to regional problems, cultures and languages.

What is needed is a training demonstration project to work out
the particular kinds of training and relationships of subject
matter and disciplines; identify research; obtain financial
support; inventory regional resources; and recruit indigenous
people from the region who have appropriate experience to serve
on the faculty.

Cooperation should be undertaken for training and for research
with the United Nations University, the International Congress
of University Adult Educators, the community college World College organization, the International Federation of Library
Associations, and other interested agencies.

Training for rural development
An urgent problem for adult education at the national and regional level is to increase food production. Training of field
workers is essential for the mounting of technical programmes
aimed at the small farmer, the marginal farmer, and those in
drought-prone areas. Such programmes would help rural men and
women in the application of small-scale agriculture technology
and management; in the use of fertilizers and pesticides; in
benefiting from needed agricultural reforms.

Such rural development training would aim at providing training
for self-reliance at the level of individual and community needs.
This would include training in small and cottage industries;
training of unemployed youth particularly in minimum managerial
skills to open up avenues for self-employment; training prog-

rammes directly related to the involvement of women in rural extension services and in farmer training programmes.

Particular attention is recommended to the training of rural leaders selected by the community to become village "technicians" or animateurs and the local link with extension agents or other agencies. Short-term training programmes could be provided at a regional centre for village men and women in those areas of need identified by the community, such as child care, nutrition, health, sanitation, building, and technical skills.

To develop a common approach to integrated rural development, extension workers from different specializations should take their training with agricultural personnel.

Training content

All training, particularly for middle management and higher administrative staff in government services, should include a sound knowledge of, and experience in, communication techniques. Training should increase the sensitivity of adult educators themselves and of allied field workers to the problems of the less privileged by both careful selection of personnel and by content and practice that stresses empathy and awareness of the human factors of development.

The training of instructors in literacy programmes, both professional and non-professional, should include techniques of animation and participation, of evaluation for self-correction, and attention to administration and reporting skills.

Training should emphasize the mutual exchange of experiences between the teacher and the "taught" and the development of participatory methods and activities that teach learners how to participate in decision-making.

Recruitment and attitudes

To recruit and provide the necessary organization and teaching personnel to carry out essential development tasks, attention is drawn to the following proposals:

— mobilize a variety of professionals, para-professionals and
    volunteers who are usually associated with departments
    and agencies not primarily concerned with education;
— use non-formal short-cycle modes of training which are more
    cost-effective, more flexible and responsive to specific
    needs, and better carriers of new ideas and innovative

practices;
— establish interdepartmental collaborative programmes in order
  to train heterogeneous and multi-disciplinary groups that
  think in terms of the educative aspect of all development
  strategies;
— encourage the acceptance by full-time adult educators that
  other professionals may be better placed to identify key
  development tasks and objectives; and that, not infrequently, the educational aspect — although not indispensable — will appear in a supportive or instrumental role.

3. THE CONTENT OF ADULT EDUCATION

The agenda of adult education must change as the human agenda
changes. This agenda now includes the goals of integrated cultural, social and political development, not only efforts to improve economic productivity.

While not denying the interests of individual learners in education for development the Design is concerned primarily with activities that foster improved social performance. To ensure that
education is used cooperatively as a major vehicle for progress,
adult educators are urged to cooperate with other agencies in
defining the role and content of development education and to
promote it through mass media, seminars, workshops, etc., at
national and local levels.

Range of priorities
When there are scarce resources there must be priorities. The
range of priorities for education for development include measures to meet basic human needs; to provide food and to eliminate
poverty; to enhance human growth and to diminish marginal survival; to encourage the arts and cultural expression; to maintain and restore environmental quality; to foster world cooperation and communion among people.

No one would pretend that there is complete agreement on all of
these subjects. However, these are the concerns that touch on
the family of mankind and should be studied as problems of, and
opportunities for, all human beings as well as from the more
restricted perspectives of national or regional or ideological
association.

New curriculum for development
It is now the task of adult educators, with international input,

to translate the priorities and imperatives of the world agenda
into a new "curriculum" for the formal and non-formal educational
system, for the learning of all adults in a variety of ways, and
for the continuing education of adult educators themselves.

It is recommended that the International Council for Adult Education create a Commission for the New Curriculum to identify
those social, political and economic forces and issues that are
crucial to development.

Participation skills
Attention is urged to content that emphasizes participation in
social development particularly of those who have been disadvantaged and restricted by the alienating force of poverty and illness. Social advance is facilitated, not impeded, by the enlargement of people who are intelligent, capable, and responsible
participants.

Educational programmes are advocated that enhance the power of
individuals to participate effectively in the life of their community and nation. In recognizing that participation is both a
method and a skill that can be learned, the content of adult
education can give a major role to activities that provide ways
and means for people to learn how to participate.

Interpretation of world issues
Recommendations emphasize the need to development education that
increases people's awareness of the interdependency of world
issues and that promotes action on the part of governments,
groups and individuals.

Earlier sections of the Design for Action have noted that the
role of adult education in and for development needs to be effectively interpreted to governments, teachers, students and the
general public. Such materials, using a range of media, can
stimulate dialogue on the inter-relationships between national
development goals and the imperatives of food, health, cultural
expression, scarce resources, the environment, lifelong learning, self-determination, and the implications of the New International Economic Order. Such programmes of interpretation and
study can be initiated from national and regional agencies with
funding assistance, when applicable, from international intergovernmental organizations.

In keeping with the above, it is recommended that adult educators work more closely with development specialists from other

disciplines to increase their own awareness of development issues
and to enable other specialists to appreciate the contribution
of adult education. In this way, both groups together can plan
and carry out more comprehensive and integrated development education programmes.

Education for eco-development
Eco-development means development that takes into account environmental protection and enhancement of ecological systems. Environmental destruction threatens the survival of humankind.
The adult education community must respond to this crisis by
accepting responsibility for a programme of action that mobilizes
public awareness about the realities of environmental issues and
the accelerating depletion of the world's resources.

The need exists to facilitate the exchange of ideas, approaches,
and programmes by such means as:

— collecting and exchanging information on environmental educa-
      tion such as UNESCO/UNEP programmes and the Belgrade Char-
      ter on Environmental Education;
— assistance to adult educators in developing and implementing
      programmes related to environmental education;
— ensuring adult education participation in international and
      regional conferences on the environment;
— cooperating and collaborating with UNESCO/UNDP in the adult
      education and social development components of their pro-
      posed pilot projects on eco-development in Tanzania, the
      Senegal River Basin, Kuwait, the Adriatic, India, and
      Colombia;
— instituting a continuing programme of international and reg-
      ional meetings to mobilize adult education experiences,
      resources, and programmes for eco-development.

Cultural development
The task of adult education in contributing to endogenous development is to promote, conserve, and use local and indigenous
cultures as the content and curricula of its programmes. To
revitalize traditional values and systems is not a step backward in time but rather to make sure that new development policies are humanely based in rich, authentic, cultural forms. In
promoting knowledge about and appreciation of the history, traditional cultures and artistic values of society, adult education
should also ensure that people are encouraged to express their
creative abilities so that a flourishing popular culture exists.

Respect for and understanding of the diversity of customs and
cultures and languages within nations and regions — as well as
internationally — is essential for cooperation, peace and mutual
learning. Sub-groups within a society should be able to express
themselves freely, educate themselves and their children in their
native tongues, develop their own cultural forms, and learn languages other than their native ones.

Adult education leadership is needed in the revitalization of
such cultural centres as museums so that they become community
learning centres that encourage existing popular cultural expressions as well as communicate the life and creations of the past.

4.   LEARNING NEEDS OF PARTICULAR GROUPS

In view of the importance of development education for raising
the consciousness of members of society towards continuing education and social awareness, adult educators are urged to participate in the learning needs of certain groups such as the following.

— Priority should be given to the provision of financial and
    administrative support to youth programmes both in urban
    and rural areas to develop responsible leadership skills
    and activities that stimulate interest in the cultural
    life of society, in social and economic concerns, and that
    give young people a sense of self-worth through service to
    others.
— Cooperative relationship with the school system is vital to
    ensure community learning opportunities for both parents
    and children.
— Ongoing contact with administrators and teachers in the for-
    mal education system can result in participation in the
    devising of curricula, teaching methods and techniques
    that stimulate learning about development education.
— Traditional practices and attitudes toward women need chan-
    ging through education directed, in many instances, to men.
    Since women are the majority of the adult population and
    constitute the largest percentage of illiterates, it is
    essential that their consciousness be raised concerning
    their actual condition and their potentialities for deci-
    sive social and economic roles.
— Adult education organizations should give attention to the
    educational and other problems of migrant workers and im-
    migrants in their countries. The involvement should not

be limited to immediate learning needs such as language
courses, vocational training, and schooling of children,
but go beyond this into inviting participation in and contribution to general adult education activities.
— Adult educators should learn more about the implications of
  urbanization for their work and in particular the role of
  adult education in assisting urban dwellers to participate
  in the planning and governance of cities.
— Some nations have a great diversity of cultures and languages
  and are faced with the problem of reconciling the needs of
  development within the preservation of cultural diversity.
  The role of traditional cultures, and of cultural traditions of immigrants, needs interpretation within the development context.
— Workers, farmers, peasants, media specialists, trade unions
  and employers need direction and stimulation in order to
  develop an appreciation of their role and responsibility
  in the imperatives of national and international development issues.
— Rural development education should stress to farmers the importance of environmental conservation, such as of land
  and water, and its role in immediate and future development.

5. MEDIA AND COMMUNICATION

Any achievement of the objectives of adult education for development depends upon the learning, participation, growth and change
of individuals and societies; which in turn depends upon information and two-way communication between individuals and groups
and governments and policy makers. In a sense, all education is
communication of information and knowledge and hinges on the
access to such communication and participation in it.

Certain recommendations at the Dar es Salaam Conference relate
to communication in two forms: the use of broadcast and print
media and face-to-face communications for specific adult education programmes; and the use of information networks for communication among adult educators themselves.

Communications policy
The emphasis on participation and liberation, which runs all
through the recommendations on which the Design for Action is
based, prompts proposals for serious study of the control of
broadcasting and print media and of the pre-conditions for the

use of media in human-centred development such as freedom of
expression and legitimate participation and feedback.

National and international agencies are urged to recognize the
political pre-conditions for educational policies that foster
liberation and that educational media alone cannot achieve results that are in total conflict with the values of the society
in which they are used.

International and national agencies must realize that the combination of group learning with broadcast and print material can
increase public consciousness of development issues. Therefore,
support should be given to such projects especially when they
make use of inexpensive technology such as radio.

Questions for mass media
It is recommended that the International Council for Adult Education investigate the issues involved in the control of broadcasting and the kinds of structures which give balance to the
interests of the public and of governments.

Some aspects of recommendations are put in question form: Is
media truly in the service of development programmes? Is radio
broadcasting really directed to the concerns and conditions of
rural people when most broadcasters are urban-oriented and
trained abroad? Are mass campaigns really committed to using
all forms of communication for two-way participation, communication and evaluation, or are they merely passing "the message"
from the top down to the masses?

Recommendations state that such questions be seriously studied
at the national level along with the need for coordination of
the use of communications media among those involved in development work. National workshops are proposed for development planners, policy makers, educators and communicators to promote and
devise a more functional integration of communication, education
and research.

In view of the present inadequate coverage of development issues
by national mass media agencies, adult educators should create
pressures for more and better coverage of national and international issues.

National and international action
Noting that the integrated use of educational media for development has been demonstrated to be highly effective and has enabled

education to be accessible to large numbers of people for whom
formal education facilities are scarce or not available, it is
recommended that governments and international agencies support
educational projects for human development that combine the use
of broadcasting, print and face-to-face learning.

In order to achieve more effective educational media programmes,
governments and adult education agencies are urged to support
and participate in structures and policies that ensure adequate
coordination between adult education and extension agencies including those run by governments, universities and other non-
commercial bodies.

In view of the danger that educational media projects can be
used to pacify the poor and widen the gap between the more and
less advantaged, it is recommended that the media employ techniques and methods which will allow individuals to become collectively aware of their present condition and the changes that
can be brought about, and which emphasize participation, initiative and action.

It is essential that adult educators — and not only technical
personnel — be involved in research on the implications for education for development of communication satellites and the use
of spin-off technology for under-developed regions of the world.

Media training needs

A pre-condition for the effective and appropriate use of broadcast and print media is national commitment to professional
training in specific skills: the training of writers, producers,
broadcasters, editors, printers, technical and maintenance personnel. As well, there is the urgent need for the training of
field workers in the use of media and in the skills of group
leadership.

The necessity of professional media production services to integrate such ingredients as technical hardware, the materials
produced and their use and distribution dictates the need for
continuing national and regional courses and workshops for adult
educators and communications personnel together. The understanding of how these ingredients work is a necessary part of the
overall training of administrators, researchers and educators,
as the following recommendation indicates.

Mass media, including newspapers, radio and television, should
be used to further the aims and objectives of literacy programmes

such as by encouraging participation and sustaining motivation, and by assisting instructors and group leaders in the actual learning situation. The reinforcement of knowledge and skills demands more concentrated study and evaluation as to the role of the various educational technologies, publishing of adult literature for neo-literates, fixed or itinerant community libraries, radio discussion clubs, special newspapers and magazines.

Folk culture and development

Traditional and popular communications of cultural values and aspirations form an existing network of "folk media" such as songs, dances, festivals, drama, etc., that can act as carriers of new ideas without distorting their authenticity. They can be used along with the electronic and print media to motivate people to learning and to understanding the reason for social change. Traditional cultural expressions also disclose the ways in which people have carried on their own learning in an oral culture and thus show how oral methods can be adapted to the teaching of literacy and to non-formal education.

Communication among adult educators

The participation of adult educators in their own continuing education and professional development is a need that echoes through recommendations from national, regional and international meetings. Since adult education has not been widely recognized as a coherent instrument and resource for development in policies of national governments and international organizations and agencies, funding for the necessary communication exchange of information, documentation, and publications and for face-to-face meetings and inter-country visits, has been minimal.

The multi-disciplinary nature of adult education, covering as it does nearly every aspect of human endeavour, finds expression in recommendations for more specific information about, and dissemination of, development issues, projects and innovations relating to research, health, rural development, environmental education, the media, pedagogy, learning theories, training programmes, etc. Many recommendations focus on the desirability of and the need to learn from other countries through publications, newsletters, and inexpensively available research reports and "state of the art" reviews.

Opportunities for operational seminars are also recommended for national and international specialists to work on the requirements for a particular project. There are recommendations for conferences and seminars at local, regional, national and international levels for practitioners of development to:

— identify practical problems that they face;
— define the characteristics of the process of aid to develop-
    ment;
— formulate hypotheses for solutions to their problems and to
    develop better mastery of the different roles that their
    work demands of them.

To facilitate cross-cultural understanding and collaborative
efforts in adult education development, it is recommended that
governments, national and regional associations, NGOs, and international agencies should actively encourage and fund:

— more effective exchange of regional and international infor-
    mation on adult education research, innovations and action
    programmes;
— the regional exchange of practitioners, planners, researchers
    and adult educators;
— expanded regional adult education networks for planning and
    development.

A COMMITMENT

At the conclusion of the Dar es Salaam Conference, Chairman
Malcolm Adiseshiah spoke directly of the commitment necessary
to ensure that action is taken on recommendations.

> I call on each of us to commit himself and her-
> self to action to make adult education an integ-
> ral instrument for the kind of development —
> the liberation of Man — to which we have pledged
> ourselves for the balance of the Second Devel-
> opment Decade. The springs that nourish this
> pledge are our own will and behind the indivi-
> dual will that each of us brings to the task
> is the community of adult education to which
> all of us belong.

In the spirit of this pledge and out of concern that only four
years remain in the Second Development Decade, the final statement recommends:

— that the Design for Action be placed on the agenda for study
    by all international, regional, national bodies, and by

all institutions;
— that each body and agency be encouraged to take action on the
   steps most appropriate to it;
— that, in addition to reports required from each country by
   UNESCO respecting progress on the implementation of the
   Recommendation on the Development of Adult Education, progress be monitored yearly by national and regional organizations concerning action on all recommendations that
   apply to them;
— that financial sources be obtained and used in each region,
   and internationally, for the process of assessment and for
   refining and improving the objectives for action for adult
   education;
— that before 1980, regional and international meetings be
   called to appraise the results of the implementation of
   the Design for Action and to plan for future action.

Appendix: List of Conference Papers

CONFERENCE PAPERS

His Excellency Julius K. Nyerere,
President,
United Republic of Tanzania

Development is for Man, by Man and of Man**

Ben Mady Cissé,
Secretary of State for Human
Development,
Republic of Senegal

The People's Involvement in Development

Majid Rahnema,
Iranian Ambassador-at-Large
and Special Adviser to the
Prime Minister

Education and Equality: A Vision Unfulfilled

Amir Jamal,
Minister of Finance and Planning,
Tanzania

Implications of the New Economic Order

Lucille Mair
Deputy Representative,
Permanent Mission of Jamaica to
the United Nations

Meaning and Implications of Expanded Concepts of Development for Action

N. A. Kuhanga,
Minister for Manpower Develop-
ment,
Tanzania

Adult Education and Development: A Tanzania Case Study

---

* Some presentations made in working groups were delivered orally and no papers are available. Correspondence about Conference papers should be addressed to: International Council for Adult Education, 33 Prince Arthur Avenue, Toronto, Canada.

** Adopted unanimously by the Conference as The Declaration of Dar es Salaam.

319

Malcolm Adiseshiah, Vice-Chancellor, University of Madras, India	Structures — International and National — and Develop- ment
Malcolm Adiseshiah, President, International Council for Adult Education	Adult Education and Develop- ment: Presidential State- ment.
Malcolm Adiseshiah	Valedictory Statement: Our Pledge
Lalage Bown, University of Lagos, Lagos, Nigeria	Report of the Rapporteur General

BACKGROUND AND WORKING GROUP PAPERS

Abd-El Shany Abboud, Maitre de Conférences, Faculté de Pédagogie, Université Ains-Chams	Lifelong Education in Islam L'Education permanente dans l'Islam
John Agard, University of Papua, New Guinea	Reflections on Non-formal Education for Rural Develop- ment in Papua New Guinea
George F. Aker, Florida State University, Tallahassee, Florida, USA	The Learning Facilitator
Barbara Barde, Ontario Educational Communica- tions Authority, Toronto, Canada	Is Adult Educational Broad- casting Responding to the Needs of the Audience?
Martin Byram, Tutume Community College; Ross Kidd, Botswana Extension College	Folk Media and Development: A Botswana Case Study
Edris Bird, Resident Tutor, University of the West Indies, Antigua, West Indies	Adult Education and Develop- ment in the Small States of the Eastern Caribbean

John Bowers,
Agricultural Extension and Rural
   Development Centre,
University of Reading,
England

Functional Adult Education
   for Rural People: With
   Emphasis on the Quality of
   Communications and the Role
   of Action-Research and Feedback

Catherine Buyoya,
Institut Africain pour le
   Devélopment Economique et
   Social au Burundi

Les Fiches Pédagogiques pour
   l'Education des Adultes

Paz Goycoolea Buttedahl;
Knute Buttedahl,
International Council for
   Adult Education

Participation: The Transformation of Society and the
   Peruvian Experience*

Helen Callaway,
Oxford University, England

Research for Development:
   Adult Learners Within their
   Cultural Setting

Lamartine Pereira da Costa,
MOBRAL Foundation, Brazil

Post-Literacy Consolidation
   Programmes

James De Vries,
University of Dar es Salaam,
Department of Rural Economy and
   Extension
Morogo, Tanzania

Agricultural Extension and
   the Development of Ujamaa
   Villages in Tanzania:
   Problems of Institutional
   Change

Romesh Diwan,
Professor of Economics,
Rensselaer Polytechnic Institute,
Troy, New York, USA

Development, Education and
   the Poor: Context of South
   Asia

Tony Dodds,
International Extension College,
London, England

Educational Alternatives by
   Distance Teaching

Draft Statement Prepared for
   Conference Discussion

Education for Development

---

* Published in <u>Convergence</u>, Vol. 9, No. 4, 1976.

Lars Emmelin,   Environmental Education Pro-
Environment Studies Programme,   gramme for Adults*
Sweden

E. A. Fisher,   The Collection of National
Programme Specialist,   Statistics on Adult Educa-
Unesco Office of Statistics   tion

Melvin J. Fox,   Some Thoughts on Language as
Ford Foundation Representative   a Factor in Basic Education
  for West Africa   in Africa

Pierre Furter,   Recherche et Formation Extra-
Université de Genève,   scolaire pour le Développe-
Suisse   ment dans le Contexte de la
                                         Dependance

Habeeb Ghatala;   Choosing Media for Continuing
Elizabeth Ghatala,   Education
Weber State College, Utah, USA;
Nsang O'Khan Kabwasa,
UN Economic Commission for Africa

Reginald Herbold Green,   Adult Education,
Institute of Development Studies,   Basic Human Needs,
University of Sussex,   Integrated Development Plan-
England   ning: Some Issues of Strat-
                                         egy, Programme, Policy**

Budd L. Hall,   Breaking the Monopoly of Know-
Research Officer,   ledge: Research Methods,
International Council for   Participation and Develop-
  Adult Education   ment

Madan Handa,   Integrated Development: Mass
Ontario Institute for Studies in   Education and Participation
  Education,   as a Strategy for Develop-
Toronto, Canada   ment

P. G. H. Hopkins,   Workers' Education for Devel-
Chief Technical Adviser   opment: Case Study of the
                                         President's Citizenship
                                         College, Zambia

---

 * Published in <u>Convergence</u>, Vol. 9, No. 1, 1976.
** Published in <u>Convergence</u>, Vol. 9, No. 4, 1976.

Solomon Inquai,
Botswana Extension College

Mass Campaigns in Botswana

Yusuf O. Kassam,
Senior Lecturer,
Department of Adult Education,
University of Dar es Salaam

Formal and Non-formal Education in Relation to Social
Justice

Jacqueline Ki-Zerbo,
Unesco Regional Officer for
  Africa,
Senegal

Education en Matière de Population et Alphabétisation
Fonctionnelle

Mubanga Kashoki,
African Languages Director,
Institute for African Studies,
University of Zambia

Cultural Pluralism and National Integration in Zambia

David Macharia,
Institute of Adult Studies,
University of Nairobi

Coordination and National
Organization

Daniel Mbunda,
Director,
Institute of Adult Education,
Dar es Salaam

Education Mass Campaigns:
Tanzanian Experience

P. L. Malhotra,
Principal,
College of Vocational Studies,
University of New Delhi

The Role of Short Cycle and
Community Colleges in
Development

V. S. Mathur,
ILO Asian Regional Organization,
New Delhi

Workers' Education and the
Organizations of the Rural
Poor

Eli Meena,
Institute of Development Studies,
University of Dar es Salaam

Adult Education and Development: Policy-Oriented
Research

Louis M. Mongi,
Prime Minister's Office,
Dodoma, Tanzania

Importance of and Methods by
which Popular Participation
can be Increased in Development Decisions

J. Opare-Abetia,
Resident Tutor,
Institute of Adult Education,
University of Ghana

The People's Education Association of Ghana: A Model
for National Development

G. A. Orie,
Deputy Principal,
Egerton Agricultural College,
Njoro, Kenya

The Role of Formal Agricultural
Education in Rural Education

H. Perraton,
International Extension College,
Cambridge, England

Learning About Anything:
The role of face-to-face
meetings in distance education.

Kathleen Rockhill,
University of California,
Los Angeles

The Uses of Qualitative Research in Adult Education
to "Enlighten, Enoble and
Enable"

John W. Ryan,
Director,
International Institute for
   Adult Literacy Methods,
Iran

Methods in Adult Education:
The Pursuit of New Ends and
the Exploitation of New
Means

V. K. Samaranayake,
Acting Director,
Institute of Workers' Education,
University of Sri Lanka

Workers' Education for Nat-
ional Development: A Case
Study of the Institute of
Workers' Education

Erik Smith,
Senior Adviser,
ILO

ILO/DANIDA Programme for Workers' Education in Management in Tanzania

Per G. Stensland
Adjunct Professor of Education
New York University

The Educational Core of Development*

Janaki Tschannerl,
University of Dar es Salaam
Tanzania

The Function of Adult Education: An Overview of its
Social Character

---

* Published in <u>Adult Education</u>, Vol. 25, No. 2, 1976.

Leo Valdivia
University of Edinburgh

Research Priorities for Adult
Education in Latin America

Francisco Vio,
University of Sussex, England

Peasant Participation in Adult
Education: The Experience
of the Peasant School of
Talco, Chile

John R. W. Whitehouse,
Chief,
Workers' Education,
ILO, Geneva

A Labour Education Approach
to Workers' Participation
for Development

Abdelwahid Abdalla Yousif,
University of Khartoum,
Sudan

Training the Adult Educators:
A Priority Within the
Priority

CASE STUDIES:
NATIONAL AND REGIONAL PROGRAMMES RELATED TO DEVELOPMENT

Viet Nam: Report on the Situation and the Experience of
the Development of Compli-
mentary Education

Nguyen Van Luong,
Deputy Director,
Department of Adult Education,
Hanoi, Democratic Republic
of Viet Nam

India: Adult Education and
Development

Amrik Singh,
Secretary,
Association of Indian Univer-
sities

Yugoslavia: Workers' Universities within the Framework of
Yugoslav Adult Education

Ana Krajnc,
University of Ljubljana
Yugoslavia

Papua-New Guinea: Reflections
on Non-Formal Education

John Agard,
Senior Lecturer,
Community Education,
University of Papua New Guinea

Guinea-Bissau

Mario Cabral,
Commissariado do Estados da
Educacao Nacional e Cultura

Mali: Alphabétisation et Dével- oppement Vue à Travers l'Ex- périence Malienne	Bablen Traoré, Chef de Division alphabétisa- tion; Ahmadou Touré, Chief de Divi- sion recherche linguistique et pédagogique a la DNAFLA
Arab League: Adult Education in the Member States of the Arab League	Mohi El Dine Saber, Director-General, Arab Educational, Cultural and Scientific Organization, Cairo, Egypt.
Iraq: Baghdad Conference on Literacy Recommendations for Development	Ayif Habib Al-Ani, Ministry of Education, Baghdad, Iraq
Philippines: Adult Education and Community Development	Socorro L. Sering, President, Adult and Community Education, National Organization of the Philippines
Hungary: Characteristics of the Hungarian System of Adult Education	
Mozambique: Literacy and Adult Education in the People's Republic of Mozambique	
Indonesia: Adult Education and Nation-Building Towards National Resilience	Djoko Sanjoto

———

Perspective on Development: Special pre-Conference issue of
Convergence, Vol. 9, No. 2, 1976.

INDEX